INSIDE JOB

Deep Undercover as a Corporate Spy

Kenneth C. Bucchi

Penmarin Books
Granite Bay, California

Editorial Offices:
Penmarin Books
2011 Ashridge Way
Granite Bay, CA 95746

Sales and Customer Service Offices:
Access Publishers Network
6893 Sullivan Road
Grawn, MI 49637
(800) 345-0096

Penmarin Books are available at special discounts for bulk purchases for premiums, sales promotions, or education. For details, contact the Publisher. On your letterhead, include information concerning the intended use of the books and how many you wish to purchase.

Visit our Website at **www.penmarin.com** for more information about this and other exciting titles.

Printed in Canada
1 2 3 4 5 6 7 8 9 10   03 02 01 00 99

Library of Congress Cataloging-in-Publication Data
Bucchi, Kenneth C.
    Inside job : deep undercover as a corporate spy / Kenneth C. Bucchi.
       p.   cm.
    ISBN: 1-883955-28-9
    1. Bucchi, Kenneth C.   2. Private investigators—United States
Biography.   3. Undercover operations—United States Case studies.
4. Drug traffic—Investigation—United States Case studies.
5. Drugs and employment—United States.   I. Title.
HV8083.B77A3   1999
364.1'77'0979527—dc21   99-44302

Disclaimer: The events and people described in this book are real. However, names have been changed to protect the innocent.

This book is dedicated

to the memories of

Debbie, George, Ethel,

Neil, Billy and Eleanor

Preface

When I accepted the job of undercover corporate investigator (UCI), I believed I'd found the panacea for my professional doldrums and the magic elixir for the angst I would feel whenever a job became just fun enough to be considered ethically and morally ambiguous. Well, let's just say I was half right.

As a UCI for one of the premier investigative agencies in the country, I quickly learned that there were few ends compelling enough to justify the unlimited means at my disposal to catch the bad guys. No police agency, except for possibly the Internal Revenue Service or the Air Force Office of Special Investigations has as much unbridled power as the UCI. In this line of work, a pinch of self-restraint and a dash of conscience is a fail-safe recipe for mediocrity and a sure-fire formula to take the fat out of your next paycheck.

Not one to shrink from a challenge or accept failure without a fight, I leaped at the chance to do something that, on the face of it, seemed almost philanthropic . . . well, as benevolent as one can be while lying through his teeth and acting as corrupt as those he is charged with investigating.

Although I wrote this book because I felt it was a subject of great importance that most people knew precious little about, the writing itself had the cathartic effect of exorcising many of the demons hatched during my years as a UCI. As a result of this therapeutic exercise, you will be exposed to a blow-by-blow account of what was arguably the wildest

corporate investigation ever conducted and certainly the most bizarre you'll
ever read about.

The insanity of the situations and the palpable dangers of the investigation will undoubtedly keep you riveted to each page, but it is my fervent
hope that the questions it will have you asking and the concerns it will
have you raising will incite you to action. As I'm sure you've already noticed, the Bill of Rights has been in a state of erosion lately, and the manner in which such investigations are conducted is comparable to pouring
salt over a rust-ravaged Volkswagen Beetle.

Oh, and by the way, if you're reading this sentence at your place of
business, you can rest assured that Big Brother is reading right along with
you.

Acknowledgments

I would like to thank my wife, Joanna, for her love and devotion, and my
children, Jack and "The Bean" (Noah), for making us a family. And to my
mom and dad (Dorothy and Ben) for supporting and loving me through
thick and thin.

I would also like to thank my agent, Jason Scoggins of The Gersh
Agency, for treating me as though I were his only client. His unwavering
belief in my abilities infused me with the confidence that I needed to
successfully navigate the rather circuitous Hollywood studio system and
eventually sign deals with Atlas Entertainment, Universal Studios, 20th
Century Fox, and NBC.

Thanks also to my publisher, Hal Lockwood, and Atlas Entertainment's
Doug Segal, for immediately grasping the synergistic, multimedia potential of my work and for having the faith in me to realize that potential.
Finally, I would like to give special thanks to my editor, Virginia Ray, for
providing clarity to the work itself.

INSIDE JOB

Deep Undercover as a Corporate Spy

Chapter 1

I was just thirty-one years old when my life began to spiral out of control in a Mach 3 plunge toward the abyss. Coincidental tragedies that included the death of my sister, the breakup of my wedding engagement, and the loss of my job had my stress level rivaling that of a suicidal postal carrier on a Sears catalog day.

Given my contempt for all things therapeutic, I did what came naturally. I went in search of a new identity, one with less self-blame and less pain. I bore no illusions about the deteriorated state of my mental condition, and when I finally came to grips with the notion that my life held no more great escapes, I stumbled onto a nebulous classified ad in the *Los Angeles Times* that read simply, "Undercover types wanted." My résumé was in the mail that afternoon.

Although I had more than enough experience in my career that qualified me for criminal investigations, including three years of undercover federal drug interdiction, six years as a commissioned officer in the United States Air Force, and three years as a private investigator, it was the latter that got me through the gate. This was early April, 1993, and the company was Krout and Schneider, Inc., a world-renowned detective agency in the little-known field of undercover corporate investigations. Their lengthy application process included an exhaustive background investigation, but the fact is, the firm was not given access to as much as a scintilla of my government file. After all, why should the government release classified documents about me to a schlock PI firm when they had already been granted authority through the courts to deny even General Noriega's attorneys access to them? But all that comes later. For now, at least, the firm was satisfied with the Feds' answer. Not that they had a choice. And besides, they were desperate for "undercover types" like myself.

The offer of a full-time position as an undercover corporate investigator (UCI), was not immediately made, however. The company had a condition of employment that they simply referred to as their "pre-employment screening." And so I found myself driving one of its employees deep into the bowels of Los Angeles, the purpose of the trip as yet unknown to me.

*   *   *

When my purple Porsche 911 slant-nose convertible crested the antiseptic glass enclave of Bunker Hill and descended into downtown Los Angeles, I became intoxicated with the sweltering stench of urine that seemed to boil up from the pavement, its sour aroma lingering in my sinuses.

As we rolled into a crumbled parking lot in L.A.'s much maligned downtown, my partner-apparent gulped a chunk of murky, polluted air, proudly expanding his chest like a bullfrog. With stinging eyes, I hoisted myself above the windshield and squinted at the dilapidated ruins of what was once a promising, if not thriving, metropolis.

Now afoot, we pushed deeper into the city, where sidewalks now blackened with seasoned gum and the once elegant architecture, sooty and gray, called to mind a more dignified past. The crowds seemed to thicken with confusion, throngs of the melting pot square-dancing their way through each human entanglement. Staggering from their midst, a man fumbled with a tie strung about a collarless shirt, desperately clinging to a final shred of dignity, when he detected my eyes upon his mismatched shoes.

"Why are we here?" I politely interrogated my partner, Glenn, my heart still with the hapless fellow.

"It's kind of a pre-employment screening," Glenn responded, seemingly oblivious to the depraved surroundings and rancid odor.

Although gaunt and somewhat gawky, Glenn could transform himself like a chameleon to suit any occasion. He had a knack for adding a pinch of quirkiness and a dash of the avant-garde to the otherwise bland roles he was compelled to perform. With one foot perpetually in the art house and the other firmly entrenched in the outhouse, Glenn played each investigative scene with classic film noir panache. He was clean and sharply dressed, but you always had this sense there was dirt beneath his fingernails. His hair was neatly groomed and professional, but his manner was neither. Glenn was a manager of Krout and Schneider, but he was about as rogue an investigator as there ever was and certainly the most stylish.

He nonchalantly flipped me a pager and continued in his typical machine-gun-burst fashion. "You're a clothing retailer from back east. Doesn't matter where, really. Pick a city. Hell, you're from Boston, right? Make it Boston then, I don't care. You want designer shit and lots of it. Cheap! You follow?"

"Sure. Knockoffs."

"All kinds. But we're mainly concerned with Dinky."

"Dinky?"

"Donna Karen, New York? DKNY? Dinky? I'm sure you've heard of it."

"Oh, sure. Dickney. My Mom's big on that overpriced shit."

"It's not shit. And it's not called Dick. It's Dink. *Dinky*. And it's certainly not low end. At least not as far as you're concerned. They're our latest client. . . . Well, sort of."

I replied, "The acronym for Mothers Against Drunk Driving is spelled M-A-D-D. It's still called mad. They don't call it DAM. They probably should, but they don't."

"What?" he asked, squinting at me. "Forget it. Where the hell was I? Oh, yeah, your cover. So you're big-money grip. You're lookin' for high volume at curbside prices."

"Uh-huh." I nodded with anticipation. "Okay. . . ." I leaned further and further inward. "Annnd?"

"That's it," he replied succinctly. "You know as much as I do now. Dickney. *Dinky* wants us to investigate allegations that this store's selling hundreds of thousands of dollars' worth of imitation name goods each year. It's not just the money, either. They wanna make a big statement. Deterrence. Teach 'em a lesson. Kick their asses publicly all over L.A. Crap like that."

"So where's the proof gonna come from? You wired?"

"Right here." He tilted his pager away from his belt.

"Cool. Is mine transmitting? And where the hell's the surveillance?"

"Nope." He stretched and yawned. "Yours isn't wired for sound. And the surveillance guys are waiting for us a few blocks away in the garment district."

Before I could probe any further, a hunched Latina stormed between us, cursing me in a sharp Spanish cadence. I spun about like a tourist, somehow believing I would get an explanation for this unprovoked abuse. When I returned to my intended path, my eyes quickly froze upon a haggard old man fuddling with a snagged zipper, his forehead pressed like a fulcrum against the darkened window of a popular bank. The only saving grace, perhaps, was that it was his own zipper he was yanking on. My concentration on the job at hand was fast eroding. I suppose I just wasn't used to being bombarded with so much dereliction in such a short period of time.

"Watch your step, Ace," Glenn warned. I was just about to collide with a semicomatose man sprawled across the sidewalk, his decomposing pants gently fluttering in the arid breeze. I found myself becoming seduced by the city's gritty charm.

"Why do they hide their beer cans in a brown bag?" I asked, spinning around 360 degrees while continuing to speak. "Does anyone really think they've got a soda in there?"

"L.A.'s got a big homeless problem, Ace. I don't think drinking in public's high on the cops' priority list. Know what I mean, Vern?"

"Homeless," I commented. "That always cracks me up. Aren't they pretty much jobless, carless, and penniless, too?"

"Not to mention careless, hapless, and hopeless. They should just call 'em omniless."

"Hell. Call the great outdoors their home and you've cured the problem. The way I see it, it's a problem in semantics, not economics."

"Huhhh," Glenn snickered. "You ever notice that even the craziest of 'em are lucid enough to wait for the "Walk" sign before crossing the street?"

"No shit, huh." I pretended to be more knowledgeable than I was about such things.

"Yeah. That cracks me up all right. . . ." his voice trailed off.

We headed south on Spring Street, dodging the beleaguered and shunning the shysters hawking their shoddy street merchandise, when suddenly we were startled by staccato bursts of automatic gunfire.

"Let's go," he yelled with a contorted face, jerking my armpit in the relative direction of the noise.

"What are you, nuts?" I wailed, reluctantly scampering after him.

As we sped down Fifth Street toward Broadway, I was bewildered by the disinterested expressions of those we passed. "What the hell we gonna do against automatic weapons? Hell, any weapons? These are pagers, not tasers!"

He stopped abruptly, extending his palm toward me in the universal symbol for "Halt." Instinctively, I reached for a weapon I didn't possess. I moved up slowly, hoping to find others in the area who were doing the same. I knew enough about such situations to know that if the looky-loos were lurching toward the scene of the crime or timidly leaning in from the periphery like hyenas drawn to a fresh carcass, then all was relatively safe.

"That's a wrap," a baritone-voiced woman shouted.

"Cool, huh?" Glenn said. "This shit goes on down here 24/7. I love this stuff."

At least now I understood why we had parked so darn far away. All the parking lots in the surrounding area were overflowing with a plethora of movie-related paraphernalia. My mood and heart quickened. Before me was all I'd ever wanted to be, in all its grandeur and pretense. My concentration loitered in their midst, a hidden passion titillated beyond self-restraint.

Police and barriers regulated traffic for an entire block. One side of the street was inundated with the controlled chaos of cranes, cables, lights, cameras, rain machines, and of course, the stars. Curious onlookers on the opposite side of the street were hastily ushered away by agitated production assistants who voiced concerns that their dopey expressions would be reflected in the store windows being filmed.

"God. What I'd give . . . ," I blurted.

"I hear ya," Glenn offered before taking a deep breath and moving on. "Not that I couldn't watch this all day, but . . . ."

"Yeah, I know. Damn."

Our pace picked up as we drew closer to the garment district. Paper and other debris churned across our path, collecting like autumn leaves at the base of each filthy curb. Abandoned buildings—and there were many —were blighted by cheesy posters of upcoming movies and obscure musicians. Even the "Post No Bills" signs were plastered with advertisements.

As we passed a sunken, dank doorway, I observed a well-dressed man kneel to pick up a discarded, crusty sandwich. After a cursory examination he took a large bite, returning it swiftly to the pavement. The crunching sound that ensued turned my stomach immensely.

"Look at that guy," I said, directing Glenn's focus to the curious man.

"What about 'im?" he replied, rubbing his nose.

"He just ate a sandwich off the ground."

"So?"

"So? Look at him. *He* needs to eat garbage?"

"Why? Because he's dressed well?"

"Of course, 'cause he's dressed well. Why the hell else would I care?"

"Maybe it's his first day on the street. Everyone hasta have a first day, you know. And they probably all look pretty good for a while."

I thought for a second. "I suppose."

"Look over there." He pointed to a large glass building.

"The garment thingamajig, right?"

"Yeah, the Cal Plaza Building. We're gonna go to the fourth floor, meet with the guy, make the deal, and get the hell outta there. Dig?"

"Wait!" I interrupted. "What the hell do I know about this crap? How much am I paying? And for what volume?"

"We're not paying diddlysquat yet. Just negotiate per piece. Figure around four bucks per, on average. Thereabouts. I thought we went through all of this!"

"Sure, whatever," I said apathetically.

"You'd best start takin' this shit more serious."

"Pleeeease. This is the garment district, for cryin' out loud. You know, talk wispy and carry a big purse."

His voice stiffened. "The bigger the purse, the bigger the weapon inside. Remember that!" he said, poking his finger into my shoulder.

Although his tone was serious, I was convinced he wouldn't cast me, an unknown quantity, into a potentially dangerous situation. Nevertheless, that all-too-familiar drumbeat of pessimism throbbed at my temples, and droplets of sweat trickled down my spine and from beneath my armpits, cooling my skin as they met a gentle breeze. Yet as fast as the concern surfaced, it dissipated. After all, this was the garment district and I, an ex-"Company" man, had been through much worse. Once again, ignorance was an ally.

Just before we reached the building, a swollen and rumpled man, draped over a rickety cane, approached us with one leg dragging behind him. "God bless you, sirs. Can ya spare forty-three cent?"

I did so without hesitation, beguiled by the exactness of his plea and feeling grateful that he imparted blessings from God.

"First time in the Big Orange?" Glenn asked

"How's that?"

"Why you givin' money to Lon Chaney there?"

"Would you hire him?" I said curtly.

"Fuck, no!"

"That's why. 'Cause he sure as hell ain't gettin' no job any time too soon!"

"You know why he uses a cane instead of crutches?" Glenn's tone became irreverent.

I answered smartly, "No, but I'm sure you'll tell me."

His voice showed even greater frustration. "Because a cane implies a handicap, not an injury. It seems more permanent than crutches. More in need of pity. You have to become a connoisseur of people."

I took great exception to this but didn't show it. As I didn't reply, he added, "It's not as if you don't need every dime you've got, either."

"What's that supposed to mean? I'm doin' pretty good with J. R.," referring to the investigation firm I pretended to still be working for.

He stopped abruptly, pivoted to face me, and stabbed the air in front of my face with his index finger. A finger, I might add, that had a Bic pen clipped to the back. "You haven't had a case in weeks! You're desperately in need of work, what with your fancy car and all."

He paused a moment, then continued pummelling me verbally. "Look, jackoff, you can play that 'I'm lookin' for more rewarding work' crap with Gino (the company VP) and Gordon (the case supervisor), but don't play that shit with me! Unlike those twerps, I've actually worked undercover cases! I know what's up from what's . . . well . . . from what's not up! Now, you gonna be straight with me or what?"

I broke into a smile and replied, "When the bullshit stops working, that's generally my fall-back position." I was jokingly candid. And I was learning. It had only just occurred to me that this ridiculous jaunt through Babel probably had a purpose. Maybe he was attempting to demonstrate that everything had a different angle from which it could be viewed and that maybe, just maybe, I didn't have all the answers. Or maybe not.

"Good," he responded, the edge lifting from his voice. "I know J. R. let you go because of that book thing you're working on. The CIA stuff."

He kept speaking despite the disturbed look on my face. "It's just between us, so don't worry. Fact is, Gino needed someone *yesterday* to cover our collective asses on this big case we've got goin' in Oregon. They're our biggest client, and we've already lost two pussy operatives up there as a result of injuries and ineptitude. Gordon'll offer you piddlings at first. Don't go for it. They'll pay through the nose to get you up there. I'm tellin' ya all this 'cause I suspect you're what we've been needin' and because you'll quit in two weeks if you're working for anything less than thirty bucks an hour."

"The job's that brutal, huh?"

"Boise Cascade? You shittin?" His rhetorical question implied a self-evident answer. He immediately picked up on my nondiscerning squint. "The plywood place?" he followed, my upper cheeks clenching even further. He could tell that I still had no idea what company he was talking about.

Impatience swelled his voice. "It's a giant saw mill in Medford, Oregon. They make plywood . . . for houses." His words had a nudging quality to them. "For boats." A pause. "Nothing, huh?" Another pause. "Well, see, there's this thing called a forest. And it's full of trees. They take the trees and . . . "

"Don't worry, I'll figure out who the hell they are in due time. How hard could it be?"

*   *   *

When we entered the building where our transaction was to go down, I fell in love at least seven times merely strolling through the lobby, smitten by the artsy women dressed in multiple hues of black. The escalator was aesthetic like everything else in the building: slender, pretentious, and impractical.

A few "buyers" stalked the halls in search of new styles for the summer season. Shop owners remained coyly inside their glass cubicles, curling their toes as they waited in anticipation of the big sale.

"Cool ties," I observed of some window dressing, almost forgetting why we'd come.

"Dinky. Dinky," he reminded me.

"Where the heck is this place, anyhow?"

"Just around the bend. You ready?" His manner grew more tense.

"They're fashion dweebs. I think we can handle it," I stated with confidence.

He whispered back, "Fashion dweebs selling hundreds of thousands of dollars' worth of illegal name bands is not something I'd take lightly."

"Bands?"

"What?"

"You said *bands*. Selling illegal name *bands*."

"Brands, jerkoff. Take this shit serious."

"I am. I just didn't understand what you said, that's all. I'm lookin' to *buy* name brand shit, not sell it, right?"

He grunted, "That's correct, Inspector Clouseau." Thrusting his pen-clad finger in front of us, he stated, "It's the store on the right, just after the leather place. See it?"

"Sure do. Looks like he's got a big-ass bodyguard. He must take this shit real serious, too." I was referring to a brawny man with a triangular torso. He towered about 6'6" and had a decidedly protruding forehead; the quintessential steroid abuser.

"You mean the big dude with the greasy hair goin' in the back room, right there?" he asked.

"Who else?"

"That's our buyer."

"You mean seller, don't you?"

"You know what I . . . Just stop that shit, already."

I was sure Glenn must have been kidding. There was no doubt in my mind that the short, stocky man was the seller, not the big bodyguard.

I pulled back the solid glass door, which bore a sign boldly proclaiming "No Samples," and strutted in with Glenn close behind. My shoes announced our arrival as they tapped the lightly colored hardwood floor like a freshly caught flounder flopping on a ship's deck. Clothing was sparsely displayed on all four walls.

The place had a sense of exclusiveness about it. I felt dormant shopping impulses arouse within me, and my wallet felt lighter under that influence. I could almost feel it creeping from my back pocket. My fingers touched the clothing caressingly.

"Just remember why we came, Ace," Glenn reminded me once again.

"Just getting into character," I whispered.

"Gentlemen," a soft Latino voice intoned from behind us. "This ways." His English began to melt as he directed us with a daintily up-turned palm. His slicked-back hair, less salt than pepper, made him appear commanding, if not despotic. A slight scar darting across his forehead spoke of battles fought and won. Although his manner was almost debonair, he could never completely mask his true abrasive nature.

"This ways, Glenn," I mocked lightly.

Without introduction, we were led through the showroom. As we walked toward the dimly lit back room, I could feel my muscles tightening, especially in my gut. I didn't know what exactly precipitated this response, but my body seemed to be having a Pavlovian reaction to some imperceptible danger. Reacting to those symptoms of anxiety, I began feeling nervous. I held the door open for what I expected would be our inevitable assailants, repositioning myself to the rear as they filed past.

"After you," I insisted to the Latino, whose eyes quickly shifted between his partner and me. A slight nod from the other defined their relationship and implied that more than etiquette was at play in their wanting us to go before them.

"You don't minds if we frisks?" the tall one asked in faulty English, although the decision to do so was foregone.

"Just me?" I wondered aloud.

"You only ones I don't know," he replied, his misspoken phrases seeming more and more deliberate.

I lifted my arms above my head, maintaining eye contact with the tall one. The Latino's pat-down was thorough, requiring an adjustment of my anatomy when he was through. "Thanks," I commented. "Now you know why I drive a Porsche."

The tall one's indifferent gaze held my eyes firmly. "Throw his beeper out," he demanded in a monotone.

"How 'bout his?" I directed his attention to Glenn's pager. Glenn's jaw muscles began to ripple and quiver like an arrhythmic cardiogram, but he remained quiet.

"I trusts him."

"But not his judgment?" I asked, the answer already implied.

He suddenly loosened up, slapping his thighs and gingerly folding his angular body into one of the few chairs in the room. He announced magnanimously, "I will do business with you!"

I smirked at Glenn, who had a look of gratification enveloping his face. I then answered rather perfunctorily, "But not I with you, you gangly, Ichabod Crane–lookin', broken-English-lisping, can't-buy-a-vowel *piece of shit!*"

Turning away naturally and not as if anticipating delay, I added, "If you can't trust his judgment of me, then how the fuck can I trust his of you? You know, I've always believed that a person who trusts nothing should never be trusted with anything."

As I clutched the ornate glass doorknob, icy metal chilled the back of my neck, the distinctive double click of a Beretta 9 mm halting my progress out the door. Truth be known, the only reason I knew he was brandishing a Beretta 9 was because I happened to catch a glimpse of it in the grimy mirror that hung on the wall to my right.

Startled, the normally unflappable Glenn blurted, "What the shit is this?"

I spun about swiftly, my left arm striking the gunman like a windmill, chopping down on his inner elbow and curling up beneath his triceps muscle, the heel of my right hand meeting his nose flush like Dempsey's prosthetic half-shoe to a teed-up pigskin.

It was the double click that gave him away. When you draw back the slide of an automatic weapon, you either place the hammer in the half-cocked position or engage the safety to prevent unintended fire. But you never lower the hammer completely; it defeats the purpose of loading a shell into the chamber in the first place. The double click, for the most part, is a movie effect intended to arouse the audience and invoke thoughts of imminent peril. Had he pulled the trigger at that point, nothing would have happened except for possibly an involuntary defecation on my part. At least that's what I was betting the farm on. This episode also told me that they considered me unseasoned, which gave me a slight edge—the element of surprise.

With the bridge of his nose mashed and pulpy and blood streaming into his eyes, it was easy to relieve him of his weapon by simply applying upward pressure on his triceps and downward pressure on his forearm. Just as I heard his shoulder pop from its rotator cuff, the gun impacted the floor. I pushed him gently to the floor with the sole of my right shoe.

Glenn stared down between his two shivering legs at the man's blood-ied face; coagulating blood in the man's eye sockets reminded me of cucumber slices on a lady's facial. Shaking his head, Glenn whispered: "Are you . . ." his voice climbing ". . . out of your *fucking mind*?!"

He let a handkerchief float down on the man's face, where it came to rest on the tip of his nose like a bank robber's disguise. Then Glenn, with one finger raised and oscillating, calmed the other man with a "Shush, shhhhh." He pressed his hand against his own forehead, as if searching for the right emotion.

I picked up the Beretta and popped the clip, drawing back the slide to expose an empty chamber. "So. Not only am I untrustworthy," I said, the decibels of my voice continuing to rise, "but apparently you think I'm stupid as well!"

"Well," the man in charge addressed Glenn, "It seems your buddy is passing the tests."

I got a terrible sinking feeling. "Oh, boy," I uttered, my eyes darting about the floor. "It sure as hell seemed like the real deal, I'll tell ya."

Glenn gazed at the seller and shouted, "I like 'im!" He was referring to me, thank God.

"Really?" I replied, stunned.

"You made a good decision!" Glenn appeared pleased. "No crook worth his salt would've done business with these guys after the way they treated us. If you'd have dealt with them, they'd have thought you far too anxious. I wish ya hadn't fucked up the poor bastard's face, though. It's gonna be tough explainin' that one to Gino baby."

"Oh, God," the man on the floor groaned, his voice nasal and scratchy. "What the fuck happened?"

"When you fell, you hit your face on the chair," I answered, attempting to limit the company's exposure. "You probably weren't expecting me to take your gun so quickly. Sorry 'bout that, bud."

"I still gets pay?" he asked, sounding insecure.

"Sure, buddy," Glenn responded. "Like it never happened. Like it never happened."

"Gracias, Señor."

Glenn smiled at me, flicking his head in the relative direction of the door. We parted company without the usual exchange of pleasantries and fled the building.

"So that's why you didn't bother to tell me about the prices."

"You're just now getting that?"

"No. I mean . . ."

"Not a word to Gino or Gordon about the nose mashing and the blood and the . . . Well, you know. Just keep it simple. I'll tell 'em you did great. We'll leave it at that."

"Fine by me. Does that mean I got the job?"

"You're darn tootin' you got the job!"

"Cool."

Glenn laughed like a maniac all the way to the street, and when I dropped him off at the office that evening, he offered me some words of wisdom. "What you did in the city today was in spite of K and S."

"I don't follow," I said before releasing the steering wheel. The tacky sound the dried blood made was in stark contrast to the ordinariness of our conversation.

"Good investigating, as you demonstrated today, begins with good cover building. K and S thinks you can develop a cover in the office and stick with it throughout the case. They haven't the first fuckin' clue about what it means to think on your feet. Improvise! Hell, you know what I'm sayin'. Tell 'em as little as possible 'bout the minutia of the investigation. Get the results they want, but do it your way!" He slapped the upholstery while leaning into my car.

"I'll try," I responded. As soon as the words left my mouth I could tell they lacked the requisite enthusiasm, but I still wasn't completely convinced this wasn't another attempt to test me.

"Don't try! Do it!"

I nodded affably and shook his hand good-bye.

"You'll do all right. Just remember, it's your ass, not theirs." He started to walk away, then pivoted abruptly. "Oh! Call me about any major problems you have, not Gordon. Okay?"

"Done."

"Good luck. You're gonna need it."

*   *   *

I would speak with Glenn often during the first couple of months I was in Oregon, but I would never see him again in this function. He was fired just a couple of months later, after nineteen years of devoted service to the company. He was also the last supervisor at K and S who had the first clue about what it took to be a good undercover corporate investigator. I would come to find that the agency was less concerned with fair and equitable investigations than it was with fulfilling their clients' political agendas. But all that comes later. For now, at least, the only thing that mattered was that I was going to get the opportunity to prove myself where others before me had gone and failed.

Chapter 2

With little time even to exhale after my Los Angeles "interview," I soon found myself on a plane bound for Oregon. The purpose of this visit was to meet with the district attorney's office as well as representatives of JACNET, short for Jackson County Narcotics Enforcement Team, to discuss the scope of the investigation and the limitations of my authority. The bottom line was that I was not a cop, and therefore not afforded any legal authority outside that specifically granted me by the powers-that-be under this particular operation. Every drug buy I would make was to be strictly controlled and monitored with continual surveillance; a rule that was skirted virtually from the outset.

I met Joe, a twenty-two-year veteran of the drug wars and the leader of JACNET, in a small park during a torrential downpour. Joe's gray, receding hairline reflected a career of pent-up stress and frustration. His girlish figure had long since matured, and his stature had shrunk and collected about his waistline. The physical erosion was but a part of the story, however. Joe could hold his own with the most courageous of young officers, and had something they couldn't: experience.

With my customary can of Diet Coke held daintily with the tips of three fingers, and donning a black leather trench coat, blue sunglasses, and a dark brown cowboy hat, I walked without an umbrella toward Joe and two other men, all holding nondescript beige umbrellas above their heads.

"Ken?" Joe inquired with a finger drawn toward me in the shape of a pistol.

"Joe," I acknowledged, with my fingers held out in the form of a "peace" sign.

Without introduction, Joe led me a short distance away from the other agents. "Where the hell's your umbrella, son?"

I answered with my best Bill Murray imitation. "I don't think the heavy stuff will be coming down for quite some time now."

"That sense of humor generally keeps you dry during a monsoon, does it?"

"A bad sense of humor can make you feel pretty wet, too," I replied.

Joe scratched his head, grunted, and then continued. "Anyway, I hope you're better than your predecessors. Those idiots were paying for shit up front and hadn't even seen the stuff, for God's sakes," he vented.

"Dealers feelin' out prospective buyers for basic street sense," I added.

"No shit, huh. Any moron could see that, right? I wanted to smack 'em." He raised his voice while twisting away from me. "Do you know what one of those little pricks did?" He waved his finger in my face. "He feigned the use of meth. You believe that shit? The little sonofabitch tells me it's the only way to get 'em to sell to him."

He spoke with a driven voice before exhaling profusely. "I should've smacked 'im. One good whack. Just once! Right in the kisser. Jackoff tried to convince me that that was even possible. I told the little prick he could go to jail over a stupid stunt like that!" Joe shook his head downward and let out another short breath. "You, though. You're different. I can tell. Were you in law enforcement at one time?"

I was a bit startled. "Law enforcement? Yeah, something like that," I responded with something approaching sarcasm. "So. What's the drill?" I inquired.

"No drill. I've read your dossier, and you sound like a good fit. Not like the last two pussies your agency sent us. Their collective backgrounds didn't amount to squat. You don't learn this job in a classroom."

"My dossier? Who are you, J. Edgar Hoover?"

He didn't react but to smirk. "Your reputation precedes you, what with the Air Force and P.I. stuff and all. I'm pretty sure you understand how to build a cover and win a dealer's trust. I just want you to keep in mind that this is not Colombia or Los Angeles."

"I'd say those were synonymous."

"No shit, huh. Anyhow, take your time in that place." He was referring to the mill. "There's a lot of nepotism goin' on . . . ."

"You make it sound like incest."

"I'm sure there's a little of that too. But the point is, they're not gonna
embrace an outsider with a Northeastern accent drivin' a fuckin' Porsche.
In a couple months, when they've gotten to know you . . ."

"A couple months? Apparently someone else's reputation preceded me.
Try a couple weeks, fat boy. Three, tops."

"See. That there . . . See, that's . . . That's the thing right there." He
mumbled, turning toward his colleagues as if they were listening. They
weren't.

Still speaking in their general direction, he continued. "You're a loose
cannon. I can tell. Not that I mind that especially, but it can create problems. Hell, in some ways I kinda like it. Fuck it; let me ask you outright.
Let's just put the cards right out there. Is there another agenda I should
know about? At Boise?"

"None that you should know about."

"Ahhh. Okay. Best left unsaid, huh? Well, just remember, there's this
minor detail called the U.S. Constitution we frat boys need to be concerned with."

"Frat boys? Ohhh. No, no, no. No, I said 'Fat boy,' not 'frat boy.'"

"Uh-huh." Joe frowned, confused. "Well . . . Well, this here," he slapped
his belly, "This is a lotta years of . . . Hell, why am I explaining this to
you?" He laughed. "Besides, fatness runs in my family."

"No," I said with a steep grin. "The problem is, no one runs in your
family."

He sniggered, more nasal than vocal. "You've used that line before,
haven'tcha?"

"Oh, yeah," I said with a wry smile. "But back to what you were saying
before. You're right, the Constitution is a concern of *yours*." Before he
could react, I added, "But don't worry. They'll all be predisposed to commit the crime when it comes time. At least when I get 'em on tape. So
what is it: wire, hat, or pager?"

"Sorry to say, we're a bit behind the times here. We're supposed to be
getting pagers real soon, though. Or so they tell me. But we don't have
'em yet, no."

Pagers were the latest form of the commonly known "body wire." They were the perfect piece of surveillance equipment. The good ones even functioned like pagers.

My mouth fell open and my jaw angled as I nodded my head in a way that implied "bush league." "So? How much notice do you need to set up your surveillance team?"

"Preferably a day or two. But if it's a good score, we can normally get by with just a couple hours. It varies, though. With money the way it is, we generally don't have enough manpower for our *own* caseload, never mind additional bullshit like this. Oh, and in case I forget: There's only a small cache of people at JACNET that know who you are, so always ask for me. Got it?"

"Gotcha."

Joe slapped his hands to his thighs and said, "Hate to cut it short, but I've got a meeting with the DEA. Anything else before I go?"

"No, there's nothing I can think of," I responded, offering my handshake. "I think it'll be fun working together."

"Roger that. You too. And good luck."

Then Joe began vigorously frisking himself. "Oh wait! Shit, I almost forgot. It's these markings here. Here, take a look at these."

Joe pulled a pair of enlarged photographs from his jacket, holding them close beneath the umbrella to avoid the rain. The pictures were extreme close-ups of forearms bearing two wide, brown tattoos but did not give any clue as to where they were taken or who the subjects were.

"What am I lookin' at?"

"Seems a lot of our suspected dealers out there have these puppies. We think it's some sorta tattoo. You know—identifies the person as safe to do business with. Like a gay man's earring"

"Where were these photos taken?"

Joe hesitated with his reply. "Why you ask?"

"Well," I couched my response carefully so as not to offend him, "If it was recent, we got a minor problem. What with the Constitution and all. I know how important that puppy is to you." I then added with an inflection, "It's been a pretty cold winter, and if it wasn't *winter* . . . then the information's outdated. Either way—inadmissible."

"Don't worry about it. It was indoors. The cameras were inside."

"Inside?"

"Yeah." He shrugged. "Inside."

"People without shirts. Bar none. No shirts?"

"Tank tops."

"All of 'em? Even the women? I can tell one of the photos is a woman's arm."

"They're not bein' used in court. We just use these kinds of ahh . . . ahhh . . . well, you know, ahhh . . ."

"You don't have to explain to me, frat boy."

"You sure are a cocky one, I'll tell ya."

"Thanks for noticing, but whatta ya say we try'n keep this conversation above the gutter if we can."

"Oh, boy!" he bellowed before coughing. "You're always on, aren'tcha? But no. You know, I'm just sayin' this kinda stuff helps us know who to look at. Focuses the case, if you will. We get the job done sooner this way, even if we haveta cut some corners with this sort of photo surveillance. When ya think about it, it's in the interest of the taxpayers."

"Hey, no problem with me. Just remember you said that when you ask me how I came to know something *I* can't explain. It's not entrapment if I don't actually use the information against them. My bullshit's like your bathroom cameras: I don't necessarily use the information to help convict them, I just use it to separate the good guys from the bad guys. It helps *me* focus *my* bullshit . . . I mean, investigation."

Joe just stared back at me, not quite sure how to respond.

"So," I broke the silence. "The tattoos. You were sayin'?"

"Oh, yeah," he shook his head. "They're common. With the drug crowd. At the mill. I don't know what I'm sayin'." He quickly broke into a vigorous laugh before responding in a raspy voice, "Ahhrrr, shit! You're great! The last guys never even questioned these photos. Hell, even the D.A. hasn't questioned 'em! You crack me up! You're good. You actually know what the hell's goin' on!"

"Well, I'll look for 'em." I offered yet another handshake. "Should help, I think."

Joe smiled. "Good luck, again. And by the way, it was your guys who took the photos. Not that it matters, but I thought you should know."

"I'll remember not to jerk off in the bathroom from now on."

Joe laughed and swatted a hand in my direction. "Maybe you're not as cocky as I thought."

"It's called modesty!" I shouted over my shoulder while waving good-bye.

Oddly, throughout the interview Joe never once attempted to include me beneath his umbrella. As I walked away across the rain-swollen field, Joe watched curiously, attempting to glean what must have been, at least in his mind, the hidden message behind my not bringing an umbrella to an outdoor meeting in the middle of a downpour. It would nag him for weeks to come.

I flew back to California and awaited the verdict. I didn't have to wait long. Krout and Schneider was contacted the next day by Boise Cascade and informed that the authorities enthusiastically embraced the operation and that I was to report for work the following week.

Chapter 3

Boise Cascade of Medford, Oregon, is one of the largest producers of plywood in the world. Krout and Schneider had been contacted by Boise's head office in Boise, Idaho, and asked to conduct a major undercover investigation at the Medford mill. The main target: employees who romanced a seductive powder called crystal methamphetamine or crystal meth.

I had been told that the mill identified the problem through anonymous tips, but would later discover that high-tech, miniature cameras were installed in bathrooms throughout the building. Drug dealers weren't the only ones caught with their pants down, if you catch my drift. For obvious reasons, Krout and Schneider treated this filming practice as a heavily guarded secret.

Working in tandem with JACNET, I would soon be buying drugs from employees while wearing a surveillance wire.

The money used during these transactions was the client's, so they wanted the biggest bang for their buck. Because it was necessary to allow the drug dealers to walk away from each buy none the wiser, no arrest would be made until the end of the case. Consequently, the buy money could not be recouped. This was necessary to allow me the opportunity to make as many buys from as many employees as possible without blowing my cover. JACNET agreed to this term with the condition that we would up the ante with any dealer who chose to increase the quantity of each sale. I was supposed to request more drugs from the dealer than his source would "front" him and work my way up the food chain.

For the client, nothing could be more fiscally irresponsible. Their best bang for their buck was just enough sales to make each case indictable. In Oregon, this meant only two buys per dealer. Anything more was overkill and a complete waste of money for the client. Upping the ante after two purchases was certainly the best way to work your way up the food chain and catch a bona fide drug dealer, but not at all prudent if the only thing you were attempting to do was clean up your workplace. An indictment also ensured that an employee would be unable to appeal a termination. Needless to say, Krout and Schneider was not forthcoming with JACNET concerning this arrangement.

Ferreting out drug dealers and users was not Krout and Schneider's only goal, however. From the start, I had little doubt that the termination of unwanted employees was high on the menu.

Only a couple of key personnel in the front office knew who I was and what I was doing at the mill. This meant that I was vulnerable to being fired by any shift foreman who felt I wasn't performing my job up to standards. In effect, the same secrecy that protects an operative can also be his undoing. Because most new employees were expected to have prior work experience in the field, I had to learn my job and learn it quickly. With the average case costing the client more than a quarter million dollars, it was imperative that an operative avoid the ax.

The twelve-hour drive to Medford, Oregon, was arduous at best, especially as I was doing it in a Porsche. Less than a mile from the Medford exit off I-5, my car suddenly and unceremoniously died.

I took advantage of this freak incident to grill the tow truck driver on every nuance of relevant information he had to offer. His reservoir of indigenous knowledge helped me locate the perfect apartment, every genre of nightclub within a twenty-mile radius, all the German auto mechanics, and, for personal reference, movie theaters.

When I stepped outside the Red Lion Inn the following morning, I was struck by the beauty and cleanness of the place. The smog and degradation of L.A. the day before was replaced with air I couldn't see and concrete I couldn't smell. The serenity was almost surreal. Birds, not to be confused with pigeons, chirped—period. The mountains were smothered in pine, painting smooth the jagged terrain. Clouds, not smoke, mixed into the milky blue, drifting slowly on an indiscernible breeze.

I scoped out the exterior of the mill a day before I was to report for my first day of work. I was amazed at the parade of logs that seemed to stretch for miles, piled to incredible heights. Water cascaded down the mountain of tree trunks as a sprinkler system sprayed over them around the clock to prevent rotting.

I drove about a mile down a side street and then another down the main drag, never breaking free of the carnage of trees. As I turned into the gigantic main parking area, I was mesmerized by the gargantuan front-end loader that scooped up logs in its jaws and placed them onto a conveyor, where they would meet their end in the saw's wrath. The blades sliced the logs like one might pull a potato into a curlicue. The half-folded wood poured into the building's mouth and disappeared from sight. A sweet malodor rose from a colossal man-made pond located at the center of the asphalt, where hundreds of floating logs were kept fresh for the slaughter.

Soon, my freshly tuned vehicle was overwhelmed with the crossing traffic of heavy equipment hard at work producing plywood. *Vabooom*! My car shook violently, rattling my teeth. A front-end loader had dropped a thirty-ton log just fifty feet behind me.

"Shit," I screamed in panic, restarting my already idling vehicle. The blood-curdling sound of grinding flywheel blades quickly ensued. "Damn," I screeched, as I jammed the car into reverse. Burning rubber and granulating gear teeth, I fishtailed my car out of the parking lot. It was only then that I realized this wasn't to be the typical undercover assignment. One lapse in judgment and I could find myself permanently maimed—or worse.

*   *   *

I arrived at the mill at 11:00 P.M. the following day to begin my first day of work. Initially, I was captivated by the enormity of the facility and the penetrating heat. I passed by a huge, perpetually spinning saw reminiscent of the old "Rocky and Bullwinkle" cartoons, feeling all eyes upon me. I strutted with an air of cockiness, having known this kind of fishbowl before.

Sawdust hung like snow in the parched air, lingering on rafters and thickly coating the cement floor. The two-story ovens, heated to excruciating temperatures, stood juxtaposed with all-wood surroundings. It seemed like an all too dangerous mix to me, a suspicion that was eventually confirmed in the eye of a fiery storm.

Wet wood flowed into the mill at its north end (the green end), where it was pulled off the conveyor belt (the chain) by some rather muscular fellows and was then sorted into grades. The grades denoted the quality of wood and were determined by the number of knots on any given piece. The fewer the knots, the better the wood, and therefore the higher the grade, "A" being the best.

From there, it was transported by forklift, or Hyster, to the two-story ovens (dryers), where the sap was dried from the wood. It then went into an ominous-looking machine called a feeder that sucked the wood in like flies on a frog's tongue. The fast-moving men and women who worked the line were also called feeders, and it was their job to pacify the beast with a steady supply of wood. The core then shot from the dryer like cards from a Las Vegas dealer and was pulled into appropriate carts by pullers, who moved at a rabbit's pace, building muscle and shedding fat with incredible efficiency.

Even the simple act of walking through this sweatbox had its share of peril. A constant flow of unusable wood and debris flowed down a gorge known as "The Hog," which ran through the mill's concrete floor toward a treacherous chipper that turned all things organic into dust. Striped yellow pathways were like force fields protecting workers from the speeding Hysters, which worked under the immense pressure of extremely tight timelines. Although I was compelled to wear earplugs, they were of little consequence in this eardrum-bursting environment.

The first employee I met was a grizzly man named Harry. At five feet, eight inches tall and 230 pounds, covered from head to toe in hair, Harry's name fit him well. His girth was a neon sign declaring him "Speed Free." I instantly removed him from my hit list.

"Harry," he said, holding out his hand.

"Nothing a little electrolysis wouldn't cure," I acknowledged with a smirk, offering him the strongest grip I had.

He held my hand firm, studying it for texture, pretending to be amused by my wit. I anticipated this and was careful to coat my hands with a thin layer of super glue for just the right roughness. It worked. In fact, I did that every day for about three weeks. By then, my hands had acquired real calluses.

"Worked the mills before?"

"Yeah, back East. But nothing like this."

"Don't worry about it. You'll catch on soon enough. Come on, follow me! Let me show you around."

The safety briefing Harry provided was just that: brief. Green and red buttons that activated and shut down bone-crushing machines seemed less important to Harry than the proper method of donning the wood puller's safety attire. He also spent considerable time dispensing lascivious remarks about any woman with a bra size greater than a "B" cup, and precious little time on warning me about those areas in the plant where one might lose, let's say, an arm.

I was almost immediately handed off to another long-time Boise employee, Dave, and given a weeklong instruction on how to stay awake while plywood core, like sheep across the proverbial fence, poured past me. There was little to do on this automated chain, known as "the auto stacker," except count knots and press buttons. Eight buttons represented eight different grades. The stacker did the rest. Press the appropriate button and the machine placed the wood onto the correct chain. Simple.

I clenched my teeth whenever I felt the urge to yawn, not wanting to offend him. In my zeal to learn the job, I'd forgotten it was actually crystal methamphetamine I was attempting to flush out. Being tired was probably a good thing when carving a path to the powdery game I was after.

"How the hell do you stay awake on this damn shift?" I asked Dave while we sat in the stark break room during one of the evening's two ten-minute breaks. His job, sitting in a chair and watching wood flow by, was extremely hypnotizing. Tending the automated wood grader, one of the few in the facility, was a coveted position, however. During the humid summers, when temperatures often soared to 110 degrees near the dryers, sitting in a comfortable chair was a most enviable position.

Dave, a slender fellow with long, black, silky hair, fumbled for a good answer. "I guess you just get used to it, I suppose."

"Damn. I was kinda hopin' the answer was much more simpler," I responded, trying not to sound too articulate. I probably succeeded.

I could feel his gaze upon me. Even the slightest hint at wanting drugs could spook a paranoid dealer, especially when he didn't know you very well. I was throwing the bait out a bit early, and I knew it. However, because the two operatives before me had wasted so much of the client's time and money, I was anxious to bring home some good news. It being my first case and all.

"Maybe some Dexetrim," I quickly covered.

He brushed his hand toward me. "Nah. Don't worry about it. You'll get used to it, dude."

"Maybe. I just hope I get used to the paltry change I'm makin', and this insane work. If I get stuck on the heavy chain (pulling heavy plywood), I sure hope I can handle it." Then I thought, "*Paltry* was probably too smart a word to use." Constant internal microanalysis over what I said and did was an occupational hazard, but nonetheless, inevitable.

"Money troubles?" Dave asked.

"I could cash my check with the fuckin' paperboy."

"Then why'd ya take it? The job."

"Ahh, lots of reasons, I guess. Mainly because I'm tryin' to finish college, and if I'd stayed in the Air Force they'd have made me commit to three more years before they'd have paid for it. I'm also writing a book. Actually, I've already signed the deal. No money up front, of course. The military, with its insane schedules, made it impossible to find time to write."

My response was completely unrehearsed. It had suddenly occurred to me to swing 180 degrees from what my supervisor instructed and present a cover that was more in keeping with who I really was. This would enable me to speak more naturally and better explain why a native Bostonian, who traveled to this job from California, was now working at a mill in Oregon, driving a sixty-thousand-dollar exotic sports car.

"So what's it about? The book?"

"An illegal drug operation by the government. It's sorta complicated."

"Oh, they've been doin' that shit for years." He acted as though it were common knowledge. This was typical of the disenfranchised and prolegalization fringe. He probably had the latest edition of *High Times* in his glovebox.

"I wouldn't know. I only know about this one time, here. They oughta just legalize the shit, anyhow. We could pay off the fuckin' deficit if they did. But that'll never happen. You know what I'm sayin'?"

"I hear ya," replied my colleague.

"So where's the party tonight?" It was Friday, so I figured I'd check out some of the local hangouts.

"I don't know; I'm married. But I think most everyone goes to the Rock 'n' Rodeo Club or the Hideaway. You heard of 'em?"

"I've been to the Hideaway, but I'm not much on that country crap."

"That's where all the babes hang out, dude."

"Oh, yeah? Then maybe I'd better get me some of them there snake-skin boots," I said facetiously.

"I would if I were single. Hey, if you need any help stayin' awake to-night, let me know."

The hooks were shiny, pronged, and fully exposed. All I needed to do now was chomp down on the bait. And if I did, just like the operatives who came before me, the worm would be snatched from deep within my throat, and the wound would be a brand mark for all to shun. I would be plagued with the label "NARC," a tattoo that was virtually impossible to shed.

I immediately changed the subject to avoid the trap. "Whoa. Time to get back, dude. Wouldn't wanna piss off the boss my first week here."

The seed was planted, and I knew that the presumption of my speed use would now come up in conversations and soon spread throughout the mill's underworld.

* * *

I was soon moved to the swing shift, 3:00 P.M. to 11:00 P.M., to begin my regular schedule. Two short weeks of training on the graveyard shift were little preparation for such physically treacherous and ultradexterous work, but that's all the training I would be afforded.

After the dryer tender, who was the foreman, provided me with an-other "thorough" safety briefing, I was ready to begin pulling dryer, or plywood core.

For days I was deluged with information on wood grades and pulling techniques, and fatigued by the grueling physical labor. Eight-foot by three-foot strips of plywood core surged by the four bins in my charge. Even if I were able to read the grades, which I wasn't, or to pull all the wood and place it into the appropriate bins, which I couldn't, I still achieved full aerobic conditioning in the first ten minutes of each fatigu-ing shift.

Technique was everything. The wood was simply too heavy, too fast, and much too fragile to manhandle off the line. Corners of perfect-grade wood tore in my grip, altering their quality and changing their grade. My inability to slide the wood smoothly through my gloves, or snap it into the corner of the cart, found me splitting it on the floor, the cart poles, and even into other strips of wood. Frustration consumed me. Refocusing my attention from ferreting out drugs to learning the job at hand became paramount.

One day, about three weeks into my new shift, I actually felt comfortable enough to look up from the chain. What I saw next was completely incongruent with this entire godforsaken environment. She was totally miscast, and she had just interrupted my concentration—something highly discouraged in a plywood mill, I assure you.

Without looking, I flipped the corner of a low-grade piece of pine, getting air beneath the wood, and snapped it along the rails of the bin as I was taught. What I didn't do, however, was keep it away from my body. Although I was wearing more than adequate protection, a large sliver—if a pencil-size hunk of wood could be termed a sliver—ripped through my forearm and exited from the side.

"Oh, boy," I uttered, trying to remain composed. "Sliver!" I yelled, as I was taught. The line was immediately shut down and the remaining pullers spread out to cover my bins. If the line were shut down for too long a period, the wood flowing through the oven could eventually catch fire.

"What's wrong?" Stan, a hyper, thirty-something dryer tender, asked.

"This." I showed him the wound.

"Fuck. How the hell'd that happen?"

I had no answer. "Follow me," he directed, leading me across the building, blood dripping from my sleeve. Everyone seemed to take notice, so I smiled through the agony.

I waited in the First Aid Room, wondering why I wasn't being rushed to the hospital. "So, what happened to you?" a short man whom I had never seen before, asked.

The obvious nature of my problem precluded an answer once again. After all, I was pulling wood, in a wood mill made of wood, and I had a hunk of wood protruding from my arm.

"Let's see what we can do here." He casually removed a jackknife from his back pocket, dipped it ever so briefly in a jar of alcohol, and began boring a cavern into my arm. As the knife foraged far beneath my skin, a cold sweat painted my face white. The digging went on and on for about forty-five minutes, and the pain was almost unbearable. The occasional glance at my skin being lifted and separated from the attached tissue like a bruised apple had me seriously reconsidering my latest career move.

"Just a little more," he said for the umpteenth time.

"Just leave the rest in me," I pleaded meekly. "Really, it's okay."

"Don't get squeamish on me. I've almost got it all."

"Uh-huh."

By the time he finished, he had retrieved all but a small piece, a piece that remains with me to this day.

When I went to remove my T-shirt at home that evening, it mysteriously snagged at my waist. A sharp sting told me something I didn't want to know. The sliver in my arm paled in comparison to the dagger protruding from my stomach. Lacking the proper instruments to extract the wood effectively, I grabbed the only tool in my studio apartment that had the ability to grip: a rusty pair of fingernail clippers. The curved surface is appropriately designed to cut fingernails but not the flat—at least at that time—surface of my stomach. The clippers were so sharp that I butchered the surrounding skin each time I pulled at the deep sliver. My skin formed a one-inch teepee as I pulled one last time at the pesky splinter. The anticipated half-inch sliver grew to almost two inches and had penetrated straight into my stomach—no angles here.

When I called in my nightly report to the home office in California, I referenced the injury, adding that I was concerned about possible exposure to HIV and AIDS. The next day, when my supervisor, Gordon Stiller, read the transcripts from my report, he said not to worry and that the practice of removing slivers in this manner was not a legal liability issue. As a caveat, he asked that I not write any more reports on the subject. In hindsight, I see that this was but the first in a long line of politically driven decisions at the expense of safety, equitable treatment of employees, and ethics.

These daily reports were uniform in nature, their categories stemming from a long list of events the operative was supposed to scrutinize, such as safety, use of profanity, alcohol consumption, harassment, theft, poor management, and of course the sale and use of illicit substances. The unscrupulous operative, I soon discovered, would fabricate events in order to avoid a reduction in his bonus at the end of each case. For every missed or partial report, an operative's bonus was cut by ten percent. Since the average case involved approximately six to seven hundred events, false reporting was inevitable. This particular case in Medford, by the way, was code-named "Sawdust, Case number 601950010."

Another week passed. One day at the mill Stan screamed out, "Bucchi! Yeah, you," he called. I reacted like any bewildered greenhorn would. "We've got a tie-up on Dryer Four! Lend a hand!"

Tie-ups were caused by drying wood that crumbled as it passed through the dryer rollers, causing all wood aft of the clog to bunch up behind it.

"Yes, sir!" I saluted smartly, exhibiting just the right measure of timidity.

Only days before this I was sent to the mill's life center, where wood in all stages of degradation was transformed into the fuel that powered the mill, and, for that matter, part of the town. I was instructed by Harry to get a "bucket of steam" for one of the dryers that was on the fritz. Supposedly this was used to restart dryer motors that stood idle for extended periods of time. Something sounded odd about the request, but then again, everything was odd about this place.

When a grave-looking man handed me an ordinary-looking bucket with a bolted-on lid, I became even more suspicious. He shoved it in my face and said crassly, "Be careful. If this top comes off," he slapped his hand down upon it, "your face'll look like a sausage and pepperoni pizza."

There is a strange psychology at work in such situations. You're more uncomfortable with questioning the ridiculous nature of the request than you are about being made the fool. I went along.

In order to return to the main mill, I was compelled to walk down a tunnel system that submerged beneath the parking lot into the mill's underbelly. Although this added the new element of fear to my situation, it also provided me enough time to better assess it. Gingerly turning back the bolts, I lifted the top. Of course, nothing happened. Even as I write these words, I realize how silly I must have appeared just taking the bucket from the man in the first place. Standing there all alone, I nonetheless felt embarrassed—for myself. But still, there is something to be said for being new that can make such silliness possible, even probable.

I stormed up the stairs leading to the mill, my shirt covering my face, screaming that I had been badly burned. My thespian skills must have been highly polished back then, because several people charged to my aid, causing me much guilt. However, one of those concerned philanthropists made the deception worth perpetrating. When Harry peeled back the shirt from my face, his expression told me all that I needed to know—we were even. And with all the witnesses, most laughing hysterically, I knew that I had made great strides toward acceptance in that place.

When I responded to Stan's orders this time to assist on the dryer problem, I was handed a long pole with a grappling hook at its tip. The object was to latch on to the snarled wood and rip it from the dryer, and in so doing clear a path for the backed-up core. Seemed legitimate enough.

When the colossal dryer doors were thrust open, steam poured out, cloaking the immediate area in a cloud of gray. The initiation party slipped into the veiling precipitation in a predatory manner. Several pairs of hands gripped me like a vice. I wrestled with them momentarily until the voice of futility sobered me. They removed my protective arm guard and pressed my forearm to the metal oven rail, studying me as the skin sizzled. I knew that to cry, scream, or call out for help would make my stay here one of struggle and frustration. So I grinned and grunted, but never once pleaded, concentrating only on the number of dollars this torture would cost my company and on the faces of my assailants.

Returning to the chain was hard enough without the pain and the charred skin, but now, because the dryer doors had been left open for so long, the wood spewed out heavy and wet. I could feel my tacky skin stretch and tear beneath what I had thought was a natural fiber. I was wrong. Turns out the shirt I was wearing was made from petroleum-based synthetic fibers.

"Oh, my God," Tari, the beautiful woman who had distracted me only days earlier, sympathized. "What happened to your arm?"

"It's nothing. I snagged it on the dryer."

"You're not the first, and you certainly won't be the last, I'm afraid. How many did it take to help you get it snagged?"

"Half the shift, I think."

*   *   *

Tari was remarkably beautiful for a mill worker and the best dryer puller on the chain. Beneath the leather apron, nylon-mesh arm guards, and double-ply leather gloves lay a woman of tenacious independence and rugged femininity. If she had a vice, it was her lust for money and those who possessed it. Such a disclaimer would deter any respectable gentleman of wealth but attracted the likes of me, as I considered it an opportunity lying in wait.

I was assigned to this dryer, Dryer Four, on a permanent basis, sporadically assisting Dryer Three (heavy wood), which faced us, whenever help was needed. Although the dryer I was assigned to generally had a smaller variety of wood, it was by no means easier. In fact, the speed at which the wood spat from the dryer to the chain had most workers clamoring to be placed on any dryer but Dryer Four. Those who didn't request a change were typically *blazers* (speed addicts). Indeed, it seemed that only those soaring on speed could keep up with the frenzied pace.

Four to five people were assigned to our dryer per shift, depending on the speed of the wood. Three were pulling dryer and the remainder were left to assist the feeders. My immediate co-workers, who I would later discover were both using and dealing large quantities of crystal, were as follows:

Shannon, a tall, red-haired woman in her early thirties, was somewhat emaciated, and she could be sweet and personable one moment and downright vicious the next. She was brash in every sense of the word.

Melba was the physical, mental, and emotional antithesis of Tari. She was extremely butch, with short hair and a stout physique, and almost always spiteful. A quick visit to the bathroom, however, generally remedied that little character flaw.

Bob Adams, with two DUIs under his belt and one more on the way, was perfectly suited for Melba, the woman he regularly committed adultery with. Aside from Tari, he was the best puller on the line and the easiest to get along with. His adroit sense of humor made him a pleasure to work with but a bitch to spy on.

On Dryer Three was an eclectic group of people who defied most initial impressions. First there was Phil Haggle, a speed freak who would volunteer for the front of the chain just to avoid overdosing on crank. You see, the person at the front of the chain was rotated every time he or she completed a cart because of the grueling nature of the work. Besides counteracting a speed overdose with a depressant such as alcohol, a person could avoid the adverse side effects, such as aneurysms and strokes, by maintaining a high aerobic heart rate. So in between breaks, when he would drink beer in his truck, Phil would find other ways of limiting his risk, such as working harder. Not a bad side effect for Boise Cascade, wouldn't you say?

Phil was also an habitual liar and moocher. And when he spoke to you, he invariably mumbled. I suppose it was a habit born out of constantly saying things that were either offensive or illegal.

Chief, a nickname affectionately given to a hefty Native American named Tony, had an uncanny ability to chant, dance, and pull wood all at the same time. When I first met him, I found him to be obnoxious, crude, and defamatory, but I would later discover these were only some of the qualities that made him so endearing. Under the caviling humor and misogynistic personality he was a real Teddy Bear at heart.

Rick, who was arguably the biggest thug I have ever met, was a six-foot, three-inch tall, 250-pound mass of browbeating. His physical prowess was matched only by his perpetual jealousy of Shannon, his constant snorting of crank, and, lest I forget, his certifiable paranoia. I always knew when he was at the front of the chain, even before I would look up. He snapped eight-foot strips of raw plywood core against the back of the metal cart so hard it sounded like a thoroughbred's hooves striking a firm track in sharp cadence.

The only female on Dryer Three was an insecure, arrogant drug dealer by the name of Linda, who had enough chutzpa to fill the Gaza Strip. She was oddly pretty, with chiseled features that made her appear cold, if not hardened. She distrusted me from the beginning, leading me to believe she had something to hide. Although I swore to never stoop to this level, I have to admit that I deliberately targeted her for termination. I not only saw it as my duty, but essential to my self-preservation. It became personal, and when that happens you can't settle for a draw. She went from despising me as a potential narc to fearing me as the competition.

During the early stages of the investigation, these were the main players.

Chapter 4

"I'll never learn this damn job," I shouted over the suffocating noise, pretending to be frustrated with my inability to master the task at hand. I hurled several pieces of perfectly good wood to the concrete floor, the resultant racket drawing attention from everyone within earshot. Cheers and jeers rose above the normal fracas of the mill.

Such behavior could be punished by termination, and because only a few executives knew my true identity, I wasn't immune to this disciplinary action. However, the threat of termination weighed less heavily on me than the desire to make a big first impression.

Shannon cursed me from across the chain, expressing strong dissatisfaction with my performance. I understood that teamwork was key to this whole operation, but I was new, and expected some consideration. Regardless, this was another opportunity for me to set the playing field.

"What did you say to me?" I hollered.

"You heard me, you fuckin' lame-ass sonofabitch! I'm tired of catching your leftovers!"

I immediately stopped pulling the wood and allowed it to swamp her at the end of the chain, where it was her responsibility to pull whatever Tari and I missed. Tari wasn't one to miss a scrap of wood, though. She continued to pull her grades without skipping a beat, glancing up occasionally to see what it was I was doing.

Shannon ranted and raved all the way to the front of the chain, bowling past me to press the emergency shut-off button. By now, wood was buckled and tangled at the end of the chain, hanging over the edge on both sides and looking much like the wings of an airplane immediately after impact with the side of a mountain.

"What the fuck is wrong with you?" she continued to rant.

"I'm fine," I said, trying to remain even-tempered. "How 'bout yourself?"

After she launched into a loquacious unchained medley of obscenities, I backed her against the chain, placing my lips close to hers. "If you ever pretend to tell me what to do again, *bitch*," I said, with the appropriate pregnant pause, "I'll have you fucked up so bad the coroner's chalk mark'll be a straight line."

To accentuate my point, I thumped her in the head with my fingers, which were formed into the shape of a pistol. "So take that Gumby ass you call a figure to the end of the chain and clean up your *fuckin' mess*!"

I was in Oregon, a place where any drug dealer worth his salt wouldn't be caught dead getting pushed around by a woman. I harbored no fantasies about this line of work. I either learned to become a drug dealer or I failed—the mantra of the UCI. And failure was not an option. For me, the only difficult thing was remembering who I was when speaking to my mom. The word *fuck* often became *fuckryin' out loud* when talking to her on the phone.

"Fuck you," she shouted for the sake of our captive audience. "I'll have *you* taken out! Do you know who my father is, asshole?"

I discovered that her father was the supervisor of the day shift. I would later take advantage of her threat by accusing her of *narc*ing on me. It was always wise to appear more fearful of narcs than the real dealers were fearful of you. Accusing others made you appear paranoid, like someone with much to hide.

Amid her verbal onslaught, I leaped aboard a piece of plywood core traveling rapidly down the chain. Mimicking a surfer, I was whisked to the end of the chain. The entire area erupted with applause, reaching a crescendo as I hurdled the pile of wood that had collected at the end of the chain and landed firmly with both feet on the concrete floor. With not so much as a genuflection to my appreciative audience, I trotted back over to Shannon and faced off with her once again, further intimidating her into capitulation.

I soon moved to the rear of the chain. Workers were typically able to talk to one another, provided they weren't at the front of the chain, where the rapidity of the job precluded conversation.

"You're doin' fine," Tari shouted over the deafening noise as she demonstrated the proper way to pull dryer. "Don't listen to that hag! If anyone gives you a hard time, tell 'em to cram it! Hey! I trained most of these idiots! Including her! Don't let her tell you she picked it up with ease! She didn't! None of 'em did!"

After some small talk, or, as it were, small shout, and some obligatory flirtation, I decided to set the wheels in motion. "You know, it's kinda hard to talk in here! Wanna go for a drink after work?"

"Sure! Meet me in the parking lot at the end of the shift!"

*   *   *

On my way out the mill at the end of my shift, I was greeted by Rick. His bulging eyes said all I needed to know. "What's this shit I hear about you and my girl?" His eyes were full of rage.

"The way I hear it, she ain't your girl no more. And even if she were, it's between her and me. Now move your fat ass!"

He smiled and placed his hand on my shoulder, digging his thumb under my collarbone as a means of demonstrating his brute strength. It was an effective demonstration. I spun my arm around his like a snake striking a rodent, countering with a claw grip to his throat. Personally, I've always found that a throat hold is best because it compels your opponent to react defensively before he can counter.

I released my hold quickly, not wanting to force him into a fight. He raised his hands in a defensive posture, mouthing words of assault, but never attacked. I stood, arms at my sides, and stared through him. I was convinced that he was merely a mirage of intimidation. I brushed past him without confrontation. No one saw the incident, so he was not obliged to pursue me. It was a successful confrontation as I gained some of his respect but not all of his animosity.

Torrential rains drenched the midnight air when I met Tari in the dimly lit parking lot on the south side of the mill. "Jump in," she invited.

"Damn, it's comin' down! So where to?"

"Dilligaf's. Know where it is?"

"No. But I'll follow you." I ran to my car and proceeded to follow her to one of the mill workers' local hangouts. Dilligaf's was purportedly owned by two lesbians and got its name from the cliché-turned-acronym, "Do I Look Like I Give A Fuck?" Although a place where uncouth mill workers slammed down grotesque amounts of alcohol and gambled away paychecks at the pool tables, Dilligaf's had a strict rule against the use of profanity. When I walked in, I was taken aback by the tidiness of the bar and the cordiality of its patrons.

"So," Tari greeted me. "Whatta ya think?"

"I like it. I really do. You play?" I invited her to a game of pool. The experiences of my misspent youth paid untold dividends when it came to creating a credible cover, and pool was always at the center of that ruse. Any drug dealer worth his salt could shoot a good stick, and I, when I was on my game, was unbeatable, especially when the stakes were high.

"Not very good," she answered sweetly. "But I'll shoot you some stick."

I knelt to extract the pool balls from the well at the end of the table and asked, while peeking above the cushion, "So, Tari? Where's a guy go around here to combat the slumbers?"

Something about the way she gazed at me told me I could move more quickly with her. She nervously twisted her stick like a Boy Scout attempting to make a spark as she leaned her chin over the felt tip. She bore a look of distrust, squinting and smirking as she pondered the genuineness of my seemingly innocuous question. "I don't do any of that shit anymore."

"Glad to hear it, but that's not what I asked."

"I don't run in those circles any longer, so I don't know the players."

"But ya do know the circles?"

"How do I know you're not Five-O?"

"Because a cop wouldn't use words of entrapment. Hey. Don't worry about it. No big. I'll find out myself."

"No," she replied, switching gears abruptly. "It's okay. I just wanted you to know . . . well, you know. You can't take chances these days."

I escorted her to an adjacent table, leaving the balls scattered about the slate in mid-game, and ordered a couple of beers. "It's simple, Tari. I watch all the "Cops" type shows and study them intently. I know all the do's and all the don'ts. I'm in this . . ."

She quickly interrupted, "Name some."

"Some what?"

"Some of the do's and don'ts."

"Okay." I shook my head repeatedly while I gathered my thoughts. "Sure. Okay, let me think here. Yeah. Okay, here we go. First of all, never make a buy in a bar parking lot. Or an empty lot, for that matter." I began by bending the truth in my favor. A packed parking lot was preferable for the authorities because it allowed for easier concealment of a surveillance team.

"Never conduct business at your residence. Not only do most of the arrests on "Cops" occur in the home, but that opens the door for them to seize property in the process." If the mill's drug dealers thought I had a major problem with conducting drug deals out of my home, it would likely cut down on the number of unwelcome people who would show up on my doorstep unannounced.

"Always buy small, and buy often, instead of large one-timers." I knew that the mill was out to catch as many people as possible selling and using drugs. The money being spent was theirs, so they wanted the biggest bang for their buck.

"You take more chances that way, don'tcha?" she suggested.

"In some ways, but the penalty's much smaller."

"Okay. I suppose."

I could see the gears churning in her head. She was looking for reasons to trust me. "Make the other guy use words of entrapment," I continued. "Make them say they're not a cop." It was a common misconception among dealers that such things would taint an arrest.

"Uh-huh. I've heard that. Sure."

"Good." I nodded. "Never use the drugs in their presence." I thought to myself, a buyer who didn't use was always suspect, so I had to preempt their trepidation.

"You're gonna have trouble with that. It makes people real nervous when . . ."

"Fuck 'em," I spouted off before lowering my voice again. "Fuck 'em. I'm not goin' to jail because someone's too stupid to realize that Five-O will snort with 'em one moment and arrest 'em the next. 'Cause they will. You can bet your ass on it. They will. Happens all the time."

"That's true. I've known people who have . . ."

"Anyhow. Where was I? Oh, yeah. Be more open than secretive." I realized that I had little time to begin making buys, so I could not appear as cautious as one might expect a prudent dealer to be under the same circumstances.

"Why would you want . . . ?"

"People whispering draw more attention than someone yelling. At least in this business."

"Ain't that the truth."

"And most important, make the buy at your place of work. On "Cops," you never see anyone busted at the worksite. Let's face it, it'd be a huge hassle to set up a sting on private property. And think of the cost to put a cop undercover in a company for months at a time." For obvious reasons, the company could not fire the dealers unless the deal was initiated or consummated at the worksite.

"You speak well for a mill worker," she analyzed.

"While I was in the Air Force I completed three years of college on the taxpayer's dime. I came here so I could earn enough money to complete my degree in a year. If I'd have stayed in the service, I would have owed them another three years."

"So what's in it for you? Recreational use?" She turned her bottle upward, keeping one eye on me.

"Money, pure and simple. I have a shitload of Air Force buddies in California that I used to deal crank to, and I can turn several ounces a month with them."

"Is that how you can afford that little Targa?" I'm still not sure why, but her pretending to know, and yet not knowing, the model of Porsche I drove seemed to say a lot about who she was, and led me to believe that such a pretense could be usurped for my own benefit.

"It's actually a cabriolet, but that's not important."

"What's that?"

"Nothing. Yeah. That's how I can afford it."

"Why would they come all the way up here for the stuff if they could just buy it down there?"

"Ahhhh." I drew my head back and then quickly snapped it forward. With my face mere inches from hers, I continued, "You've asked the million-dollar question. If they get caught on a drug charge, it's ten years in Leavenworth. In the military, drug crimes are federal offenses. No slaps on the wrist. They can't risk trying to find another source, what with the OSI running around and everything. And therein lies the beauty. They're more than happy to pay me three times what the shit's worth."

The OSI, or Office of Special Investigations, is the Air Force equivalent of the Drug Enforcement Administration (DEA) and the Internal
Revenue Service (IRS) all rolled into one. They operate autonomously
from the rest of the Air Force, often IRS-like, without regard for due
process or fair play. Extraneous detail tended to convey a sense of legiti-
macy, so I provided her this take on the OSI.

"Sounds like you've got it all under control. So why do you need me?"

"I thought I'd explained all that."

"Explain it again. I don't wanna get in any trouble."

"I know. And you won't. I just wanna lead. I don't want you involved
in any way, shape, or form."

"Do you know Carcass?" she blurted.

"Who?"

"Carcass. Ahh, ya know, Ahhrr. . . . Renalto Sisson. Works over on the
Spreaders." The Spreaders were located in the "finish end" of the mill
where the core shot through long spinning rods laced with glue, reminiscent of a newspaper printing press. The resultant core was then laid between sheets of wood by a hypercoordinated individual who slapped the
core down, arranging it like pieces of a puzzle to form the final product.
Just as this core was set into place, two other Spreaders swung another
piece of wood over the layer's head and the process was immediately repeated. A good team could produce a piece of plywood every six seconds.
It was arguably the most strenuous job in the mill.

"He's real thin. Hence the name Carcass."

"Oh, yeah." My brows floated up my forehead. "I've seen him. Kind of
anorexic, right? Real speed freak, huh?"

"Big time."

"He doesn't mind being called Carcass?"

"No. I mean, yeah. Of course he would. Which is why we call him
Caracas, instead. At least to his face. It's kind of a running joke, sorta. We
call him Caracas, but we really mean Carcass. He thinks it's a compliment
'cause his friends tell 'im it's a real cool place to live in Venezuela. And it
doesn't hurt that Venezuela's in South America. You know, cocaine. I don't
know; it's weird. It's just one of those things that stuck and now we sorta
don't even think about why we call him that. If he gained fifty pounds,
we'd probably still be callin' him Caracas."

"Caracas, huh? I kinda like that. Invite him out after work Saturday. I'll bump into you two here. We'll shoot some pool, drink some beer, et cetera, et cetera." I patted myself on the chest and added, "I'll take it from there. If it goes well, I'll compensate you for the information."

"No! No, you won't. I don't want anything to do with this. The only reason I'm helping you is because you're not like the rest of the slugs at the mill."

"Oh, yeah? How's that?" I giggled, considering the absurdity of the notion that I was somehow better in view of the fact that I was posing as a drug dealer.

"You're not a mill rat. You're educated, and you're not gonna let yourself rot here."

"Personally, I don't see anything wrong with working in a mill. It sure beats the hell outta the lazy bastards who want the government to give 'em everything. I don't think anyone has to apologize for working hard. How do you think all the houses get built in this fair nation of ours? It's honorable work, if you ask me." I defended the mill against her low self-esteem and false pride, which were at work in the suggestion that I was somehow too good for the mill. *She* was working there, yet she was only a year from her Masters degree. She wanted to hear from another so-called educated person that the work at the mill was admirable, so I capitalized on the opportunity to solidify her trust. I not only built upon our fledgling friendship but, by disagreeing with her, made her feel more confident in my veracity.

This was undoubtedly the toughest part of the job for me, yet the part I was best at. I could build legitimate friendships with a variety of people under completely false pretenses. The irony was that I would have to someday betray that very trust I so intimately created. A dreaded necessity, especially in the case of Tari.

The following evening, I arrived at Dilligaf's about an hour after Caracas and Tari. "Tari," I began as I tapped her on the shoulder. "How's it goin'?"

"Hey, Ken. You look good. I wish I lived so close to work that I could go home and shower before goin' out." She then swiveled about. "Say, have you met Caracas?"

"No. At least I don't think so. God, I've met so many people since coming here."

"Well," she began, "Ken, Renalto. Caracas, Ken."

"Do you prefer Carcass or Renalto," I asked.

He let out a light, airy laugh. "It's Caracas, not Carcass."

"As in the city?"

"Yeah, as in the city," he said with obvious discomfort. His eyes rolled up into his head, as it appeared he considered the similarities in these words for the first time.

"So? Which do you prefer?"

"Doesn't matter. You shoot pool?" he asked politely. Caracas had a feminine quality to him, barely detectable, but there. He was an anomaly of sorts, emaciated and pseudointellectual, performing a job that should have had the motto "Only the brawny and profane need apply."

"You're terrible," Tari said with a snicker as she brushed past me.

"Occasionally," I responded to Caracas's offer to play some pool. "Why, you wanna put up on a table?"

"Sure. We can shoot these guys in partners if you'd like."

"Sounds good! I'm always looking for places to invest my money. Especially where there's an assured and profitable return," I boisterously insinuated.

"You must be pretty good to be so confident."

"My money never goes anywhere if I haven't considered all the potential pitfalls. Take these chumps, for instance. They haven't run more than three or four balls in a row, yet they're putting on a big show with their superficial attempts at impossible shots. No one's laughing at 'em, so I'm assuming this place's full of chumps. Look at 'em. They have yet to set up a second shot. We'll beat 'em like a red-headed stepdaughter."

Caracas looked at me curiously, attempting to glean the hidden message. A cat-and-mouse game ensued, with both of us bobbing and weaving our way through the turnstiles. "So?" Caracas probed. "What's your best advice for short-term investments?"

An opening, I thought. "There's a mill filled with people being made to work at an insane pace. I'd kinda like to tap into the resources that facilitate it. Know what I mean?"

"You sound awfully bright for . . ."

". . . a mill worker. Yeah, I know. So I've been told." I threw a smile toward Tari. She returned the gesture. "I'm getting my degree. I'm only one year short of my bachelor's . . ." I continued to explain as I had with Tari.

Caracas strolled over to the bar and grabbed a bowl of popcorn, spinning the stool before he sat down. "I know lots of people," he chuntered with a mouthful of corn. "I can be of some help. There's an underground network, but you don't get in without an invitation."

"I sure need one of those, 'cause I don't know who to trust. I've heard that the mill has narcs tryin' to bust everyone," I said, sounding paranoid.

"That rumor's been floatin' around for years. They just say that to scare everyone. Don't worry, I know alotta the bosses who do crank. That bitch that gave you a hard time . . ."

"Which one?" I said in a sarcastic tone, turning my back to the bar and laying my elbows on the counter. My black leather trench coat parted, revealing the handle of my Colt '45 automatic. Only Caracas could see it, so I wasn't concerned about getting into trouble.

"Shannon," he answered with concern in his throat. His eyes volleyed nervously between the gun and his Budweiser before I dropped my arms and closed up the jacket.

My response was perfunctory, as though I was unaware of his discovery. "Oh, her."

"Yeah. Yeah! Her father's a real blazer, dude."

"How do ya know . . ."

"I used to date her."

"My condolences."

"Thanks. Hey, look. I can put you in with the right people. I'm pretty connected," he said as though he were attempting to impress me. "You know a guy named Phil Haggle?"

"I know *of* him."

"He's in tight with a guy named Rick. Big red-headed dude on Dryer Three. Know him?"

"We've met." My optimism was fading fast.

"Well, get to. Phil won't move without Rick says so."

"Gotcha. Thanks, dude."

We played several games of pool and never once lost. By night's end, we were up about eighty dollars apiece. I billed four hours of overtime and my drinking expenses back to the client nonetheless. Hey, I don't make the rules.

*   *   *

A week passed and still there was no buy. My supervisor, Gordon, was breathing down my neck almost daily. His favorite line, "You gotta get close to these guys," reverberated in my head twenty-four hours a day.

Even though my contract stated that bonuses were based upon such things as good attendance and accurate reporting, Gordon made it crystal clear that they were not. Drug dealers and users were the main staple, and all that mattered to Krout and Schneider.

Over the next couple of weeks, I made a point of squaring things with Shannon. She was my surest avenue to Rick, and he, my best bet with Phil. After some early stomach-wrenching conversations, I actually began to find Shannon's company quite entertaining.

*　　*　　*

It was Friday night and Shannon was in true form. With virtually every sentence two feet below the gutter, it was easy to see what preoccupied her mind. She knew that I had become quite chummy with Tari, whom she despised, but it had no effect on the volume of sexual innuendoes she heaped on each conversation.

During a rare lull in the action, I chitchatted with Shannon. "Why aren't there any women working on the Spreaders?" I was attempting to steer the conversation toward more relevant matters, such as sexual discrimination, for instance.

She slid her rear end along the chain in front of me and spit a sunflower seed at my feet. "Because no woman wants to be called a Spreader. Except for me, of course. I spread like fuckin' peanut butter," she flouted without humility. "Plus they have this initiation thing that goes on for about a month where they grab the new guy's crotch all through the shift. Everyone here 'cept me thinks that sucks. I call those two things fringe benefits. I'd work there in a heartbeat if the work weren't so fucked up. *Man* is it fucked up."

While I shook my head and laughed, she added, "You goin' to Mutts tonight?" Mutts was another local bar conveniently located near the mill.

"You?" I asked.

"Sure. Rick'll probably be there, though."

"So."

"Yeah!" She smiled like a shark. "So fucking big deal, right?"

"I may be a bit late, so wait for me."

"Why? Gotta make a score?" Although she spoke in jest, I was well aware that it was common for a user to feel out potential new sources.

I was equally vague. "It's gonna be a long weekend."

She wiped the perspiration from her forehead. "Good shit?"

"I wish I knew. I'm not even sure I can trust the dude. To be honest, I hate dealin' with people I don't work with."

She moved in tight. "Why's that, stuuuddd?"

"If someone you work with doesn't show up for a couple days," I paused and bobbed my head back and forth, "unexpectedly like, you can just bet if he tries to sell ya some crank, he's wired. Probably strikin' some sort of fuckin' deal with the pigs."

"So why the hell you doin' it?"

" 'Cause no one round here has the balls to sell me *shit*."

"And *he* does?"

"I didn't say he was a *he*. And anyhow, he's an idiot."

Torrents of air exploded intermittently from her nose as she attempted to control her laughter. "Go with me right from work," she insisted, smacking me on the upper thigh. "I'll fix ya up. I've got testicles like medicine balls."

She was wise. She knew that I wasn't wearing a wire at work, it was much too loud and far too dangerous. So if I left straight from work—no wire.

I had no other choice but to accept her offer. To do otherwise would have set the investigation back months and destroyed any credibility I might have already established. She also realized that I was new in town and that whoever sold to me first would likely become my steady supplier.

Tari was on her day off, so I didn't feel that my slipping out to the local dive with one of her enemies would have any negative repercussions.

This was one of the more tricky aspects of corporate investigations. Unlike law enforcement officers, I had to buy drugs from as many employees as possible. Once I had enough evidence to terminate an employee, it made no sense to continue spending the client's money. It would be overkill. Buying from the competition when your main supplier was treating you right may have made smart fiscal sense, but it made no sense to dealers who were selling you good dope. Buyers tended to reduce their exposure by dealing with as few people as possible. Only a narc wouldn't fear the risk, because, for a narc, there was no risk. So if I planned to buy

from Tari or any of her friends in the future, I would have to come up with
a good line. If I didn't, they would soon be drawing lines around me on
the sidewalk.

Mutts was located less than two miles from the mill, down a dark,
twisting road. My Porsche stood out like the sorest of thumbs in a parking
lot full of shotgun-toting pickup trucks. The one-story bar was merely a
shed for storing alcohol, pool tables, and poker machines. As I walked
through the cratered parking lot, the door of a large blue pickup truck
swung open in my path. Somewhat startled, I pitched sideways.

"Hey!" Shannon greeted.

"Damn, girl! 'Bout gave me a heart attack."

"Here," she said nonchalantly, placing a small bindle—a small, spe-
cially folded piece of paper containing narcotics—into my shirt pocket.

"What's that?"

"Blaze. Shhhh." She twitched her head about like a game hen.

"No shit. I mean how much?"

"Later. Not here."

I followed her into the bar, ever cognizant that I wasn't operating under the sanctity of law. I couldn't refuse the speed for obvious reasons, but
I couldn't report it either. Although I had been given guidelines for making uncontrolled purchases of small quantities of narcotics, an exchange
of money was necessary to constitute a sale. As it was, I was now unlaw-
fully in possession of illegal narcotics.

If a sale had taken place, I was required to lock the drugs in a container
that JACNET had provided to me weeks earlier, and for which I had no
key. I kept this secure box unlocked in the trunk of my car and therefore
had to be alone to open it to avoid detection.

Once the drugs were secure, I would call Bud, my liaison in Medford,
and he in turn would immediately contact JACNET. I would then meet
with the task force in some clandestine location where I would turn over
the drugs along with copious notes of the incident. This procedure was
authorized only when it was impossible to avoid: when faced with life-
threatening situations, when drugs were stuffed into a pocket, when contacting the task force was too risky, or while at work. And only in the
beginning, when establishing my credibility was paramount, outweighing
any potential legal complications.

After a few very impressive pool games that seemed to sway Rick in my favor, he reached over my shoulder with an icy Budweiser and said, "This one's for you, New York." Although my accent is more in keeping with my roots, Massachusetts, everyone at the mill seemed to think the eastern seaboard was ninety percent New York City and ten percent Florida. I let it slide, believing that he preferred to be right more than accurate.

"What's happening, big man?" I nourished his fragile ego.

"You shoot a mean stick. You and I could win us a heap of dough, couldn't we?" I knew what he meant to say was that I could win him a heap, but of course I played along.

"Let's get some pairs goin', then." I bounced the rubber end of my stick off the floor and reached for the chalk. "Next!" I announced, knowing the egos would come flocking if a *New Yorker* challenged them.

After polishing off five straight tables, Rick and I stood side by side near the table and guzzled to our success. Then, without provocation, two young guys, neither taller than 5'9", rudely plowed through us and headed for the opposite end of the table. Rick's eyes distended. I was sure he would attack, but he didn't. He tossed me some line about being on probation, so I took it at face value and forgave their bad manners. After they intimidated the next two players in line, they racked the balls and became our next victims.

"Okay. Now stick it [the rack] up there again and do it right this time," I said to the one who had just racked the balls.

"How 'bout I stick you up there and do you right, faggot," he sneered, standing directly behind the racked balls at the end of the table. He made whimpering noises in my direction as though suggesting I was afraid.

"I don't get it. I'm a pile of sticks?"

After a prolonged vacant stare one scoffed ineptly, "Fuck you, bitch."

"Fornicated Use of Carnal Knowledge of a female canine? You're either very desperate or possess no English skills whatsoever."

"One more fucking word . . ."

Rick put his drink down and appeared to ready himself for action. I was confident that he would cover my backside, and my front side for that matter, if something were to happen.

I knelt to the table in my normal stance for breaking the balls, which loaded excessive topspin on the shiny cue ball. With one fell swoop, I sent the cue ball careening across the worn felt and into the racked balls. The rack parted like the Red Sea, sending the pearly white sphere hurtling into the air to greet my opponent's perfectly positioned testicles.

"So let it be written," I said mockingly. "So let it be done."

He buckled like a switchblade, to the pleasure of all who watched. Except for his partner, that is. He instead opted to avenge his friend's misfortune by taking on Rick. Giving up eighty pounds and a whole lot of common sense, he attacked with flailing fists.

When I saw Rick recoil into a protective posture, I grabbed the guy by the back of the head and slammed it into an unpadded wooden beam. He collapsed like an imploded building. To my astonishment, he attempted to regain his feet before the bartender and doorman could shake him to his senses. With the regular patrons, mostly Boise employees, vocally demonstrating their partisanship, the two punks were rudely escorted through a partially open door.

After stuffing twenty bucks into the rear pocket of Shannon's jeans and listening to a couple more hours of depraved conversation, Rick and I left in his truck for the local strip bar. That was our intended destination, anyhow. Instead, he spent the next two hours wallowing in the mire of his lost love while I listened and advised. Strangely enough, I felt compelled to help him. As would become my habit, I began taking personal interest in the people I would later help to indict. I suppose I saw them as two separate and distinct issues.

After saying good-bye to Rick, I called Bud and had him contact JACNET.

Bud was a genuinely good and moral man to the core. He was a seventy-year-old veteran of World War II and a hero of the Army Air Corps. He grew up in a time when very few people dealt in illicit drugs, and when they did, a kilo of anything was tantamount to a conspiracy on the scale of the French Connection. This innocence, coupled with his regimented past, caused him to take this stuff a bit too seriously. Surreptitious meetings in crowded parking lots with wires, guns, and talk of drug dealers only tended to exacerbate his already overactive sense of 007.

This didn't change his effectiveness, though. In fact, my diminished sense of secrecy struck a good balance with him and his hypersecretive wife, who happened to be a very hospitable host and a fine cook to boot. Bud contacted Joe and had him meet with me at 2:00 A.M.

I met Joe in an empty parking lot of the local "everything store" called

Fred Meyer's. I pulled alongside his Ford Taurus, which was parked at the side of the building. My headlights recessed back into the hood as I slid my car in close to his passenger door. Considering the remote possibility that someone saw me, it would appear as though I was making a score.

"Hey, guy," Joe greeted. "Whatcha got for me?"

"Didn't Bud tell ya?"

"He wasn't sure, exactly. Said something about you being all shook up."

"Shook up?" I blurted. "No. It's just a small bindle. She charged me twenty bucks."

"Who's she?"

"Shannon."

"The one you've been writing about in your reports? The loose one?"

"That's her. She just slipped it into my pocket and said, 'Here you go.'"

"You didn't discuss prices before this?"

"You kidding? She's hardly touched the subject. Prior to this evening, the strongest substance she's talked about is Excedrin. So, no. No. This caught me completely off guard."

"That's good. She's beginning to trust you, then. When ya supposed to pay for it?"

"Already did. I wasn't about to let her claim she just gave me the shit. I gave her a twenty right then and there." I stretched the truth somewhat so as not to lose the essence of what had actually transpired.

Bending the truth for the greater good may have served the interests of Jackson County but only served to weaken the U.S. Constitution just that much more. It also offered me the unneeded temptation of knowing how easy it would be to create a means worth justifying.

"Good. Make sure we get that in the conversation whenever we make our first buy with her on tape. Okay?"

"No problem." I was sure I could work it into a conversation such that she wouldn't pick up on any of the details and simply acknowledge the transaction.

Joe took a small vial with a rubber-sealed opening at one end from the glove box and placed the drugs inside. With both of his thumbs pressed on the vial's center, he caused a faint snapping sound; a clear liquid rushed over the suspect substance. The liquid instantly turned blue, identifying the substance as highly pure crystal methamphetamine. Joe explained how its wetness suggested that it was reasonably fresh from the lab and that Shannon's source was probably closely connected to the cook.

"This is good. This is *really* good."

"Oh. Before I forget. Her friend, this Rick character, says his mom works in one of the local DA offices. I'm not sure which one, but he says he had her check me out for him."

"Don't worry; they won't find out anything. You're not in any computer systems outside the task force."

"That's comforting, but it still pisses me off that she would even check. Know what I'm sayin'?"

"Don't worry. If it's true, she won't be employed for long. After you leave, of course. I can promise you that."

"Good."

"Well," he said as a prelude to departure, "you've broken the ice. When everyone sees that she doesn't get in any trouble over this, they'll get easier to approach. Just don't spread it too thin. You'll make a lot of people nervous if they know your takin' so many unnecessary chances. Now go and get some sleep."

"Roger that. Thanks for comin' out."

"You got it, my friend."

"Oh, Joe!"

"Yuh?"

"The marks on the forearms? In the photos?"

"Uh huh?"

"I think I've gotta bead on them."

"Yeah? Whatta ya think they mean?"

"I can't tell ya what they mean, but I can sure as hell tell ya how much they hurt." I rolled back my sleeve to expose the burn.

"Holy shit. That looks painful. How'd they . . . ?"

"It's not important *how*. What matters is that it probably means I'm halfway to gaining their complete trust. Wouldn't ya say?"

"There's such a thing as being too trustworthy. Get that thing looked at right away, you hear?"

"Yes, sir."

"Good work."

"See ya, Joe."

I phoned in the report at around 3:00 A.M. One of the titles read: "Sale of Narcotics," the golden grail of the UCI. I heard back from Gordon at 9:00 A.M. that same morning. His enthusiasm was masked only by his knowledge that the two other operatives who went before me were unable to make a single buy and that I had made my first buy weeks ahead of schedule. Because the amount of a bonus was in direct proportion to the number of employees identified by the UCI as being involved in inappropriate workplace activities, he didn't want to tip the company hat prematurely.

The first recorded buy was set for the following Saturday, just before work, in the Boise parking lot. The dealer, Phil Haggle, was the means by which I would solidify the confidence of the other, more prolific dealers. In the big scheme of things, Phil was a lightweight, a dealer motivated by an insatiable drug habit and not by profit. In many ways, this made him less predictable and consequently more dangerous than the larger suppliers.

My previous deal with Shannon and some veiled suggestions of a long-term and profitable patronage were enticement enough for Phil to chance dealing with me. Over the past couple weeks, he had thrice dropped small bindles of crank into my shirt pocket. This was apparently the way paranoid drug dealers decided it was best to avoid prosecution—drop the drugs into a pocket and collect for it the following day when no drugs were present. I never mentioned these exchanges to the police. If nothing else, I figured the drugs might come in handy if I ever needed a prop.

In order to push things along more quickly with Phil, I stopped wearing shirts with pockets. Also, something about him told me he wouldn't be reaching into my pants pockets any time too soon.

At 2:15 P.M., I met Joe and another agent of JACNET in the Fred Meyer's parking lot. This spot was selected for its proximity to the mill and for its conglomerated, often tumultuous traffic.

"You'll wear the wire in the ball cap," Joe said, displaying an Oakland A's hat. "I know it looks bulky, but believe me, no one's ever suspected it contained a wire. Here, try it on."

"Feels fine. I've done this before, you know. I have to admit, though, I prefer the body wire."

"We've got a body wire."

"Then give me it instead."

"We sometimes lose the transmission when the wire dips below the window of the car. If the buy is outside your vehicle, then it's not a problem."

I capitulated. "I guess we go with the hat the first time, then."

"You prefer the wire, do ya?"

"Of course."

"Okay. It's the wire the first time, then. I wantcha to be comfortable first time outta the chalks."

"I know this is old hat. No pun intended." He then thought for a moment. "No, wait. We're not goin' with the hat, are we? Forget the pun."

He cleared his throat. "Let me go through what we need to make this case indictable. First of all, try to make him do most of the talkin'. Talk about what you'd agreed upon when you spoke with him at the mill. Have him speak on the quality and quantity of the meth. When you give him the money, count it out. We'll need it to indict. Am I forgetting anything?"

His partner, Mike, added, "Yeah. About where we're gonna meet afterwards to get the drugs and wire. And have him sign for the money." I was required to sign a few sheets of white photocopies of the specific bills being used in the drug transaction.

He then turned to me and said, "And get him to talk about future deals and maybe his ability to score quickly. And larger quantities; don't forget to ask about that."

"Here's the thousand dollars," Joe said, passing me ten large bills. "That's a bit much for an ounce of crystal, by the way."

"Yeah, I know. But I wanted to get the ball rollin'."

*   *   *

I drove into the mill parking lot, careful to make my presence known to all the employees who came to work an hour before me on the mill's overlapping work schedule. The more the dealers saw me meet with Phil, the greater my chances of getting into the underground.

While JACNET hid from sight on the lush farm next door, I waited with unabashed impatience, thumping my fingers on the dashboard as I listened to Glenn Frey's *Smuggler's Blues*, a song I played before every drug deal.

I could just imagine Joe's face when he heard the music begin to play. He probably frowned at Mike and said something to the effect, "Is that song saying what I think it's saying?"

*   *   *

Phil's beat-up Japanese pickup truck clanked into the parking lot ten minutes late for the appointment. I came up from behind the vehicle, reading the make and license plate number just below my breath. Joe furiously copied the number down, gulping back his spit as he drew his binoculars to the windshield once again. Mike peered through the bushes at Phil's truck, snapping picture after picture with an ultra-zoom lens.

"I don't do business this way, Ace," I growled, yanking the passenger door open. "I say two-forty-five, I *mean* two-forty-five!"

"I had to get gas," he mumbled.

"You're givin' me gas!"

"You got it, man?" he said, referring to the money. His crystal methamphetamine–induced paranoia shrunk his voice to an inaudible, convoluted mutter.

"Fuck you! Get gas on your own time, bitch. I don't know how you country fucks do business in Hoboken, but those of us from the civilized world do it on time. Comprende?"

"Sorry. Here," he said unintelligibly.

"Look, you're gonna have to speak up or speak more clearly, or something. How the fuck can anyone tell what the hell you're saying, anyhow? You got the meth?" I needed him to speak more clearly for the tape.

"Yeah. Right here." He passed me a cigarette pack with an ounce of crystal methamphetamine inside.

"Good. At least now I can understand you." I inspected the drugs. "This is that brown-speck bullshit, isn't it?"

"It's not bullshit. The brown-speck around here has long legs." Long legs referred to the length of time the high would last.

"Next time, bring me rose, white, or peanut butter. Okay?" I was attempting to determine whether Phil was dealing with more than one source.

"This shit's better, dude. But I'll see what I can do."

"Here's the grand," I said, counting the money out in denominations of a hundred. All the while I kept thinking, "If I was a drug dealer, the first thing I would look for, besides a wire, of course, would be counting the money out loud." If ever his paranoia would have served him well, it was now. But now, when he needed it most, it was as pacified as a cooing baby.

Phil took the money and then clumsily removed a Ruger 9 mm automatic from beneath his seat. "If you ever fuck me, man . . ." he mumbled, timidly displaying the weapon in a pathetic attempt to intimidate me. He apparently misjudged me as a run-of-the-mill drug dealer.

"A nine millimeter," I verbalized for the sake of my covert audience. "You ever pull that on me again you better be willing to use it, fuck head. Now put it away before I stick it up your ass and turn you into a Popsicle. *Now*, you little prick!"

I glanced out the window and noticed Joe leveling his weapon at the car from behind a rock wall. "Now," I repeated forcefully.

"Just remember," Phil muttered unimpressively, sliding the gun back beneath his seat. He then got out of the vehicle and started walking toward the mill as if nothing happened.

I trotted up from behind him. "You pull that gun on everyone the first time?"

"Yeah. So don't take it so personal."

Still walking slightly behind him, I tilted my belt buckle forward and turned off the transmitter. I circled him to the front and began walking backwards. "Tell everyone who knows about your little gun threat tactic that you got your scrapes and bruises from me after the deal went down."

Phil stopped suddenly in his tracks. "What? What bruises?"

"These," I calmly replied before releasing a barrage of punches. Beaten to his knees and then to his back, Phil wallowed in a mire of his own blood and venom.

I ended my assault with the obligatory kick to the gut and then said, "Have a nice day." Phil curled up like a fetus, quivering spasmodically on the warm, dampened pavement. Several employees noted the incident, but none interfered, knowing as they did Phil's penchant for living dangerously.

I quickly drove to a nearby vacant parking lot to make the exchange with JACNET. I watched carefully for tails as I sailed down a long stretch of road and into the barren lot.

"We lost your signal when you passed behind a group of pickups. What was said?" Joe immediately asked upon my arrival.

"He really didn't say much of anything," I answered.

"He pulled a gun on ya, huh?" Mike seemed surprised.

"Yeah, he sure did. He said he wouldn't do it again, though, when we spoke behind the truck. By the way, what were you planning to do with your piece? I saw you pointing it in my direction."

"Me?" Joe asked, pointing toward himself. I acknowledged in the affirmative. "If I had to, I was gonna kill him," Joe said.

"The glasses you're wearing? For aesthetic purposes?"

"I'll take you to the gun range sometime, sonny." Joe giggled. "Excellent job with the conversation. One more buy with him, and we've got an indictment. Let's see if we can get to his supplier."

Mike slapped me on the back. "We should use this tape as a training tool. Great job. You really nailed him."

In corporate investigation terms, things were moving along quite smoothly; or so I was told. In retrospect, however, I should have listened to that inner voice that said I was moving way too quickly and getting far too involved with the employees I was investigating. That advice would have served me better if I'd had the restraint to heed it.

Chapter 5

It was 8:02 A.M. when the phone rang. I had been up all night typing my report and phoning it in to the home office. Not to mention the four hours I spent writing Chapter 14 of my first book, *CIA: Cocaine in America* (hey, a little self-promotion couldn't hurt). If the voice on the other end were anything but sweet, I was prepared to hang up without delay. It was Tari. We talked for about two hours. Her favorite response to almost anything I said, "That's right, that's right," played perfectly on my delicate sensibilities.

It was at this stage in our relationship that Tari decided to tell me about her committed relationship with a fellow co-worker named Keith, a person whom I immediately took a disliking to, if for no other reason than default. For the most part, Tari treated him like excess baggage, as forgettable as a worn-out plaid Samsonite. He was a Hyster driver, and as I would soon discover, a very dangerous and jealous one.

When Tari asked if I would meet her for lunch in a rather surreptitious manner, I was intrigued, if not a bit aroused. Of course, I kept telling myself that I could garner a lot of valuable information by meeting with her. My rationalization reflex was in peak form that day.

The information was indeed priceless, but could I disclose the source? Did I want to? Over the next few weeks, Tari and I continued to rendezvous in remote, if not romantic, locations. Conversations about drug-dealing employees eventually devolved to sexual volleyball. She served; I pretended to block.

Not until Tari mentioned that she occasionally used drugs at the mill did I begin to seriously question the prudence of my latest strategy. Although Tari would sporadically offer to supply me with coke or crank, I refused her carte blanche. Not simply because our relationship was a bit more than platonic, but because I knew she was offering it only because of her feelings toward me. The information, however, that's another story.

I kept Gordon apprised every step of the way. His words of wisdom, "Gotta get close to these guys," played like a vinyl record in the middle of a sandstorm. I was on my own. When it came to Tari, however, he kept insisting that, according to the rumor mill, she was, in his words, "a player." This made it that much more difficult to maintain the facade that Tari was offering this information to me without motive and that she herself wasn't knee deep in a powdery quagmire.

I can still remember driving around endlessly with the top down, hoping the air would wash away the clutter that was clouding my judgment. I repeatedly sought refuge from my guilt in the anonymity of a darkened theater. Still, I couldn't escape the investigator's dictum that this was a repugnant means only marginally justified in the wake of a bittersweet end.

After making the requisite two recorded deals with Phil Haggle, I set my sights on bigger game. I quickly found my prey in the cross hairs of, would you believe, a wood-chipping machine?

Due to poor scheduling, we would occasionally find ourselves with an additional puller on the chain. As a result, we were given an all too infrequent "sweep break." When it was my turn to clean up, I grabbed a broom and carved the shortest and lightest path I could to The Hog—a gorge cut down the middle of the mill—and pushed a load of scrap wood, sawdust, and superfluous debris into the conveyor. Weaving my way around stacks of plywood, and being careful not to be detected by a dryer tender (a foreman), I made my way to the phone booth located near the Spreaders. The phone booth was well insulated and virtually soundproof due to its proximity to the noisy surroundings. The unintended effect, of course, was that it made a great location for employees to conduct drug transactions. I had the room bugged virtually from the outset.

Once there, I phoned in to my answering machine some names and information that I feared I would forget by day's end. The deafening silence of the booth gave me an eerie sense of heightened awareness. As I looked through the small square window on the door, displaying the appropriate paranoia for my always vigilant audience, a surreal vision caught my eye. An obese Hyster driver named Paul fell into The Hog like a Dali clock melting on a desert tree branch.

"Note to file," I said mechanically into the telephone receiver, "Safety problem with Hog."

As if waiting for the adrenaline to kick in, I hesitated to see what everyone else was doing. The noise and the nonstop work seemed to drown out what I'm sure was some real intense screaming and cries for help. I don't recall throwing the door open or even running across the floor for that matter, but the next thing I knew I was holding onto his forearm and gripping the metal safety fence with all my might. My arms and chest were stretched and flexed like a gymnast performing the iron cross on the rings.

The only part of The Hog with any measure of safety was the last twenty feet or so. Anywhere else along the way, you could literally walk into it unobstructed. As it was, Paul somehow managed to flop his considerable bulk over the fence and into The Hog.

Working against the flow of the wood piling up around him, I pulled with every fiber of my strength. Just as I was about to lose my grip, Stan darted out from nowhere and pressed the emergency shutoff button. The removal of the rhythmic crunching sound from the cacophony produced by the mill quickly drew everyone's attention.

People came from every direction to assist me out of The Hog, but mysteriously, no one offered Paul so much as a helping hand. I should stipulate that it was a mystery to me at the time, but Paul's character would soon clear up any curiosity I might have had.

When I smelled Paul's breath, I became infuriated. "Motherfucker," I vented, pushing through the crowd. As I pursued him back to the Hyster, it also occurred to me that he had yet to thank me for saving his life.

"Hey!" I said. "You're welcome!"

He glanced down at me for a moment, my shirt torn and sweat dripping from my brow, and quickly drove away. Stan came up from behind me and placed his glove on my shoulder. "You were expecting a thank you, perhaps?" A toothy smile drew across his face. "He's an asshole. Don't worry about it."

"He's drunk; you *know* that?"

"Yeah, and if you'd have let 'im chip we'd be done with his sorry ass. He sued us, you know. That's why he drives a lift."

"So fire 'im."

"Boise's too ascared of another lawsuit from that jackoff. He used to work your chain, then he had alotta operations or somethin'. You know, carpal tunnel. He's a fuckin' pussy. He couldn't pull to save his life. I think Boise's ascared that if they fire him he'll claim they retaliated against him for suing them." Stan went on in the vernacular of southern Oregon to say that Paul's lawyer was partial to polyester suits, Brill Cream, and slow-moving ambulances.

"I should've let 'im chip. I will next time, I tell ya." I blew out a burst of air. "Who am I kiddin'? No chipper's gonna suck that lard ass through. It'd probably shut down the mill with a power surge. The guy's a movin' safety hazard, you *know* that?"

"Look around. Who isn't?" he said slovenly.

"Yeah, but accidents aren't caused by people blazin'. They're caused by people too tired or too drunk to react." As I watched for his response, which appeared agreeable, I was hastily summoned back to the chain. I was confident, however, that the seed was planted and that Stan was a player. My suspicions would soon be confirmed, but not in the manner I would have preferred.

When I returned to the chain, I told Tari what had happened. After she expressed her sadness over Paul not being ground up, she recounted a similar situation that recently resulted in an employee's foot being severed. According to Tari, and later confirmed by my company, an employee high on crank let his foot dangle where it didn't belong and had it sheared off by a rail that lowered into the floor at the feeder end of the dryer. Having heard this horrible story, I deliberately made my way over to the feeder end that same day and quickly devised a way to prevent such an accident from reoccurring in the future.

My proposed solution was a hinged metal lip that would come up as the rail lowered into the floor and would prevent a person from accidentally sliding his or her foot across the opening while the rail was in transit. The day after I included this suggestion in my report, Gordon called and said that I was not to offer any more solutions to safety problems unless I consulted with him first. When I asked why, he said that there was a lawsuit pending and that such an obvious solution would make Boise appear liable. They never enacted a single safety measure for this particular problem during my entire stint at the mill.

It was early June and the temperatures soared to a hundred degrees or more on the chains. Chief tried to bring rain inside the mill with his colorful rain dances, and Phil was mumbling in anyone's ear who would listen. Shannon and Melba periodically dashed to the bathroom with frowning faces, only to resurface bright and cheery. And Bob and I, well, we entertained Tari with our play-by-play descriptions of our fellow codependents—I mean, co-workers.

Phil continued to play Russian Roulette with his heart as he volunteered again and again for the front of the chain, desperately attempting to stave off the inevitable heart attack brought on by a crystal methamphetamine overdose. Melba and Shannon, I was told, would shave a bit off the top of their private stock in exchange for Phil covering for them at the front of the chain.

When it came time for Chain Three to "break" Chain Four, Phil was a logical candidate since he was visiting us on a regular basis at the behest of the Bobsie Twins. Linda, who I had yet to formally meet, came along with him. When it was her turn to break the front of the chain, Phil drifted over to Linda sideways and mumbled something in her ear. Whatever he said apparently did not sit well with her.

"Get the fuck away from me, you stupid sonofabitch!"

Phil responded like a sick puppy dog, moping back to his position on the chain. It wasn't long, however, before he found himself back by Linda's side, muttering what were surely guttural solicitations in her ear.

Linda's reaction this time was surprisingly cool, causing the rest of us (Tari, Bob, and myself) to roll our eyes and shrug our shoulders. Then it happened. An event I'll never forget as long as I live. I cringe and pucker even as I type these words.

As Phil bent over to slide a large piece of "strip" wood—the only long bands of wood pulled on Chain Four—into his bin, Linda, who was at his backside, allowed a piece of wood to drift past her just far enough so that when she pulled it back toward her bin it dragged across Phil's derriere, depositing a sliver so large that it nailed his cheeks together. Phil's scream could be heard round the world.

The sight of blood trickling from his ass made it very difficult to yell "sliver" because of the laughter that kept seeping into our voices. While we attempted to collect ourselves, Linda leisurely walked over to the emergency shutoff switch and turned off the dryer. She acted completely indifferent.

"Sliver," she barked. She might just as well have been yelling, "Burger! Medium rare!"

I think this was her way of saying, "Don't fuck with me." Very effective, wouldn't you say? I couldn't pull wood or sit down for seven months without thinking about Phil's buttocks. Needless to say, this was not a job for the in-house splinter remover. Phil was rushed to the hospital by ambulance.

"I don't like Phil any more than you do," I said to Linda. "But if you ever try a stunt like that on me or mine, I'll kill you. He's a putz, but he didn't deserve that."

"Don't cut in where you don't belong and you won't haveta worry about it."

"One," I raised a single finger. "I'm not worried. And two," again, another finger. "I belong wherever I decide I belong."

"Then watch who you expose your ass to."

"You're gonna find my ass a lot tighter than Phil's and my shit a lot stinkier, I assure you." I then altered my tone. "But enough with the ass metaphors. You wanna get laid after work?"

I knew the dramatic shift in gears would throw her into a tailspin and prevent the showdown I was not prepared to fight. After all, until this very moment I knew precious little about her, never mind the fact that she was a player, and one with the unmitigated audacity to erase the competition with such a brazen display of testosterone. And the symbolism . . . forget about it!

"Sure," she replied.

"Sure, what?" I thought. "Oh."

* * *

I met her that evening at a nightclub that was holding its annual "Best Body" contest—for men. You would think that might be a bad thing for a flaming heterosexual like me, but in fact nothing could be farther from the truth. Like many smart women who have gone to sports bars, where there are usually many more men than women, I discovered that any event which draws a four-to-one ratio of screaming women to desperate men can't be all that bad. Unless of course one of those two hundred women is Linda.

Believe it or not, I went to another one of those muscle-flexing affairs at another club only days later and met one of the sweetest girls I've ever known. Her name was Macki, and we became the best of friends during those eight or nine months. We still talk from time to time, mostly about movies; the ones in the theaters, the ones she thinks I should be writing, and the ones I think she should be performing in. I'd elaborate further on this wonderful soul, but her privacy and the nature of this story do not permit it.

After drawing my attention to her boyfriend, who was flexing his pecs for a far-too-sympathetic crowd, Linda assured me that he would bring those muscles to bear against me if I ever screwed her.

"I thought that's why we were here," I quipped. "I'm confused."

"You better be glad Jeff didn't hear that shit!"

"So why we here?"

"You wanna piece of advice? Stay the fuck off my turf."

"So we're not gonna fuck. That's whatcha tellin' me?"

"Keep it up, asshole."

Sympathetic applause interrupted her speech. When it ended, Jeff was already approaching our table.

"Go ahead, smart ass. Tell him what you just said."

"Who the fuck are you?" Jeff launched into an interrogation as he invaded my space.

I remained seated. "Put your skirt on . . . I mean your shirt . . . and let's go out back so I can explain."

"Fuck you! Let's go right here!" He assumed a stance. Not for fighting, mind you, but for exhibiting muscle definition.

"Whatever you say, Franco," I said, alluding to the great bodybuilder Franco Colombo. Then I pushed him back with the soul of my shoe in order to create the needed separation. I was all too aware that muscle and brawn were useless if not brought to bear in tight quarters.

My hands have always been fast and accurate, but never were they as fast and accurate as that night. A flurry of punches landed squarely on his face, forcing him back into the crowd. As my father once taught me, and Bruce Lee later confirmed, punching is not unlike kicking a football. You must always aim six inches behind your target and punch through the ball, I mean face. It's also important to remember not to stand around waiting for someone to say

"Great Fight" when the fight is over. Bolt for the door just as fast as you can. That's something I learned on my own stewing in the principal's office.

*   *   *

When I arrived at work after my two days off, I was acknowledged by my first name by most everyone working on the Spreaders, something that had not happened since the moment I arrived at that sweatshop. After two days of not having to breathe superheated air and scratchy sawdust or wear ten pounds of protective clothing, it was difficult to return to that oven.

As I shuffled over to Dryer Four, careful to avoid one Hyster driver who wanted me dead and another who was perpetually three sheets to a typhoon, I was intercepted by Tari, who appeared disturbed and disheveled.

"You're already on the chain?" I said. "What the hell we pullin', re-dry?" This comment referred to her physical appearance as well as her excited manner. When you were pulling wood that had already been through the dryer once, the work was especially grueling due to the fact that you were forced to run it much more rapidly to prevent burning. This experience typically left pullers exhausted and desperately searching for someone to relieve them.

"Yeah, but don't worry, we've been covering for you. That's not what I need to talk to you about."

Just then, a man, a very muscular and incensed man, rambled toward us, bruises and cuts covering his face. I knew he wasn't coming to apologize, so I met him with the same attitude I greeted him with a couple nights before.

"That's what I wanted to tell you," Tari explained, slowly backing away from me.

"I never realized how much of a contact sport bikini contests were," I called to him as he neared, hoping to rattle him.

Before I could ready myself, however, he pushed me backward with a two-handed thrust. I recovered and assumed a fighting stance as I had done in the bar that evening, somewhat like Rocky Marciano in his now famous pose. As Jeff closed in, ostensibly more prepared than last time, with his hands raised and clenched, I kicked him square in the groin and walked away.

"So is it re-dry or that long strip wood," I asked Tari as if nothing had happened.

Everything was a stage, and you always had to be ready to impress anyone who might be watching with more than a passing interest. Acting unaffected also helped to temper my own nerves. Truthfully, I was scared to death he would kill me. He certainly had the physical attributes to do so. Especially compared to my own ravaged body. The only thing that kept me from getting my butt kicked back then was attitude and experience. I was almost always outmatched physically.

"What the hell happened Saturday?" she said while looking back over her shoulder at the buckled man. "I didn't know that guy worked here."

"Day shift. He's a real asshole." She smacked me on the chest with her gloves. "What'd ya, piss off his girlfriend or something?"

"You mean Linda?"

"Yeah. You piss 'er off?"

"She's very territorial, huh?"

"Oh." Disappointment crept into her voice as her head turned downward. "You bought from someone on Chain Three?"

Wanting to probe deeper, yet not wanting to mar our budding friendship, I had a difficult course to navigate. "That depends."

"Upon what?"

"Upon what chain Phil is assigned to."

"That's her territory all right. That would also explain Phil's sudden disdain for sitting around on the job."

When I arrived at the chain some fifteen minutes late, I was expecting the customary profane assault from Shannon and Melba but was met with accolades and physical embraces instead. With sunflower seeds spilling from her mouth, Shannon said in her all too familiar, crude manner, "I can't fuckin' believe it. You fucked that Linda bitch's old man all to shit. Damn! I fuckin' love it," she erupted in adoration.

"It's what I live for."

"You need some more shit?" Shannon bobbed about in front of me.

"I've moved up. Can't use any of that bindle crap anymore."

"How much you need?"

"What can you get?"

"An ounce."

"Bring me it tonight at that little bar with the poker machines."

"They all have . . ."

"You know the one. You pass it on the way to the mall."

"The Hideaway Club?"

"That's it! Meet me there at twelve-thirty. In the parking lot."

"Why so late? We can be there by eleven-fifteen."

"I wanna go home and change," I explained, realizing that I would need time to gather the JACNET unit together.

"You're so fuckin' vain." She rubbed her nose with a gloved hand, an act that I had seen lodge a sliver where it didn't belong on more than one occasion.

"It's a curse. I'll see you at exactly twelve-thirty, agreed?"

"Sure," she said prosaically. "Whatever."

The fact that she had such immediate access to the drug told me that she probably kept a supply in her truck at all times. I called Bud from the phone booth in the mill that evening, and he in turn mustered up a couple of JACNET officers, who of course included Joe.

As is typical with all drug dealers, large or small, Shannon was late for the appointment. As I sat impatiently outside the bar, I watched a man and woman exit the building together, verbally assaulting one another. When the argument escalated to violence, with the woman physically assailing the man, I sought assistance from my clandestine audience via the body wire I was sporting.

"Flash your lights if I should do something here," I asked, concerned. Nothing happened. Then all at once the aggression reversed and the man became the aggressor.

"Oh, boy," I continued. "How 'bout now, guys? Look at this idiot, will ya. He's gonna kill her. Flash your lights if I should stop this thing. Are you guys listening? He's gonna kill her. What should I do?"

All at once the man hauled off and clobbered her. "That's it, guys," I said, throwing open my car door. "Gotta go." As I shuffled briskly toward them, calling for him to stop, two black-and-whites bounced into the parking lot, seemingly from nowhere.

"We'll take it from here, sir," one of the officers advised as he leapt from his vehicle. "Thanks for your help."

I moved back to my car and thanked Joe for calling the cops. As fate would have it, Shannon's truck rolled into the lot while the flashing lights on the police cars pierced the evening canvas, brush painting the walls with bold, transitory strokes of red and blue. I approached her vehicle naturally, detecting her ballooning eyes as the patriotic colors danced about her bleached white face.

Standing stiff and rigid just outside her truck with her hands clenched tight like claws, she declared, "I'm outta here."

"Relax, relax," I repeated with that sound you create when your lips barely part. "If you take off, they're gonna think you're drunk or somethin'."

Her response was terse, yet restrained. "Fuck!"

"Hey, what better place to avoid the cops than a club called the Hideaway."

As we walked past one of the police vehicles, a large German Shepherd practically leaped through the partially opened rear window, growling and barking at Shannon like a police dog trained in the detection of narcotics should. Our hearts deadened in our chests and our feet stuck like taffy to a loose filling. Not surprisingly, the cops' attention immediately shifted toward us.

"She's slipping the cuffs," I advised them with a faltering timbre, slowly pointing a trembling finger toward their vehicle. "She's slipping the cuffs."

"Huh?" the Sergeant said with a crooked neck.

"Your prisoner," my voice returned. "In the back seat! She's slipping the cuffs!"

"Oh, shit," the sergeant blurted out. "Hell, *I* cuffed her the first time. One of you's has to get 'em back on."

"Bullshit," another officer replied. "I ain't gettin' in there with that crackhead."

"Good luck," I offered with a waving hand. But they were no longer interested in us.

Once inside, we immediately grabbed a table, and I began working on her obvious trepidations. "Don't worry. They're too busy with those idiots out there to be bothered with us."

"Did you see that dog? They know. They're comin' in here."

"They don't know jack. They've already forgotten about us by now, for cryin' out loud."

"That was a drug dog," she whispered harshly. "Do you have any idea what that means?"

"He sniffs *drugs*?" I responded with ill-advised humor, crossing my arms on my chest to muffle the mike. "Forget about it. Sell them to me and I'm the one the dogs will be sniffin', not you. If you actually think they're comin' in here, it's your best play, now isn't it?"

I knew that this line of persuasive conversation might be flirting with entrapment, even though she was already predisposed to commit the crime, which is why I momentarily severed my transmission. I couldn't help but feel that I had compromised my integrity, even if just a smidgen.

"Here," she said, slipping me her pager beneath the table, her face wrinkling with distress. "Go to the bathroom."

I took the pager and didn't ask any questions that might make me appear even less street savvy than I already felt at that moment. The bathroom was double occupancy, so I checked the stall and bolted the door when I was satisfied that I was alone. After a few awkward and ridiculous moments (I was still on tape) standing there and waiting for the pager to do something, I decided to inspect it. When I removed the backing, I saw only batteries. After further examining those same batteries by touching the ends to my tongue, I concluded that they were indeed batteries.

Now frustrated, and feeling dumber by the minute, I began prying at seams that were apparently not designed to separate. Just as I was about to give up, which was about thirty seconds after putting a small hole in the wall, I remembered a magic trick from elementary school. In fact, I'm sure you've seen the same trick yourself. You know, the one where the magician places something in a box and then spins it about, and when he opens the box again the object is gone. However, when he spins it around and opens it for a third time, the object suddenly reappears. Well, this box required that you stand it upside down. When I did, a miniature plastic baggy stuffed with crystal methamphetamine fell out.

"Bingo," I signaled Joe through the walls. I hastily placed the hundred dollar bills inside the pager and flipped the pager around to secure the money inside.

As I was leaving the bathroom I couldn't help but chuckle at how ironic it was that the pager served both sides so well in the art of deception. The cops use pagers to appear as drug dealers and to conceal bugs, while the drug dealers use them to conduct business and to conceal narcotics. What a diplomatic invention. It bears the distinct signature of the Swiss.

When I returned to the table, I handed the pager back to Shannon and invited her outside for some fresh air. "Yeah," she sighed in relief. "Let's get the hell outta here."

Now outside, I fought hard to get the logistics of the transaction on tape precisely as they had transpired. I would need it for an indictment.

Specifically, I needed her to admit to selling me a specific quantity of drugs for a specified number of dollars.

"You got rose this time, huh?"

"It's the best," she replied.

"Crystal by any other name . . ."

"What's that s'posed to mean?"

"Nothing, I'm just being . . . I put the three hundred in the beeper."

"No shit. I thought you'd eaten it."

"I couldn't measure the crank. I trust it's about four grams?"

"You can measure it later," she sniped, twisting her head madly in all directions, still paranoid that someone was watching. "It's all there. Now shut the fuck up about it, already."

"What are you, fucking paranoid? There's no swine out here."

"Excuse me for getting nervous when I show up to make a deal with a guy I hardly know and three fuckin' police cars are parked right next to him."

"First, there were two cars, not three. And if I couldn't be trusted, there wouldn't be a cop car within five hundred miles of me. Now relax. I don't drive a sixty-thousand-dollar car because I'm careless or stupid."

"Then why do you drive it?"

"Because the pigs know the drug dealers are all drivin' jacked-up white dualies."

"Ha ha, very funny."

"So how much can you get?"

"How much you need?"

"Half a brick." [half a kilo]

"What?! You're fuckin' crazy! No one can get that kinda load. Maybe five or six ounces, but a half key . . . no way."

"Tell ya what, get me the ounces and we'll talk."

"You can move that much? Really?"

"In a day."

"I'll make some calls." She climbed into her truck and sped away.

Things were moving along so well that my supervisor began seeking my advice on a case Krout and Schneider was investigating at Campbell's Soup Company of Ohio. According to Gordon, we had two investigators there posing as security guards for approximately four months, and they hadn't uncovered a thing. Then suddenly, when the rug was about to be snatched out from under them, one of the UCIs claimed he had witnessed upwards of forty employees smoking marijuana in the parking lot at various times throughout the week.

My response was simple and brief. I contended that they probably weren't able to earn the trust of the employees but had access to the rumor mill. Believing that the accused would presume we (K and S) had them on camera, the operatives figured they would roll during the interview process. They believed this, I surmised, because of the K and S practice of leading the accused to believe that surveillance cameras had captured their every move, when in fact they hadn't.

The formula was simple: Inform the accused of all the methods by which evidence is acquired, but don't specifically attribute any of those methods to their particular case. By association, the accused will presume that all of those methods were brought to bear against them. Supplement that tactic with the insinuation that others have already talked and that their cooperation might mitigate their punishment, and you've got a recipe for diarrhea of the mouth on the part of the accused.

Play this in reverse and you can see how the latter might lead to the former. K and S had a habit of encouraging unethical behavior and then standing back far enough not to get spattered by the mud. But in all fairness to Krout and Schneider, I truly believe that this was the result of incompetence on the part of case managers and not the deliberate intent of the owners. In fact, this is an area that inside sources at K and S assure me has been rectified through the rehiring of bona fide agents like Glenn and the firing of a host of impersonators, some of which you will read about farther along.

I would later speak to the UCI at Campbell's Soup of Ohio at the behest of Gordon and confirm all that I had suspected about the case. Several months later, the TV news magazine "20/20" aired a segment dealing with this very case. I must have received twenty phone calls from Gordon after that report aired, reminding me that it was against company policy to sell the company down the proverbial river.

A week passssed and I still hadn't heard back from Shannon concerning the status of my drugs. Around that same time, a corpulent gentleman by the name of Jim joined our motley crew on Chain Four.

Jim was the kind of guy that you liked, but you never fully understood why you liked him. His pants were always in a perpetual state of descent, he was terrible at his job, and he swore like a trooper on a three-day pass in Managua. His love for the opposite sex was never elevated above his belt, and he made no bones about it. No pun intended. In fact, he was so vulgar that even Shannon and Melba were repulsed by him. Of course, had he been better looking or more charitable with his drugs maybe that wouldn't have been such a problem with them. Strangely, Tari and I got along perfectly with Jim. I guess it's because we saw through his facade, although I grant you, even Clark Kent would have struggled with that one.

Having been told by both Tari and Bob (the guy with two DUIs) that Jim had worked at the mill previously and was cool—the euphemism for "he uses drugs"—it didn't take long before we were waist deep in conversation about crystal.

Tari always had one eye on the flowing wood and the other on me whenever it appeared I was discussing illegal matters. That duality was also at play in the manner in which she would prod me about what it was I was talking to people about. She was supportive while at the same time disapproving. It was tough because I had really grown fond of her and wanted so much to tell her that I was not a drug dealer. However, she was not against drugs per se, only as they related to me. Somehow I was supposed to be better than that, somehow having higher standards than the rest of the mill workers. Go figure.

One day, Jim and I were screaming back and forth across the chain, laughing about all subjects depraved and cavorting. Melba and Shannon, on the other hand, were not so vivacious. Slowed by the initial stage of withdrawal, they were in an ugly, distasteful mood.

"I'm sick of collecting all your leftovers, you fat fuck," Shannon hollered. Her words sounded vaguely familiar, except this time they weren't directed at me. It reminded me a lot of Louis Gossett, Jr., in *An Officer and a Gentleman*, only now it was Jim's turn to hear that there were only two things that came from Oklahoma. His response, however, was not nearly as animated or as effective as mine.

"What?" Jim feebly murmured, subjugating his will to her perceived authority.

"Way ta go, tiger. Good comeback." I laughed. "Don't let her push you around, bro!" I playfully egged him on. "Go on! Get in there and mix it up!"

Jim glanced about, appearing impotent, which tended not to deter aggressors, especially in this Thunderdome.

"Get the fuck outta the way, you fat fuck!" Shannon brayed, shoving him aside and pulling the bulk of his wood off the chain as it came pouring past. It was amazing how well she could work when she was perturbed and bent on belittling someone.

"Screw it," Jim mumbled as he slinked past me with one of his legs dragging behind him, the foot twisted permanently outward, the result of a terrible motorcycle accident years earlier. "I don't need this shit. I don't! I'm new here! What the hell do they expect?"

"Hey, Quasimodo," I said impishly. "Don't worry 'bout it. When you and I get things goin', you won't need this fuckin' job."

No sooner were the words out of my mouth than I realized they were bordering on entrapment. After all, wouldn't you be a bit motivated to sell drugs if it meant you wouldn't have to work in a hellhole like this any longer? Just a little? Anyhow, I didn't want anyone selling me drugs who wasn't otherwise inclined to do so of their own volition. But such remarks so easily tumbled out. Indeed, after talking with other K and S operatives, I found that such methods of enticement were the staple of the unethical investigator.

"I'll call you tonight," he blurted before shuffling away.

Getting people to sell to me had become virtually effortless. I'm sure they thought, "How could he be a narc? People are getting paid and no one is getting arrested." Apparently the easiness of consummating deals had gone to my head, and I had become complacent. In fact, by night's end I had three deals scheduled for the following day, a Saturday. Jim, Phil, and Shannon were on tap. Shannon, however, was not ready for the big leagues yet. We were only able to agree to an ounce.

The plan, as I recall, was to meet with them separately with enough lag time in between to drop off the drugs with JACNET, have them conduct another search of my vehicle, change tapes, and then return for the next appointment with time to spare. That was the plan, at least.

To start with, Phil missed his appointment with me because he saw a nondescript white vehicle in the McDonald's parking lot (where all the deals were scheduled to take place), Shannon was late because she had to wait on her supplier, and Jim had car troubles. By the time I answered all my pages and phone calls and rearranged schedules with JACNET, we were all due to meet in the same parking lot, just fifteen minutes apart. Can you guess how this turned out?

Shannon arrived early because she wanted to case the area, Phil arrived late because he was *too busy* casing the area, and Jim was careless, so he showed up on time. So there I was, standing in the last available parking space in the McDonald's lot, JACNET nestled in the huge parking lot adjacent to where I was standing, when the three vehicles belonging to my appointments arrived within two minutes of each other. I directed Jim into the spot that I was rudely saving, figuring he was the most important deal I had going because I had already bought from the other two. I directed Phil down a ways from where I knew JACNET was parked, and, before I could direct Shannon, she parked— you guessed it—directly in front of the surveillance vehicle. I mean, directly in front.

I glanced over at Joe, who was gesturing with his hand as though he were slitting his own throat, and mumbled beneath my breath, "I got it under control. Relax."

Shannon got out of her gigantic white truck and walked over to where I was standing alongside Jim. As she brushed past, she murmured with her jaw firmly clenched, "What the fuck's this?"

"Excuse me, Jim," I apologized as I walked in tight formation with Shannon toward the bustling McDonald's restaurant. "Just go back and wait in your truck, I'll be with you straightaway."

Her voice climbed several octaves. "You're dealing with *him*?"

"Do you have half a key stuffed in your bra?" I asked rhetorically. She rolled her eyes and crossed her arms as she stopped dead in her tracks. "That's why I haveta deal with slugs like him and Phil," I barked. "He's here too, by the way."

"Great," she capitulated, running her fingers through her hair and groaning. She was clearly antsy, her foot stomping the pavement repeatedly. "What number am I?"

"You haveta admit," I bragged, "It takes alotta balls."

She smiled politely. "What number?"

"You're next. Phil can wait till the cows come home."

"Don't worry; he will. That boy needs money. Make sure you weigh it. He'd cheat his dyin' mother. And this guy," she said, throwing her eyebrows toward Jim, who was waiting impatiently by his car. "You better watch your ass. Just be careful. No one has the sheet on him yet."

"Great. Who's in your truck, by the way?" I asked of the female companion sitting in the back seat of her expanded cab.

"Just a friend. She won't be there when we deal."

I knew this meant that the drugs were being fronted to her and that whoever this woman was, she didn't trust Shannon well enough to let go of the leash. At least not as long as she was carrying an ounce of her drugs.

"Why don't you two wait in the restaurant until I'm ready. It's way too fuckin' hot out here to be waitin' in a car. You probably don't have AC in that tank, I'm guessing."

"No. You're right. Let me know when you're ready. And don't make us wait too long."

I had to keep them away from the surveillance team while I was dealing with Jim. So far, everything was going smoothly. Well, sort of.

"What was that all about? Huh?" Jim pressed.

"Nothing. Old business." I figured Jim didn't need to know all the details, since he would probably leave the moment we completed our transaction.

"Was that Phil Haggle I seen a minute ago?"

"Charity work," I replied succinctly.

He analyzed the situation for about a nanosecond and then introduced his wife. She seemed embarrassed and almost apologetic about the nature of their visit. "We just do this with our friends. We're not dealers or nothin', you know?"

"Hey, I'm not your probation officer. I don't care if you're Mother Teresa as long as the shit's good."

"We're just a little nervous," Jim started. "We've never done this before, and we hardly know you. You know what I'm sayin'?"

"We don't haveta do this. It's no big fuckin' deal to me. As you can see," I spun a turned-up palm to the parking lot before me. "I'm not exactly hurting for suppliers."

"Yeah, I know," Jim said. "I just want you to know our situation, that's all."

I knew that he was posturing himself for his defense if need be, so I had to take that bullet out of his gun. "You see, I don't give a flyin' fuck how much experience you have at this. But if you're gonna bore me with the details of your life anyhow, don't blow smoke up my dress. You *never* sell drugs, and the first time you *do*, you're gonna sell them to a guy you just met? Please. I'm not sure I wanna do business with someone that fuckin' stupid. Do you really think I'm gonna bust you and then go over to Shannon's truck and say 'okay, here's the grand, you got the stuff?' Are you that fucking dumb?"

"That's true, honey," Jim's wife quickly conceded the ridiculous pretense. "Why the fuck would he do that?"

"Can't never be too careful, you know," Jim explained.

"Careful's good. Jerking me off's not good."

"You're right. Hey, don't worry. We know what we're doin'."

I offered my handshake and, with the money in my palm, I said incidentally, "Here's your three hundred."

"Honey," he exhorted his wife while looking me dead in the eyes, "Shake the man's hand."

She offered her hand and I shook it. "Is this four grams?" I asked.

"You can weigh it," Jim reassured me.

"I will. And test it, I assure you."

"You'll see it's a lot better than the shit you'll get from them two."

"I don't wanna look at it out here," I said for the purposes of getting more of the particulars on tape. "What kind is it?"

"Peanut butter. The longest legs in the business. It'll run a marathon (24+ hours) in a single stretch (line)."

"How much more can you get?"

"Why?"

"You see the crap I'm dealin' with here today. You really haveta ask?"

"I know the cook," he said offhandedly.

I couldn't believe how trusting he was. "Everyone claims to know the cook," I responded.

"He does," his wife affirmed. "He owns a wrecking yard here in Medford. Emerald Wrecking?"

"Honey," Jim turned his arms outward and implored her to be quiet.

"Just tell me you're not buyin' from a guy stupid enough to bake it at his own wrecking yard."

"No! No," Jim explained. "He goes out on his boat a couple times a year."

"No shit?" I thought for a moment. "I like it. I like it a lot."

"We gotta be goin'." Jim offered yet another handshake. "Enjoy the weekend."

"You kiddin'? I don't get weekends, dude. My days off are Mondays and Tuesdays. I work today."

"See ya." He jumped in his jalopy and puttered away.

*　*　*

I signaled to Shannon, who was sitting with her friend in the restaurant, and began walking toward her vehicle alone. When they arrived at the truck shortly after me, I knew something was amiss. Without explanation, they hopped in and Shannon bounced the vehicle into reverse and began to pull away. "We gotta go," she said tersely, leaning her head out the window.

"No problem," I nonchalantly responded. "Let me know when you wanna try it again sometime."

As I turned away, the truck stopped sharply in its tracks, shaking back and forth like Jell-O until it found its equilibrium. With a roar of the engine and a short squeak of the tires, the truck moved forward and into the parking space again. "Okay," Shannon shouted. "Let's hurry the fuck up and do this, then!"

As I entered the vehicle, the other woman excused herself without introduction. "I don't mind if she stays," I said.

Shannon acted twitchy and agitated. "No. That's all right. She doesn't mind." Her frown instantly dissolved into a plastic smile. "So? You got my money?"

With the surveillance team directly in front of us, I concentrated all my energy on keeping her looking directly at me at all times. I began by rotating in my seat to face her. If I had remained facing forward toward the windshield, she would undoubtedly have done the same. I could tell she was extremely nervous and wanted nothing more than to complete the transaction as quickly as possible and get the hell out of there.

"You got it?" I asked.

"Yup. Uh-huh."

"We agreed on an ounce, correct?"

"Yeah. Here," she stammered, passing me a small cardboard box that felt much heavier than it should have.

"Are fifties okay, I hope?"

"Sure, whatever."

"Fifty. One hundred. One fifty . . ." I began to count out one thousand dollars in denominations of fifty.

"What the fuck, over!" she forcefully protested. "You haveta count every fuckin' bill?! Just give me the shit all ready!"

"Nothing personal, but I don't want you coming back to me later sayin' I didn't pay you a thousand dollars for the ounce of crank." I stipulated the amount once again for the record.

"Then finish for god's sakes so I can get the hell outta here." I did as she insisted, and moved on to Phil.

*   *   *

After finishing up with Phil, I rendezvoused with JACNET just a few blocks away in a church parking lot, a location generally safe from happenstance encounters with drug dealers. After Joe and Mike explained how they had never seen anybody pull off three separate deals with three different dealers in a single location before, they began testing the drugs.

"Could you photograph Shannon?"

"Are you kidding?" Mike laughed. "You could count the hairs in her nose. That was . . . That was . . . Hell, man, that was terrific! Top-notch!"

"How much did Shannon say she was selling you?" Joe's stretched face told me all I needed to know.

"I knew that damn thing felt heavy," I said. "I thought it might be the packaging or something."

"Yeah," he said, his eyes rolling up at me. "About four ounces heavy."

"Oh, my god, she'll hit the roof," I said gleefully.

"You mean her friend will hit the roof," Mike chimed in.

"After this," Joe directed, "Go home and wait for her to call you. She'll wanna meet to retrieve her drugs. When you bring them to her, we'll follow her back to her source. Which is probably the residence of the woman she was with, I'm guessing."

"A slam dunk," I added.

"You betcha," Mike said jubilantly. "Three deals in one parking lot at one time. How about that."

*   *   *

When I spoke with Shannon, she was frantic, bordering on terrified. After explaining to her that it was probably not a good business practice to return a portion of the drugs after the deal was consummated, I told her that I would do so only because I wanted to keep her as my main supplier and because I was still waiting for her to come through with the half kilo. I also decided that this would be an incredible demonstration of good faith toward that end. I was keenly aware, however, that her supplier would probably never trust her again with that much crystal after this blunder.

I went to work immediately after returning Shannon's drugs to her, and when I sat down that evening to write my report, prior to phoning it in, I felt euphoric as I reflected on a day gone well.

A faint knock at my door at midnight, however, reminded me that reflections should always be reserved for events that have already passed.

Chapter 7

Peering through my peephole, I was surprised to find Caracas standing on the other side of my door. He acknowledged me with a wave of his hand the instant the peephole darkened. I suppose this was his way of preventing me from pretending that I was not at home. The question was, however, how the heck did he find me?

I drew the door back slowly, in a manner that implied I was tired. Bending my neck around the jamb and hanging my head across the threshold, I said groggily with scratchy-sounding vocal chords, "Hey, dude, what's up?"

"A bunch of us are goin' out to that new strip club. Wanna come?"

Although I've never been fond of such places (no winks), I saw it as a golden opportunity to get to know some of the guys who worked on the Spreaders. The word was they were the biggest dealers and users in the mill.

"Yeah, sure. Give me a minute here. I'll get my coat and wallet and junk."

"Why you livin' in a studio [apartment], dude?"

I could see this was going to be a long night. I responded without inflection. "I figured it'd be a good idea to get a place that would allow me to go month-to-month until I got the lay of the land." I cleared my throat. "Why do you ask? You know of any cool places?"

"No," he seemed taken aback. "I mean, I live in a house. I don't know. I can find out, though."

"Great. Do that and let me know."

As I walked out the door, he interjected, "Nice computer." This was just his way of saying, "Watch out. I notice things."

"So how'd ya find me, by the way?"

"You left a bill in the back seat of your Porsche," he answered, as if already prepared for the question and wanting to impress me.

"I assume you don't mean a dollar bill, a duckbill, a handbill, a Congressional bill, a guy named Bill or a Buffalo Bill. You mean like an insurance bill or electric bill, correct?"

"I think it was a credit card bill, actually."

"You didn't happen to pay it while you were in there, did ya?"

"I wasn't *in there*. I just peeked through the window."

"No shit."

"Why *'no shit*?'" He seemed insulted that I found him ill equipped to break into my car.

"Because you're standing here and not decomposing in some ditch somewhere," I answered, before starting down the hallway of my apartment building. I then said over my shoulder, "Don't go snoopin' around my shit anymore, Ace."

"I wasn't snoopin'."

The next thing I heard was the sound of a gun slide snapping forward. Without hesitation, I reached into my black leather trench coat to the rear of my faded jeans and spun about. With my gun leveled squarely at his forehead, I was relieved to see his dopey expression as he fumbled with a handgun, struggling to press it into a belt holster.

"Fuck!" he said, startled, dropping the weapon to the floor.

"What the hell is wrong with you?! You come here unexpected! You admit you went snoopin' through my car . . ."

He interrupted, "I didn't go through your . . ."

I immediately reciprocated, "I don't give a fuck! You do all that, and then you pull out a gun and lock 'n load while walking behind me! Are you that fuckin' stupid!?"

"I didn't. I didn't think that . . ."

"Don't! Don't finish that sentence. I don't think I could lose any more respect for you than I already have. But I really don't wanna find out right now."

"Hey, I'm sorry."

"Think how sorry you'd be if I'd have shot."

"Think of how sorry you'd be."

I stood for a moment and thought. "Naaah. I feel nothing here." I paused just long enough to make him feel bad. "I'm just fuckin' with ya, you bulimic sonofabitch. Let's get the hell outta here."

*   *   *

We met up with three other Boise Cascade employees in a parking lot just across from the newly opened strip joint. As luck would have it, a mob of protesters and media had converged on the club, smothering the sidewalk leading to the entrance. Worse yet, I actually recognized a couple of people from the church I attended in Applegate, a town approximately a half hour from Medford. The reason I chose that church in the first place was its distance from the mill, deciding it was highly unlikely that I would cross paths with a Boise employee so far away. You see, it's not just the drug dealers you have to worry about. Anyone who might mention that they saw you in a church to the wrong person is also dangerous.

I grabbed a sign that was leaning against the building and, under the guise of mocking the protesters, held it in front of my face as I neared the entrance.

Mortified doesn't begin to describe the emotion I felt when the bouncer demanded I give the sign back to the protesters. When I turned to do just that, who did I end up face to face with but one of the people I recognized from my church. Like any good UCI, I maintained my cover and, with Caracas practically in my left pocket, was compelled to rebuke the protesters.

"How is it you notice the speck of sawdust in my eye and not the plank in your own?" I shouted as I handed the sign gently to the protester and winked. "Take the plank from your own eye so that you might see the speck in my eye more clearly to remove it!"

I was hoping that the protester would see fifteen layers beneath that wink and realize that which she could not. I was fast discovering that the diametric clash between leading a good Christian life and being an effective UCI was far too volatile to continue with both. I already knew that I had to move to another apartment and change the church I attended, and the night was still young.

As we moved into the dimly lit bar, Caracas asked, "Plank? That's that new English translation Bible, isn't it?"

"Hell, I don't know," I cackled like an agnostic on a three-bong binge in Haiti. "I heard it from Steve Hagar during one of his protests."

"The dude from *High Times*?"

"Yup, that's him."

It was always good to drop such names when the opportunity presented itself, especially when you were being subtly grilled by a master chef. When we slithered into the club, swaggering in typical male fashion, like we had just canceled three hot dates to spend some quality time with the boys, I was surprised to discover that it was an all-nude, all-the-time sort of affair. It always tickled me that the men who complained most about beautiful women being teasers would spend half their paychecks on women whose profession it was to tease. Studying the libidinous expressions of the mob I was with, I couldn't help but feel compassion for the wives of the men who frequented such places. A little bit of this place and lord knows what they would demand of their poor wives when they got home. I dropped all drug talk for the next two hours and pretended to have a good old male chauvinist pig of a time—again, no wink-wink. Really!

For most of the evening, I reveled with a guy named Steve, a dark-featured and strikingly handsome sort. I was made uneasy, however, virtually from the outset by a brooding Latino who cast the upper quadrant of his two-hundred-and-a-quarter pound frame over a backwards-facing chair and stared at me intermittently throughout the evening. The only sign of life I saw from him was when a half-naked stripper, pretending to be disgusted by his advances toward her, pointed to a ring on his left hand and said, "What would your wife think?" His response was either brutally candid or he was a very capable liar: "I don't know, you'd haveta ask her attorney."

*   *   *

Around 2:00 A.M., Caracas asked me to follow him back to his "crib" for a friendly poker game. With the protesters now dispersed to their homes, as any sensible and respectable citizen would be, I crawled into my car and did as I was expected to do. Caracas lived at the end of a cul-de-sac where large evergreen trees and imposing shrubbery offered an abundance of privacy. The sprawling complex swallowed most of the yard it occupied, a remarkable piece of real estate for a man barely scraping by on thirteen dollars an hour to own. Sparse street lighting made a complete assessment virtually impossible.

*   *   *

The anticipated poker game turned out to be a strip-poker game and involved more players than I had anticipated.

"Ken," Caracas began his introductions. "Come on in and meet the gals."

I did my best to remember their names—mostly colors like Jade, Sapphire, and Amber—but was distracted by the number of healthy men I saw with irregular waistlines. I knew all too well what those bulges meant—no, not that—I'm talking guns and lots of them. Smoke filled the stagnant air and booze poured as freely as gravity would permit.

I knew that anything I did with regard to this case would be tainted if I allowed myself to get embroiled in the inevitable debauchery. My comparative sobriety enabled me to cheat at will and, as a result, maintain a reasonable level of decorum. However, I could not abate the rapid shedding of clothing around me.

"Why not your socks?" I asked one of the hard bodied women at the table as she pulled her lime green silk blouse over her head.

"I'm hot!" she replied with her shirt wrapped around her head. "Help me. I'm stuck."

The ruckus continued, with all the women seemingly content to remove their major garments first, even though they lacked underwear. From the looks of it, the Silicon Valley stretched far beyond California. "First time I've seen any of you do that without music," Steve howled.

"You're strippers?" I asked with an incredulous affectation.

"Where'd you get this guy?" the Latino from the club asked in the general direction of Caracas, all the while puffing on a fat cigar and massaging a woman's breasts.

"No," I shook my head. "I mean what do they care if they lose? They do this shit for a living."

The Latino tilted the cigar upward in his mouth and grinned. "Goooo fawkin' point! What the hell you gals gonna do for us when you lose?"

A striking blond shouted, "Wooo! I'll hang upside down on that . . . the . . . that machine [fitness apparatus] right there and you can stick it in any place it fits! How's that, you fawkin' spic?"

"That's it," he declared with a rambunctious hoot. "Any of you gals lose, we get to do ya!"

"Butcha gotta get me high first!" she stipulated.

Powder gushed from everyone's pockets until the table was besieged with a rainbow of crystal methamphetamine. After everyone indulged their nostrils and completed a chorus of sniffles, snorts and sneezes, they turned their attention toward me. "Well, 'New York'?" a sophisticated-looking Anglo man prodded. "Don'tcha like us?

"You're makin' me look bad, here," Caracas said with an undertone, nodding his head toward the sea of powder.

"I don't give a flyin' fuck what you or 'Cochise' do or think."

The Latino drew a 9 mm automatic from his pants and pressed it to my head. "Put a sheet behind his head, I don't wanna stain the wall," he said snidely, clicking the hammer back two notches to the "fire" position. "Someone frisk him," he demanded.

A scrawny fellow sitting next to me rubbed his hands up and down my body, avoiding my crotch like the bubonic plague. "Ewww. What do we have here?" He removed my Colt .45 from the back of my pants.

A rolling-eyed, slavering girl slurred, "Wow. Nice rod."

I slowly folded my arms behind my head, interlacing my fingers, and yawned. "Go ahead, 'Sitting Bull.' Or is it 'Sitting Bullshit?' I get confused sometimes."

"You think I'm fuckin' around here, asshole?" He attempted to intimidate me—it was working.

"No." My response was disarmingly controlled. "I think I am."

Before the man could wipe the shocked look from his face, I snatched the weapon from his hand and hastily drew back the slide. "Don't ever bluff me, you fat shit. If you're gonna pull a gun on me at least have the decency of intending to kill me. That clicking the hammer crap is a good movie effect for idiots that don't know shit from shinola, but it'll getcha dead next time you do it to me, jerkoff."

I realized that the gun jammed in my face was empty because the idiot cocked the hammer just before threatening to blow my head off, just like the moron in Los Angeles did. Everyone in the room was thoroughly impressed but not yet convinced. A refrain of gulps and stammered speech was a picture window into their collective street sense and the relative size of their testicles.

The Latino grabbed the other gun, the one they took from me moments earlier, and pointed it at me. "Drop the fuckin' gun," he said with an unconvincing, shivering voice.

"There's no such thing as a Mexican standoff when it comes to guns at this range, you stupid shit. Again, too many movies. If I pull this trigger, your brains are on the wall before your friends, and especially you, know the battle's even begun. In case you hadn't heard, bullets travel faster than sound. *Much* faster."

"I'll fuckin' do it, asshole! I'll fuckin' do it!"

"Then do it and stop wasting my time."

"Fuck you! Drop the gun!"

"Then do it!"

There was an endless silence except for the Latino's nasal wheezing. And then he did it. He pulled the trigger. The hammer striking the firing pin resounded throughout the house. Everyone's breath fled, and when the moment was over, I was still intact. Even though I knew there wasn't a bullet in the chamber, I was nonetheless stiffened by the moment. He popped the clip to see if there were shells in the gun, which of course there were, and then looked back up at me with the look of a man who knew he had been beaten. "My gun, please?" I asked softly, taking it as he passed it across the table. No one knew quite what to think. Their combined relief appeared to tell an even bigger story, though.

Unless I knew I was headed into a perilous situation, I always cleared the chamber, leaving the hammer in the firing position, and then loaded a full clip into the gun. It was my belief that the gun they knew you were carrying should always be your decoy. And as a decoy, it must also weigh as much as a loaded gun but nonetheless give you the advantage if removed from your person. I figured if I had the time to pull it on someone before they took it, then I probably had the time to pull back the slide, too. My guess is that the Latino didn't actually intend to pull the trigger. Drugs, tension, a hair trigger and fear of the unknown probably had something to do with it.

Steve casually lifted a Glock 10 from beneath the table and drew the slide back with two fingers. "Is that the noise you were looking for? No hammer to deal with on this bad boy."

The sound of the slide snapping into place increased my respect for the rapidly deteriorating situation. My hands sank obediently to my front, falling beneath the table. The muffled thud of the guns hitting the carpet was met with many relieved jeers.

"Your turn," Steve challenged me, casting his eyes toward a mountain of powder directly in front of me. The cockiness that had pervaded the room before I turned the metaphoric tables returned with a vengeance. The only thing missing from the festivities was the casting of lots for my linens.

I stared for a moment and then cautiously leaned toward the pile. Just as my nose met the drugs, I turned my head sharply to the left and dove beneath the table, shielding myself from Steve's line of fire. Steve lurched backwards, trying to find an angle to shoot me. Before he could, however, I lifted the table with my back and pressed a two-shot Derringer into his crotch. "Two shots," I said. "Two bull's eyes."

Reaching up with my left hand, I carefully removed the gun from Steve's now flaccid grip. I climbed to my feet, paying close attention to the apologies from the other dealers and their attempts to dismiss the threats upon my life as routine. I turned the gun on everyone in the room, leveling it at each of them in turn, and watching for their reactions as it pointed at their respective heads. Convinced that they were nothing but small-time drug dealers trying to impress their female cohorts, I turned the gun over in my hand and whipped it at Steve, planting the heel of the stock into his forehead. Blood dribbled down his face as he crumbled to the carpet. "Leave him alone," I insisted of the woman who knelt to his side. "He knows the price of stupidity."

"Chill out, man." Caracas pleaded. "Look what the fuck you did."

"What *I* did? What are you, *nuts*? And if you think that's all I'm doin', you've obviously misjudged me. I've only begun to exact my retribution."

"Hey, dude," the Latino began.

"Shut the fuck up," I shouted, an insane fire growing in my eyes. "You don't pretend to tell me *shit*! And stop calling me 'dude'!"

"All right. All right." A meek man sniveled. "Whatta we need to do here? Let's not go postal."

"Who the fuck are you?"

"Everyone calls me 'Blaze.'"

"What the fuck's your real name?" I snapped, impatient.

"It's Tom. Tom. It's Tom."

"That's real bright, Tom. Call yourself 'Blaze.' The cops'll never figure out what you do for a livin'. Is everyone around here that stupid? How do you people cross the street without getting hit by a bus?"

"Why don't you just talk with me," a refined-looking man advised. "Just focus on me."

"And your name?"

"Doesn't matter," he said in that all too annoying tone psychologists are known for using. "Let's just be calm and talk rational."

I fired a round at his feet, not intending to do harm. "How's that for rational?" I said calmly as blood began to squirt from a smoking shoe.

"Jeeez!" Caracas blurted. The man with the hole in his shoe was frozen in disbelief. The expected screams of agony never surfaced; he just sat on the floor against the wall and stared dumbfounded at his foot while blood oozed onto the oyster colored carpet. The smell of "small-town drug dealer" was palpable.

Fear sobered them into submission. Their trembling jaws and twitching eyelids were signs of drug roads less traveled. For me, the danger of being killed had been replaced with the less frightening danger of being arrested, a risk I nonetheless wanted to avoid if at all possible, however. "Raise your hand if you still think I'm a narc. Because if you do, I still got time to discuss it."

"No, no, no, none," they responded chaotically.

"Good. But if *I was* a cop, how smart was it to snort in front of me and then pull guns on me? If I was wired, you'd all be gettin' fucked in the ass for the next ten years by a guy name Tyrone! If we're gonna make money together, ladies, I'm gonna need a little more street savvy and a little less estrogen from you bitches. Am I makin' myself clear?"

"Are you out of your *fuckin' mind*?" snarled the man who was busy bleeding.

I leveled my weapon at his other foot. "You know," I started irreverently, "If I shot your other one, it might smooth out that limp you're likely to have."

"Shit, man," he winced while raising his arm to shield his face. He then drew his legs to his chest and added, "Lighten up, dude . . . man. I mean, man." Bursts of partially restrained laughter rippled across the room.

"You should really have that thing looked at before it becomes infected. Caracas?"

"Huh?"

"Would ya get him somethin', for God's sake."

Caracas dashed into the bathroom as the mood became more relaxed. Everyone seemed to understand that this was an incident non grata and would never be spoken of again.

"Get him to a doctor sometime tonight. Just tell 'em it was an accident. It doesn't look all that serious. Probably just needs a few stitches. Oh. And guys, from now on, when you're friskin' someone, don't be embarrassed to grab their nuts. It'll save ya alotta hassle in the long run."

I leaned over the table and without coercion, snorted a minor line. Having already bent the law to the point of breaking, I figured I had everything to gain and nothing to lose. Of course, with all that had happened, I decided not to use any of the incriminating evidence I had garnered, including the evidence against me.

A gala atmosphere soon returned, and when one of the naked "ladies" hung upside down on the fitness apparatus and invited all forms of sexual penetration, I politely grabbed my weapon from Caracas and left the party, my reputation firmly rooted. I would soon discover, however, that a reputation rooted in sand is readily extirpated.

On my way home that evening, I couldn't figure out why I felt so exhilarated and alert. I had been up for twenty-four hours straight and yet I was still raring to go. And then it dawned on me that I had snorted that line of crystal. "Wow," I gasped, sitting alone in my car. "I guess no one would be attracted to it if the only selling point was that it burns, drips into your throat, tastes like crap and makes you feel the way it tastes."

I took advantage of the stimulation to work on my book and typed for the next eight hours. Some of the best writing I've ever done, actually. And it was at that point, the point where I realized how incredibly beneficial such a drug could be, that I resolved never to repeat the experience.

Looking back on it, it tickles me that we humans think we can control the events of our lives to such exact degree. The best we can hope to do is to prepare ourselves for battle far enough in advance that we are ready, with God's help, to meet the challenge when evil comes a knockin'. And make no mistake about it, such challenges are the work of evil and not of God. We are never free of evil's temptation, but hopefully, with God's help, more prepared to wage battle against it. God is there to make sure we come to that meeting prepared. It just so happens I wasn't.

Chapter 8

Following my days off I arrived a few minutes early for work. Steve pulled alongside me on his Harley Davidson Nostalgia, strips of leather fringe looking like strips of bacon flopping at the tail of his leather jacket. He had never approached me before this, but now I was suddenly his bosom buddy. I didn't want to enter into any sort of illegal transaction with him any time too soon because the sordid events at Caracas's house were still fresh in everyone's mind, and I feared this would increase the probability that the incident might surface during a monitored conversation with him. JACNET surely couldn't look the other way on that one.

"Hey, my man!" He reacted to a bond that didn't exist. "How's things?"

"Things are good. Just tired, I guess." The word was no sooner out of my mouth than I regreted having said it. Telling a co-worker that you are "tired" first thing in the morning is part of the small-talk ritual engrained in the American workplace. A remark as commonly spoken as "Another day, another dollar," I suppose.

"I'm sure the doctor can fix that!"

"I told ya, I'm in it for the money." I then turned my attention toward the mill. "God, I hate this place."

"Why? It'll probably make you rich some day."

"Rich? Who the hell you been talkin' to? I'm not making squat."

"That's 'cause you're dealin' with those losers on [Chain] Four. Save for Tari, that is. Come on over to the dark side, Luke."

"*Save* for Tari? *Save for*? Are you serious?"

"Yeah, that's proper English, dude. You should use it in that book I hear you're writing."

"No book of mine will ever contain the words *save for*, I can assure you. Not in that order, anyhow. *Save for*. Wrong country, wrong century. *Dark side*? I think you mean Dark Ages." When I was done tap dancing, I turned toward the mill, hoping I had sidetracked him enough to avoid any further discussion about drugs.

"Let me know!"

"We'll talk," I shouted over my shoulder and left it at that. I then walked back into the place I hated most.

When Tari greeted me with a warm and bright smile, I realized that I was going about this all wrong. This was important work, but it didn't require that I stoop to the same level as my adversaries. Well, it sounded good anyhow. The fact is, this was not the kind of work that was very forgiving of people wanting to live a clean and sober life or anything approximating one. You couldn't just leave what you did at the office. It became an integral part of your life, whether you liked it or not, whether you resisted it or not.

As I talked with Tari throughout the day, steering clear of anything negative or illegal, I found myself thinking about what I had accomplished thus far. Granted, I was leaps and bounds ahead of my predecessors, but they were imbeciles. The question was, was I really cleaning up the mill or just Chains Three and Four? There were six manned chains and two unmanned chains in that hellhole, by the way. To continue down this prim path of scoring two buys from one person and then moving on to the next would never, in my estimation, nail a real, bona fide drug dealer. But if I was patient and refused anyone not willing to deal up each time, maybe I could smoke out the mill's kingpin.

So that was it. I began refusing—or in Phil's case, ignoring—all my suppliers, except for Jim, that is. I made another small purchase from him to secure the indictment.

"Booch?" Jim leaned over to me on the chain, both of us drenched in sweat. "My boy can get me an ounce. You want it?"

"Too risky. I'm only out for big scores from now on."

"It's better than goin' dry."

"Who says I'm going dry? Believe me, I'm wet. I'm friggin' water-logged, dude."

"How much we talking?" he asked in a loud, scratchy voice, his eyes never contacting mine. As if that actually fooled anybody.

"Not ounces."

"Keys?"

"It better have the word kilo in it."

"I'll see what I can do."

"Yeah, you do that, bro."

I was sure he would never come up with it, so I pretty much erased everyone from Chain Four off my target list. I filled the ensuing reports with categories like "Talk of Hard Drugs," "Unsafe Working Conditions" and "Poor Supervision." All of which were important to a healthy work environment, but none of which mattered one iota to Krout and Schneider. K and S cared about one thing and one thing only; criminal offenses. I don't care if you identified all of the management and safety problems in the company. If you didn't ferret out drugs and theft, the case was a complete failure. After about three weeks of "Johnny doesn't know how to supervise," I received a call from Gordon.

"Things have kinda died down there, huh?" he said with much insinuation.

"Up here," I corrected.

"What?"

"No. I'm just playin' it cool while things settle down."

"Settle down? Why? What's the matter? What's unsettled?"

"Nothing's the matter. These people aren't stupid, you know. Well, not entirely anyhow. They get to smellin' pork when a person keeps buying twice from one person, then moves on to the next, increasing his risk exponentially."

"That's never been a problem before."

"*Before* where?"

"Well, Campbell's, for instance."

"Oh, please. Don't tell me you bought that crock o' shit?"

"You know something we don't?"

"Something you apparently don't wanna know. Because I refuse to believe you haven't already seen through that bullshit."

"Crock of shit? What crock of shit?"

"What?

"You're callin' it a crock of shit. What crock of shit?"

"I said bullshit. I said crock o' shit before that."

"What? I . . . I don't . . . Who cares what you . . ."

"You gotta be a better listener. Anyhow, let's move on because it's obvious you don't wanna know."

"I don't think there's anything *to* know. He's bought from . . . I mean, he's seen about forty people doing drugs there."

"A far cry from buying drugs from forty people, wouldn'tcha say?"

"Meaning?"

"*Meaning* he's full of shit. Forty people aren't smokin' dope in front of this guy if not a one of 'em is willing to sell to him. Now stop pretending I'm as stupid as everyone else. If you have anyone at K and S that can do this job better than me, you're welcome to send 'em up here. But in the meantime, stop bullshitting me!"

"Calm down for Chris' sakes," he admonished with a stern tongue. "I don't need another one of your harangue pies. No one's saying you're not doing a good job down there."

I thought for a moment about his cute play on the words *meringue* and *harangue* but was far too aggravated to pay him any compliments. "I don't give a crap if they are or they aren't. I know I'm the best you've got, and I sure as hell don't need confirmation from some desk jockeys. If you have someone better, don't be shy, send 'em on up. This place'll eat 'em alive in a week. Oh, wait. You already know that, don'tcha? Two K and S bitches already tried and were summarily tossed out on their respective keesters. And Rubin (the UCI at Campbell's Soup Company of Ohio) is the most unscrupulous motherfucker I know. And believe me, that says a lot, because I know *me!*"

"Are you done?"

"And it's up here, not down here."

"Are you done?"

"Is that a rhetorical question?"

"Look, all I'm sayin' is ya gotta get close to these guys. Especially the Spreaders. We really think there's a lot goin' on there."

"*We* think so, huh? Sure. Whatever, Gordon. I'll get close enough to tell you what type of hemorrhoid medicine they use."

"That might be too close. Just get close enough to tell me if they use a softener."

"Does that include the females?"

"I don't think there're any women on the Spreaders, are there?"

"No, it was a joke," I said, realizing that he had the comedic leavening of Al Gore. "Anyhow, I'm working it."

"We really need to keep this thing going; that's all I'm saying."

"By 'keep it goin',' I take it you mean encourage people to sell me drugs?"

"Yeah. It's what you're paid for."

"One of the things. In a manner of speaking. But I can't buy drugs from people not predisposed to sell them."

"You work there. How many people you think do that work without help?"

I sighed in frustration. "Sounds like a whole other problem to me. But what do I know. Don't worry about it. Okay, Gordon? Things'll pick back up again."

"Good. That's what Gino wanted to hear. Whatta ya think, a few days or so?"

I sniggered. "Yeah, sure. Whatever. Is that all you were callin' about?"

"That's it. Go get us a Spreader," he said like a big game hunter. "And remind me to tell you about Glenn when I come see you."

"Glenn? Come see me?"

"Yeah, remind me."

"You're coming to see me? When? Why?"

"Nothing to worry about. I wanna get together with you, Bud, JACNET and the D.A. to do some strategizing."

"Strategizing?"

"Yeah."

I gave up on that line of questioning. "And Glenn?"

"He's no longer with us. I'll explain it to ya when I see ya."

I at once fell silent, allowing the pregnant pause to convey my reaction. "I don't think I can take another mental lap dance today, Gordon. I'll see ya."

"Don't worry about it. I'll fill you in when I see you. Good luck. And hey, you're doing a great job down there."

"Up here."

"Up there."

"See ya, Gordy."

For the next week or so I made no effort to break new ground at the mill. I believed, and still do, that to do so would have been to unduly influence someone into dealing with me. Especially when you consider the major effect news of the incident at Caracas's humble abode would likely have had on the people Gordon wanted me to target.

Tari and I had a liaison or two in the mountainous countryside around Ashland, where our relationship unintentionally blossomed like a field of poppies shortly after a nuclear explosion. The intent of the detonation is not to grow flowers, but boy do they ever grow. But, as I would learn, albeit as slow as a retarded bulldog on barbiturates, any deal that appeared free of conflict generally had an addendum that made the remainder of the contract nonnegotiable. In this case, it was her boyfriend. Not that I had a problem with a woman dumping me for another guy or vice versa, excluding matrimonial relationships, but to dump a guy who by all accounts seemed to be a nice person, excepting his wanting to kill me, just seemed wrong. Then I began to wonder about her motivations. And whenever I did that, it was only a matter of time before I moved on.

We met in one of those ostentatious coffee shops in downtown Ashland one evening to discuss what she termed an "important matter." It turned out that she wanted me to essentially talk her into dumping her boyfriend for me. Aside from the fact that he bored her to tears and that she wasn't physically attracted to him, they shared a lot in common, like an immense passion for the great outdoors. Why then did she need me to talk her into anything? I suspect it was because he was rich.

Tari was physically attracted to me and thought that I was quite funny and mentally stimulating, but for the life of me I could not see how that was any less artificial than dating a guy because he liked to go camping and could afford to get there in a Range Rover.

Keith showed up at the coffee shop at around 11:00 P.M., and appeared ready to do battle. I was sitting at a booth with Tari and had no practical way to maneuver except across her. Keith hurried to our table and sat directly across from us. He was visibly distraught. "I need to talk with you," he pleaded with Tari.

"Not now," Tari coldly snapped. "Go home, Keith. You shouldn't be here."

Without so much as a glance in my direction, he continued, "Come on. Come with me. I need to talk with you. Just for a minute. Pleeease?"

"Keith, you really need to go." Her voice showed contempt. "I'll call you."

"Give him a break," I interrupted. "Go on and talk to him."

"No. This isn't right," she persisted.

"What isn't right? If I were him, I'd be here too. I think he has that right, don't you?"

"Ken," Keith said, turning his attention and glistening eyes toward me, his speech now muddled with sobbing, "You sound like you're probably an all right guy, but this is between me and my Tari."

"Fair enough," I agreed.

Tari pivoted in her seat to face me. "It has everything to do with you."

"Fine," I said, "But would you just go somewhere and talk with him?"

"Let's go," she said begrudgingly, grabbing him by the arm and leading him out the door and down the street a short distance. When she returned without him a few minutes later, she apologized for his behavior and began attacking his manhood. When I finally had enough, I told her what I thought.

"The guy loves you. Can't you understand that?"

"That doesn't mean he hasta come down here cryin' like a baby. It's embarrassing."

"For who?"

"For him."

"He loves you, for God's sake. He's not concerned about his image at a time like this. I'd think you'd be proud of a guy that'd be willing to cry in front of another guy over his girl. Do you think he wanted me to see him that way? Hell no! He'd rather fight me than have me see him that way."

"Yeah, right. He knows you'd kick the crap outta him."

"Do you really think that's why he chose this approach instead?"

"Yeah. Whatta you think?"

"I think he realizes you'd dump him if he pulled a stunt like that."

"So he cries like a little baby instead?"

"He's an emotional guy; what can I say?"

"Why you defending him? He tried to kill you at the mill, and he's sleeping with me."

"He's *sleeping* with you?" I said facetiously. "Screw the little whiny-ass sissy boy." We both laughed hysterically. But the fact that she could stay with a man she had such little respect for really stuck in my craw. Hell, I had a higher opinion of him than she did.

Except for this one flaw—her love of money and the accompanying baggage—we were great together. At the time I thought it was a shame, but having since found the perfect woman, I am grateful for the way things turned out and for the friendship and the time that Tari and I had together.

Just before the evening ended, while sitting in my car in an Ashland parking lot, she said the most peculiar thing. "You know, there is a rumor that meth is being mixed with boat stock glue and shipped to a company that services rich clients with dinghies." *Boat stock* referred to the perfect grade of wood (no knots) needed to produce plywood for boats. The glue used for such wood also had a unique set of specifications particular to the plywood's end use. She had a habit, which I shamelessly exploited, of giving me tidbits of information on subjects that she thought I was interested in whenever it appeared our conversation was lapsing or getting too platonic.

"And?"

"Supposedly the glue is broken down with a simple recipe and the crank is extracted on the other end. It might be coke, though. But I think it's crank."

"Sounds like a lot of work for very little gain."

"Are you kidding? If it's true, they strip those babies down and they've got kilos and kilos of crank."

"Or coke."

"Or coke."

"But boats are expensive."

"Dinghies."

"Ahhh. I see. That makes sense. That'd be pretty freakin' ingenious."

"It's just a rumor."

"Where'd you hear it?"

"Keith told me. Well, actually, I've heard it from a number of people," she explained, naming some that I knew and some that I didn't.

"Spreaders?"

"Mostly. Uh-huh."

"You think that's why Keith's so freaked out over our getting together?"

"No. I mean, he's mentioned it. Like, you know, 'have you said anything to him?' Shit like that. But mostly it's the fact that he thinks you're having sex with me."

"I hope you've told him we're not."

"Why? It's none of his business. You don't ask me about he and I."

"That's because you volunteer everything."

"That's because I feel like I owe you an explanation . . . but not him. I can't explain it. I just don't have the same kinda feelings toward him that I have toward you. I don't know. It's complicated."

"If you really feel that way about him, I think you owe him an explanation."

"He'll just cry like he always does and nothin'll change. He doesn't care how I feel, just as long as I'll marry him. He's as much as said it. He says he doesn't mind if I grow to love him. You believe that?"

"Question is, do *you* mind? Forget that! *Why* are you with him? Regardless of what happens to you and I, I don't think you should even consider marrying this guy unless you feel toward him what you think you need to feel to get married. It's not fair to you, and it's certainly not fair to him, no matter what he thinks. He'll be a lot happier someday with a person who cares deeply for him than he will be with you. And to be honest, after seeing him tonight, I think he deserves that. He seems like a real genuine guy, and that's hard to find nowadays."

"If I break up with him, then what? I wait to see how you feel in a few months? "

"Oh," I said with an inflection and eyebrows crawling up my forehead, "So that's it."

"What? I should be ashamed for not wanting to give up a pretty good thing without knowing what for?"

"Do you hear yourself? You're a beautiful woman . . . smart, great personality . . . and you're playin' let's make a deal with two mill rats?"

"It's not like that. Keith and I have a lot of fun together. We share all the same interests. We . . ."

"Make a lot of money."

"He doesn't care about that."

"As long as it means he gets to keep you, he cares."

"It's not like that."

"Do you love him?"

"Yes. Not in the same way I care for you, that's all. But I love 'im just the same."

My eyebrows collapsed. "What?" I abruptly followed that up by saying, "We should get goin'."

"Great." Her voice sank. "You think I'm a gold-digging, two-timing bitch now."

"No, not at all. How much more plastic are your motivations than mine? Looks are an important factor in any of my relationships, but apparently not to you."

"He's not ugly."

"I know that. You know what I'm sayin'. It's not the most important thing to you."

"It's not your looks, either, you know. It's our conversations. You and I can talk endlessly about anything. You're smart and funny and very analytical. He's none of that."

"Well, we're goin' in circles with this. I'm none of what he is, either. That's neither good nor bad. You just need to assess what it is you can live with and what you can't live without. Nuff said. New subject."

*   *   *

Because the Ashland meeting had been on the last day of our weekend (we shared one of our days off), I would see her at work the following afternoon. Keith was on the day shift and therefore typically had limited contact with me during the brief, half-hour changeover period before my shift began at 3:00. The bizarre chain of events leading up to that afternoon, however, was to be anything but typical. Even as I write these words, I realize that nothing was truly as it seemed at that mill, especially as it related to what transpired that afternoon and what precipitated it.

Chapter 9

The phone rang at 7:13 A.M. "This better be important," I rasped with a larynx that could best be described as parched and scratchy.

"Ken, it's me," Tari's voice faltered. "I gotta see you right away. It's urgent."

"What's wrong? Did he hit you?"

"No, it's not about Keith. It's about something I told you, I think. Can I meet you somewhere? Away from Medford?"

"Sure. You know the area better than I do. Where do you think?"

"Do you know where Table Rock is?"

"No, but I can find it. Give me the directions."

She proceeded to give me detailed directions, right down to the specific boulder where I was to meet her. It required some serious walking, so I dressed accordingly. And, of course, I brought my gun. What I did not do, however, which had become a reprehensible habit, was notify any of my support team; that is, JACNET, K and S, Bud, and so on.

When I arrived at the site, I saw her pacing off in the distance at the exact location she had described. I hunkered down and surveyed the surrounding area with due diligence. Still crouched, I scampered to another vantage point, one that provided an approach from an entirely different angle. As I crept up from behind her, I cautiously scanned the perimeter. She occasionally crossed in front of me as she paced back and forth, still facing away from me.

"Tari?" I said softly.

"Ken." She spun about, the sound of relief in her voice corporeal. "Thank God you're here."

With her arms tight around my neck, words began to gush from her. "I mentioned to Keith the rumor I told you about, and then he told Steve from the Spreaders." She pulled away from me and held up a hand slightly over her head as she described him. "You know. Good-looking guy, about this tall . . ."

"Yeah, yeah, yeah. I know Steve. What about 'im?"

"Well, then he told some other guy I'd never heard of, and he . . ."

I was visibly anxious. "Yeah, yeah, I've seen this commercial before. What the hell happened?"

"I don't know, but we get these goons over this morning pushing Keith around and threatening him. He wouldn't say what it was about, but I know it had something to do with what I told you. One of 'em was an auxiliary cop or something. Keith's always tryin' to pretend he's more connected than he is, so he won't admit to me that he doesn't have a clue about what's goin' on. Oh, God, I'm scared, Ken. I'm really worried."

As I placed my hands on her shoulders to comfort her, a red light danced upon her white cotton shirt. "Down," I screeched, pulling her to the ground and dragging her roughly across the gravelly dirt to protective shelter behind the boulder. No shots were fired. We trembled with our backs to the rock and watched as the light bounced about the dirt immediately in front of us. Directing her attention to the erratic red beam, I made her understand why we had suddenly become so intimate with the earth.

"Oh, my God. Is that what I think it is?"

"You tell me."

"You think *I* did this? I'm out here too, you know."

"Yeah," I said with a dubious tone of skepticism. "I couldn't help but notice that he didn't shoot when he had you in the cross hairs."

"I swear, Ken. I swear." She slapped her thighs. "I didn't know anything about this. I swear! Whoever it is . . . *Whoever it is* is gonna kill us both! Oh, my God. What are we gonna do?" Her head smacked backwards against the rock hard enough for me to hear.

"God's certainly a great place to start," I responded with grave sincerity, twisting my head rapidly to glance above the rock. "Now let me think.

Let me think. Okay. Come on, Ken. Let me . . ." my voice trailed off as my eyes darted about the ground before me.

As the laser crossed each time, seemingly for effect, I began to learn things about our enemy's position. Assuming he wasn't standing a few feet away, the distance from where the laser struck the ground to the boulder suggested he was perched high above us. As the beam passed each time, I detected a small break, approximately two feet in width, where the light left no trace. This indicated that the assailant's vision was obstructed by an object, likely a tree, and that it was probably too far in front of him to maneuver around. I marked the soil on both sides with my finger.

"Your hubby have a laser like that?" I probed while extracting my .45 automatic from my pants.

Her eyes distended. "What are you gonna do?"

"Never mind! Answer the damn question!"

"What? A red thing like that?" She stabbed her finger toward the light as it became less nomadic and steadied on the ground to my right. "No! I don't think so. No! I'd know! I'm sure I would remember. What are you gonna do?"

I flaunted the gun in her face. "Teach 'im a lesson, I hope."

Except for an occasional shimmer, the light became stationary in the dirt. I leaned out into the killing field, doing my best to keep as much of my body within the lines that I had drawn in the dirt as possible. On my knees, I reached my gun out in front of me, the barrel facing back toward me in the direction of my head and my thumbs resting delicately on the trigger. As I extended further and further away from the relative safety of the rock, the laser beam bobbed slightly. My arms were becoming heavy and began to shake. My heart pounded in my chest and resonated in my ears. My knees scraped along the gravel inch by inch until the barrel of my gun neared the beam.

"What are you doing?" Tari demanded, her voice brimming with terror. I didn't reply. I couldn't.

Just as the light began to move again, I moved my gun toward it, the barrel still wavering precariously in the direction of my head. Taking a deep breath and exhaling slightly, I steadied the gun just long enough to place the beam directly into the center of the barrel. With a tuck of my head and a gentle squeeze on the trigger, I fired a bullet over my shoulder back along the path of the beam. The gun recoiled and flew from my grip.

The explosion rendered my hearing completely numb except for a faint, high-pitched ringing, and the beam instantly vanished.

I rolled away from the boulder and retrieved the gun, which had been hurled several feet away. Covering Tari, I instructed her to flee.

"Let's go! Let's go," I screamed repetitiously. We scampered just as fast as our legs would travel until we reached the nearest cover. When we made it to the edge of the sheltering forest, I pulled her down behind a group of large pine trees and thick underbrush.

"Did you kill him?" she said ominously.

"Just who would 'him' be?"

"For the last time, I had nothing to do with this!"

"Why aren't they firing?"

"I told you," she snapped. "For the last time . . ."

"It was a rhetorical question for Pete's sake. Chill out already. I just don't get it, that's all."

"Maybe you got 'im."

"With that little stunt I just pulled?"

"It's like a military thing or something, right?"

"Hell, no. I just made that up. I didn't hit shit. I just wanted to get close enough to scare 'im, that's all."

"Oh." She seemed concerned, if not a bit disappointed.

"Maybe they were just messin' with us. You know, tryin' to scare us into shutting up about something, or breaking us up. Or something like that."

"You think it's that glue stuff?" she asked tentatively.

"You mean that malarkey about meth . . ."

"Or coke."

I sighed briefly in frustration. ". . . Or coke being placed in the glue and then sold in boats?"

"Yeah. Then they break it down and . . ."

"Pleeease! Get a grip already. This is about you and me. It's your stupid boyfriend. Or maybe that bitch Linda or something. Maybe I stepped on someone's toes. I'm sure that's it in a nutshell." I reached my hand out and gripped her shoulder. "Now stay here, I'm gonna try 'n get to the bottom of this."

"I'm not stayin' nowhere."

My confidence in her veracity was supported by her desire to go with me into the lion's den. "Then stay close to me. And do what I tell you, when I tell you. Got it?"

"Ready when you are."

Moving along the edge of the thicket in a crouched position, we searched gingerly for any signs of danger. Mild breezes rustled through the leaves and needles, smoothing over any sounds that might suggest someone was pursuing us or skulking nearby. Tari traversed the natural obstacle course like a gazelle evading a leopard. With my overachieving, arthritic body, I was breathing heavily, but she barely showed any signs of respiratory fatigue, much to the dissatisfaction of my delicate male ego. Each time I stopped to observe what was in front of us, I would turn to find her hardly gasping and nary a bud of sweat on her perfectly smooth, milky white forehead. Her face, which appeared oblivious to my obvious exhaustion, was like a three-hundred-foot neon sign saying, "What? Why are we stopping?"

When I saw what appeared to be a deer blind in a large tree off to my right, I believed I had found our attacker's observation post. Inching up slowly on the blind, which stood about twenty feet off the ground, we canvassed the immediate area with our eyes, ever cognizant that our unwanted visitor might still be lurking nearby. As Tari walked to my side, I detected the laser on her ankle.

"Watch out," I whispered stridently, pushing her aside. "Get down."

Now on our stomachs, I grabbed a fallen branch and passed it over the spot where Tari had been standing. The beam was still shining, steady and unwavering. The odd thing about these lasers is that they generally can only be detected at the point of impact. The path that they follow can often be invisible to the naked eye, especially during the daytime. Because there was a large log merely twenty feet away that would have obscured anyone lying behind it, I immediately concluded that the gun had been dropped. I came to my feet cautiously and, in a stooped posture, moved to where I thought the gun might lie. To my surprise, resting upon a hunk of bark was a laser pointer, the type typically used by professional lecturers.

"Someone's playing a very dangerous game," I stated, slowly standing erect.

"Why?" she asked cautiously. "What'd you find?"

"This." I flipped her the pointer while keeping my attention on the shadowy woods around us. "Recognize it?"

"Should I?"

"Dollars to a doughnut it's got your hubby's fingerprints on it."

"If that's the case," she responded with a hint of dread in her throat, extending her arm to reveal a bloodstained hand, "Then this would be type A negative."

"Let me see that." My eyes protruded with terror. A cursory check of the area disclosed an even more ominous picture. A blood trail leading away from the pointer suggested a wound not readily stanched. The drops were small and sparse, but there was enough blood to warrant concern. My only hope was that the wound was caused by tree shrapnel or a short fall and not by the bullet itself.

"We should be getting outta here," I said.

Clutching her right hand with my left, I held the gun in my right hand and swept back and forth across the woods as we hastily retreated backwards toward our cars. Once in the open, we turned and ran. Slicing our arms on the occasional brier and bruising our legs on fallen tree limbs, we didn't stop until we reached our vehicles.

Leaning her head outside her car, Tari cast an arm around my neck, yanked me in and kissed me hard on the lips. "I had nothing to do with this."

Shamefully short of breath, I responded, "I know."

Her eyes filled with tears. "What just happened?"

"I don't know. We'll talk later. Let's just get outta here before someone sees us." And so we did.

*   *   *

When I went to work that afternoon, I made a special effort to look for Tari's boyfriend, Keith, before he completed the shift changeover. To my surprise, he showed no signs of injury. Although I was relieved, I was more confused than ever. In fact, not a single person at the mill exhibited any signs of having been wounded outside the normal cuts and scrapes of the mill.

That evening, after making several noble attempts at writing a report that accurately reflected what had happened, I became discouraged and opted instead to lard the report with a number of innocuous entries such as "Poor Supervision" and "Safety Violations."

I went to the movies the following day with Macki, and she helped me forget about the mill and all its depravity. At least for a few hours, anyhow. She had an uncanny knack for helping me see things through unstained glass. Things were just more innocent and insouciant when she was around.

By the time my weekend had come to a close, I had actually reached the point of relaxation. But in this line of work, I would learn that there was such a thing as being too relaxed.

By this juncture in the investigation, my wood-pulling skills rivaled those of the best pullers in the mill, Chain Three notwithstanding. I was now rotating among all six chains, which provided me access to more employees and expanded my investigation exponentially.

"How ya feeling?" Tari seemed concerned. "I thought I'd hear from you before now."

"I'm sorry. I just needed a break."

"From me?"

"No, not from you. Just all this." I swept my hand across the mill as if it were a canvas I was painting. "I just wanted to get away and relax. That's all. How've you been?"

"A mess. I didn't hear from you. I didn't know what to think. Keith's been asking about us. He thinks I'm sleeping with you. He says you're a narc."

"What is it you tell him?"

"That we're just good friends. I care for you. I couldn't lie. Not completely, anyhow."

"No, no. I mean about the narc stuff?"

My response did not elicit the emotions I had hoped for. Her face twitched and stiffened, and her eyes immediately filled with tears. She bowed her head to the chain and went about the business of pulling wood. I had obviously tipped my hat, however inadvertently, to the thing I valued most, however unconsciously. It must have confirmed in her that which she feared most: that my drug activities meant more to me than she did.

"We'll talk later!" I hollered over the unrelenting noise, not wanting to shout out that I cared for her, too.

"Booch?" Stan shouted. "Break Chain Six!"

I turned to Tari for her usual words of wisdom, but she had already bolted for the lunchroom. Her moping demeanor and slouched posture indicated that I had screwed up on both a personal and professional level. The personal level was the only one that I cared about at the time, however. It wouldn't be long, though, before I felt the full breadth and impact of the professional screwup as well.

I traversed my way around and beneath the matrix of lethal machinery and beat a path to the opposite end of the mill. The constant bombardment of clashing sounds made the building shimmy round the clock, but it was most detectable when I entered or walked through the building.

As I ducked under a conveyor chain that dropped from on high like a pool slide, I saw Chief directly in front of me. Printed on the back of his black tee shirt was a gray depiction of Jesus adorned in thorns. The shirt read simply, "He Gave His Only Begotten Son." As I swung around him, I quickly glanced at the front. The poignant words, "What Has God Done for You Lately?" prompted me to comment, "Cool shirt, Chief."

Not unlike Ray Liotta in the movie *Goodfellas*, I felt that those simple, innocuous words would be my undoing. In fact, like the movie, it was as though everything stopped and Liotta's voiceover said, "Just like that. A guy says 'cool shirt' and he could be dead."

Crossing into a sector of the mill I had previously avoided, I caught the eye of a disarmingly cute woman who was activating a piece of equipment I had not yet been introduced to. When she smiled down at me from her platform, my getting introduced to that machinery became the utmost priority. Without having ever met her, I conferred on her all the qualities lacking in this place and everyone in it. For that instant, and until we would formally meet, she was as pure as the virgin snow that settled atop the majestic pine trees in the Oregon mountains. As always, I was idealizing a person based on a single encounter. If only I could have avoided meeting her, she would likely have remained that way to this day. But as history would prove, I just couldn't leave well enough alone.

When I got to Chain Six, I was greeted harshly with "Catch those fuckin' carts," by a country hick with an extremely gruff appearance.

"I'm Scott," he started, with a demeaning bent to his voice. "And you're late!"

"Actually, it's Ken. And I came when I was broke, pal."

He slid down from the front of the chain, shuffling like a hermit crab and carrying six long pieces of wood that must have totaled nearly a hundred and fifty pounds. After effortlessly snapping them into a cart, he confronted me, invading my neutral space like an NFL linebacker. "Try spending less time flirting with Sherry-cherry over there and more time walking next time."

I smiled. "So it's Sherry, huh? Thanks, Scotty!"

"I'm goin' on break! You got the chain!" He grinned and brushed past me.

Before I could retort with the requisite profanity, wood piled at the end of the chain, folding and snapping until it jammed the entire line back to where it spilled out from the dryer. As I searched for help after shutting down the conveyor, I noticed something rather peculiar about Chain Six. With the dryer at the head and The Hog at the foot, a bearing wall on one side and the huge, as yet unidentified machines that Sherry operated on the other, it was the undisputed bastard chain of the mill. No one could fully appreciate the precarious nature of my situation unless they stood where I did. And of course, no one did.

The chain was apparently an afterthought, as if the designer said, "What are we gonna do with this excess space over here in the corner?" Although the wood took time to lumber down the chain, it was generally very heavy and of various grades. By the time I had hurled an eight-foot piece of lumber into the appropriate bin at the end of the chain, ten more pieces were barreling down on me, none of which belonged in the carts I was standing near. After subsequently dragging several pieces of wood over the top of still more pieces flowing down the chain, crisscrossing them in the process, I decided to throw the wood into whatever cart was accessible, regardless of grade. The way I looked at it, by the time the problem was discovered at the Spreaders, I would be long gone from Chain Six and Scotty would be left holding the bag.

When Scott did return, he immediately began to inspect the carts—something I hadn't counted on. His return also marked the end of my sentence on Chain Six. At least for today. As I went to pass him, however, the hand he placed on my chest said that our opinions probably differed somewhat on that issue.

"Where the hell *you* goin'?" A question framed more like a directive.

"I'm on break."

"No you're not. You're gonna straighten out this mess while I keep the chain running."

"It's a mess because you took a thirty-minute break while I was left to fend for myself! That's why it's a mess!"

I'm not sure why, but I didn't quite know how to take him at first. Even though he was stomping all over me, I did nothing to stop him. Unless, of course, you consider stumbling over my words and pretending to be a doormat a good countermeasure. Standing there with a doltish look on my face and completely ignoring his commands only served to exacerbate his already foul mood.

"What are you, *deaf*?" he began to spew. "Don't fuck with *the king* now! You're messin with *the king*! The king don't like no drug dealers! Got no place for no drug dealers on my chain! You wanna deal drugs, work on Chain Three or Four, or even the Green End, but not on my chain! You mess with the king, you get the crown . . . ," he paused as though he did not have an appropriate ending to his sentence, ". . . *up your ass*!"

As he continued his diatribe, I reflected on the past a la Grasshopper of *Kung Fu* fame. Hearkening back to a period many years earlier when my older brother Danny, my best friend Mark Rizzo and I all worked a summer job in Framingham, Massachusetts, with a truck driver who boasted of being "The King" of all eighteen-wheelers, I expected to find the necessary wisdom to deal with my present situation. Unlike Grasshopper, however, my meditation took me back to a time when I was just as stupid about such things as I was in the present.

Just before things got out of hand, Chief arrived on scene clutching a brown paper bag and gesturing for me to go on break. "Here," he said, pressing the bag to my abdomen. "It's only ten bucks. Pay me whenever you get a chance."

A quick peek into the crumpled brown bag told me more than I wanted to know. Nothing could put the fear of God into a drug dealer faster than Jesus Christ himself. Not even the police could evoke such consternation.

And, speaking of our savior, guess what was balled up in the sack? You guessed it, a crisp new tee shirt just like the one I had admired on Chief.

Facing away from Scott, my only hope was that he hadn't seen the transfer. But then he gave me a sudden shove from behind, and I was sure that he had.

"Fuckin' drug dealers are all alike!" he vented.

Although it took me longer than Bill Bixby to get green on this guy, I bounded to my feet determined to squelch his relentless aggression. I recoiled with the tenacity of a wolverine, only to find Chief grappling with him, forcing Scott's forehead down upon the moving conveyor chain. The repetitious thuds that resonated from Scott's skull were amazingly harmonious and not the type of sounds you would generally associate with the living. Plead and plead as he might, his bloodcurdling screams did not move Chief to emancipate his face from the chain's torment.

"I think he's learned his lesson, Chief," I offered impartially, in deference to Chief's obvious physical superiority. More important than rescuing Scott was being careful not to shift Chief's disappointment toward me.

As if under my spell, he relented without further incident. I moved next to Chief and offered my gratitude. "That would be the latest thing God's done for me," I said.

"Enjoy the dope!" he bellowed joyously. "Best drug on the planet!"

From that moment on, I was convinced that Chief knew what I was doing there at the mill and that he was sympathetic to the moral duplicity I was obliged to act out in this place. I smiled mildly and winked. Chief grinned and began his customary war dance, pulling wood off the chain as he hopped about on one foot. He chanted in a cadence that had a very distinct pattern to it, adding an element of authenticity to an already kaleidoscopic personality.

Before departing for my well-deserved ten-minute break, I made a passing assessment of Scott's face. His skin was like an overused eraser: shiny, flattened on one side and smooth. It had an almost glossy blue look to it. Aside from the fact that his forehead looked very tender and a lump was forming at the center, he was essentially fit for duty. At least in plywood mill terms.

Staggering to his position at the rear of the chain, he glanced from the corner of his eye at Chief. And when he happened to turn in my direction, he startled and fell backwards against a cart of wood. Profound fear and disorientation now shrouded the bully within.

"See ya, Chief," I called out before turning toward the break room. As odd as this entire mill experience had become, the very fact that I was comfortable with openly expressing my interest in drugs, yet paralyzed with fear by the mere possibility that someone would catch me with a shirt depicting Jesus Christ, was utterly and completely preposterous. As I passed the Spreaders on my way to the break room, it occurred to me that Scott failed to include them in his running commentary on areas of the mill that embraced drug use. Something as benign as that could make a UCI suspicious about an employee's impropriety. Particularly when said employee had already pissed off the UCI.

When I punched out my report that evening, I left the window wide open on Scott. In fact, I may have crossed into that gray area of casting suspicion on someone for no other reason than I didn't like him. Oh, sure, I rationalized that his ruffian nature was not conducive to a harmonious work environment, but the fact is, he pushed me on the ground and was mean to me and that was why I cast aspersions on him, not because I had probable cause to do so. This was a job that demanded objectification of all accusations, but in reality encouraged, suborned and engendered subjectivity.

Deep down I knew that what I was doing was wrong, but at the time I figured if Scott stayed the course and essentially remained an asshole, I could cast enough innuendo around his kingdom to warrant an interview at the conclusion of the case. The way I saw it, if his character were impeached and he admitted to wrongdoing, which he would, the mill would be rid of one more rodent. It was a cynical attitude, to be sure.

Speaking of the interviews, the reason they were so successful was the unscrupulous, yet marginally legal way in which they were conducted. Once an employee was dredged through the cold and formal preamble to the inquisition, which, if done craftily, would create an aura of omnipotence around the enigmatic interviewing "agency," the employee learned about all the tools used to acquire information—the cameras, wire taps, bugs, undercover investigators, fellow employees, and so on—none of which may even have applied to his or her specific case, and then, and only then, was the interview conducted.

The interviewee was typically taken to a wailing, I mean waiting, room and seated with a number of employees he or she had been known to associate with. They were then simultaneously taken into separate rooms that adjoined one another. During the interview, the interviewer frequently left the room at strategic moments, leading the interviewee to believe that he had gone to one of the adjoining rooms to verify key information. While the first interviewer was gone, another interviewer would come in and ask the interviewee some questions concerning one of the other deposed employees. When the first interviewer returned, he would come armed with some very damning "facts." The interviewee, believing his friends had rolled over on him for a better deal, would attempt to strike a deal for himself. Vague offers of "support" would be proffered and the employee would cop to a slew of illegal acts that the company didn't even know about before the interview.

I have rarely seen an employee go into an interview room and come out with his or her job. Ultimately, I was sending Scott to the Policemen's Ball without his Miranda card just because I didn't like him, not because I knew of any specific illegal activity he was involved in. If he went into that interview room, he definitely wasn't coming out employed. His only hope was to make amends. Guilty until proven amiable, I suppose. Before going to bed that night, I stuffed my Jesus shirt beneath some junk buried in my closet, right next to my Bible.

Chapter 11

I was now three and a half months into the investigation and was dreading even the mere thought of going to work. Not because of the moral conflict within me, although that had also reached the point of combustion, but because I simply hated the scorching, pounding, grueling environment. The simple act of driving past the mill or catching a brief whiff of sawdust in the air would make me agitated and queasy. The carrot Gordon constantly waved in front of my nose, about becoming a case supervisor in the event this investigation turned out to be a success, was all that kept me going.

As I began to realize that this mill was not a sanctuary for drug dealers but rather a drug den where plywood was occasionally produced, I began to see things more clearly. It was an insight similar to one of those once-popular paintings that required you have to gaze upon without focusing your eyes and, as a result, a hidden picture is revealed within. I simply needed to lose focus in order to see things more clearly.

With the presumption of guilt jading my every maneuver, I forged ahead like Joseph McCarthy. I also succumbed to the temptation of using innuendo as an instrument of personal vengeance. This certainly was the case when it came to Linda, Paul and Scott.

The tactic of building a case of cards against someone was the underpinning of the UCI's handbook. For practical purposes, K and S wanted the UCIs to use their judgment on such information. Subscribing to a variation of the old adage "Kill 'em all and let God sort 'em out," K and S strongly suggested that the UCIs "Accuse 'em all and let K and S sort 'em out." The caveat, however, was that each UCI was evaluated on the rate of "convictions" during the interview process. And make no mistake about it, if any interviewee admitted guilt, or if the majority of interviewees accused another of wrongdoing, that person was convicted and sentenced to termination—of their employment, that is.

The last element of caution was thrown to the winds if not the hurricane and no longer shackled my investigation. Talk of drugs was not merely creeping into conversations, it was dominating them. Often before I knew someone's name, I knew whether or not they were "cool." Any conversations that didn't involve something illegal was literally a waste of the company's time and mine. I wasn't there to make friends, and I no longer had to worry about establishing myself as a de facto employee.

Chain Four was full of my favorite drug dealers and presented no uncharted territory. Jim slid between Melba and me on the chain, refusing to sell her any crank and promising me as much as I could move. The only problem was I didn't know what he was telling Melba.

He kept repeating, "All you can handle, dude. All you can handle."

"You dealing with her, too?" I probed.

"No," he assured me. "She keeps wanting me to take the front [of the chain]. I told her to stick it. I have enough trouble just doin' one tour of duty up there per cycle. Know what I mean, man?"

"Sure do. She must be needin' some toot real bad. Stay away from her, she's bad news. She'd sell you out for a snootful and not lose a minute of sleep over it."

"With a snootful she won't be getting any sleep anyhow."

"What's that? I'm not sure I . . ."

"I'm cool!" he shouted. "I'm totally aware of her selfishness. It's just me and you from now on, guy. Just say the word and I'll set it up."

"Word."

*   *   *

The night was coming to a close, a rather uneventful night at that, and I had what was surely a UCI's worst nightmare—nothing to report. It was nights like this that led K and S operatives to falsify reports. As you will recall, UCIs lost a percentage of their bonus if they did not have at least five events per workday, and there were no carryovers.

"You and Jim become good buddies, I see," Melba teased.

"You know me. I like everyone."

"You buyin' his shit?" She didn't wait for the answer. "You know he's king of the bullshit, don'tcha?"

She was the only one I had yet to deal with on this chain, so I went on what I thought to be an innocent fishing expedition. "You've got better?"

"So you *are* dealin' with him?"

"Is this a quiz?"

"I just wanna know what I'm up against, that's all."

"Separate but equal. That's my philosophy."

"What?"

"You're not up against anything," I reassured her. "There's enough to go around for everyone." I answered in a way that insinuated prior dealings with Jim in order to build her confidence, but not definitively, so as to avoid any backlash from Jim. It was tricky business to say the least.

With about thirty minutes left in our day, the dryer tender decided to run previously dried wood back through the dryer, or redry it, because it had not been completely dried during the earlier runs. It was common-place to run redry at the end of a shift when enough had accumulated to justify it. The only problem with running it at the end of a shift when everyone was tired, however, was that redry was the fastest-running wood in the mill. This is because it had already been dried once before and could catch fire if left in the dryer too long.

The wood began pouring down the chain like water from a burst dam. With everyone totally absorbed in jerking wood from the conveyor, it was the job of the dryer tender and the person at the head of the chain to monitor any early signs of snarls.

"Tie-up!" Melba screamed, pointing to the stacker. The stacker was an eight-tiered machine just forward of the dryer and immediately aft of the chain that paced the wood coming out of the dryer to prevent overlapping and to avoid deluging the pullers with a solid mass of wood without sepa-ration. Separation was critical because it enabled the puller to get his hands in between each piece of wood. Without it, there was no way of getting the wood off the chain.

When the dryer shut down during redry, it was as though you were frantically thrashing about in whitewater rapids and it suddenly became placid. With the brim of my hat marinated in sweat and my shirt clinging to my skin, I looked up to see what the problem was.

"It's on number six!" Melba advised. Number six meant that the third level from the top was clogged, generally too deep to reach from the top without climbing inside. Simply put, someone had to crawl inside the machine, and they had to move quickly before the wood inside the dryer caught fire.

I climbed hurriedly over the top from the front side, leaving Jim, who was less agile, to go around back and activate the emergency override shut-off switch. This switch prevented accidental activation by someone at the dryer who might not see us crawling around in the lethal machinery. I lowered myself into the stacker and found what I assumed Melba was talking about. As I began ripping the wood from the rollers, I realized it was just a red herring, something an experienced puller should not have shut the dryer down for. No sooner did that thought cross my mind than I saw Jim's portly body crawling into the stacker from the rear.

"I got it, Jim!" I called.

"Let me just get this one right here," he replied, reaching for some slightly crossed pieces of wood. It was obvious that he was just killing time. He knew that the longer we spent fiddling around in the stacker, the less time we would have to pull redry before the next shift took over.

"They're fine. Let's go before it cooks!"

Looking down through the tiers, I saw a most disturbing event. The third tier began to cycle, and the resultant thundering sound of thousands of pounds of metal rocking forward and striking the tier above it sent me thrashing for the surface. Pulling myself up through the narrowed bars, I contorted and squeezed my body unnaturally until I was through.

"Shut it down," I screamed in terror. "Jim's still inside! Shut it down!"

Jim swore and cried out like a man about to meet a horrific death. And believe me, he was. I scrambled across the top of the stacker on hands and knees, slipping through the rollers time and time again like a dog breaking through thin ice as it desperately races for the shore. When I finally reached the back edge, the number five tier began to cycle. The metal rollers shook violently beneath me as it slammed into place with the finality of a mausoleum door. Just as I was about to leap fifteen feet to the ground, I saw Melba diving below the chain and back toward the shut-off button she was supposed to be manning. With an anticipatory flinch, I jumped to the concrete floor. The number six tier rocked forward. I rolled from the floor, my left knee buckling beneath me. In a final desperate lunge, I dove toward the stacker and smashed my fist against the emergency shut-off button. . . . Jim would live to snort again.

By now, Jim was making only monosyllabic sounds of sheer terror. Chain Three was shut down, and everyone began to gather around.

"Didn't you shut it down before going up there?" Fred, a straight shooter from Chain Three, asked while wearing a look of bewilderment.

"I went over the top," I responded vacuously before redirecting my attention to Jim. "Jim? You okay there, buddy?"

"Ooow. Wooo. Oh, no. Oh, boy. Oh, boy," he rambled incoherently.

"Did you turn off the stacker?" Stan, who was just on the scene, inquired of Jim.

Jim scrunched backwards out of the stacker, his round body compacting and stretching like a small baby learning to crawl.

"What happened?" Stan's jaw hung open, and his eyebrows caved in toward one another. "Why we still shut down? We're running redry, aren't we?"

"Would you like us to crank it up with him still in there?" I said.

"*You* know what I mean." He became frustrated and anxious. "Why the hell is everyone gathered around here for just a little tie-up?"

"That *bitch* turned the stacker on with me in it!" Jim cried.

Stan yelled back, "Didn't you turn off this emergency button, here?"

"Will everyone shut the fuck up about the damned button!" Jim wailed. "She turned the stacker on with me and Booch still in it! She tried to kill us!"

"Then why is he out here and you're still in there?" Stan poked fun.

Jim responded with embarrassment. "I think I'm stuck."

All I kept thinking was, how could a guy that did crystal methamphetamine as often as he claimed to do it get to be so fat in the first place, especially when you consider that he worked in this sauna mill. "Gotta cut back on those cupcakes, my friend," I joked at Jim's expense as I assisted the others in jarring him free from the stacker's warm embrace.

"I have glands," Jim said by way of explanation.

"Really," I said. "You would think that at least one person in Auschwitz would have had a glandular problem. But damned if they didn't all come out thin."

"They were *starved*!" he screamed back at me.

"Ohhh, so there is a connection between eating and weight gain."

"Fuck you," he replied while everyone laughed away their tension.

Stan's concerned face wrinkled like a prune. "Did she?"

"You mean 'try to kill us'?" I said. "Yeah. But I'll handle it, Stan."

"What the fuck's wrong with that bitch? She could've killed you guys. Just promise me you're not gonna kill her, that's all."

"No, but *he* might." I said, grabbing Stan by the shoulder and catapulting myself past him as I tore after Jim, who was now wobbling after Melba. Nothing could have appeared more Key Stone Cops than that scene. Both Jim and I were physically impaired with respect to our running abilities, which is probably why I've always chosen fight instead of flight, and Melba's chunky legs rubbed as she ran—another fire hazard. I caught up to them around the feeder and prevented what surely would have been a killing.

"Get outta the way, Ken. I mean it," Jim said angrily.

I patted him lightly on the chest. "Jim, just give me a sec here."

"It was an accident," Melba insisted.

"What?" I reacted. "Turning the emergency shut-off back on and then turning on the dryer?"

"I didn't . . ."

"Don't!" My voice hardened. "Don't try to tell me you didn't! I saw you crawling back and forth beneath the dryer! Underneath the conveyor! Just before the stacker came back on! So don't!"

"You stupid bitch!" Jim shuffled about like a crab as he attempted to get around me.

"Fuck you!" she retaliated, stabbing her finger toward Jim. "You don't have any more shit, right? Lose some fuckin' weight and maybe you wouldn't've gotten stuck in the damned thing in the first place!"

Before she could get more particular about what I had told her, I snatched her by the throat and, with my other hand, shoved Jim back. "Enough! Jim! You're on break! And Melba, you're feeding."

She drew a clawed hand within an inch of my face. "Go ahead," I dared her with a controlled, deliberate tone, drawing back a fist behind my head. "Go ahead. What are you waiting for? I'd like nothing more than to bury my fist in that Bull Dog puss of yours."

"Tari," I called up to the feeder. "We need ya to pull. Bring him along."

I motioned toward a young, clean-cut man I had never seen before. I would later discover that his name was Matthew.

"Get your fat ass up there," I told Melba, grabbing her by the scruff and shoving her up the stairs leading to the feeder. "Crank it up," I hollered to Tari as she neared the dryer. Dashing to the end of the chain, I did my part to yank as much wood off the chain as my aching limbs would permit.

Being the conscientious dryer tender that he was, Stan joined in and pulled wood at a feverish pace, enabling us to go nonstop without missing a single scrap of wood, and, more importantly, without having to shut down the dryer to catch up.

"Good job," Stan shouted. "From what everyone says, you probably saved his life!"

"Thanks! You really should do something about her, you know!"

"Like what?" he hollered, continuing at the frenzied pace we all found ourselves in.

"Like *fire* her, that's what!"

"Good!" He paused in between pulls. "Then we're all out of a job!"

I took this to mean that he was afraid Melba would rat on everyone concerning their drug use. Nothing could have conveyed more poignantly the collateral dangers of drug use within a company. If the supervisors are doing it, and half the employees are doing it, then everyone has leverage and an ability to blackmail. Everyone is compromised and therefore unwilling to tell management about problems, no matter how dangerous they might become.

*   *   *

"Fire," a shrill voice rose above all the other sounds. "Fire!"

Without stopping to see who was yelling, we all turned our disbelieving eyes toward the dryer and gazed in horror as smoke billowed from the top of the last stage of the two-story oven. The smoke quickly turned to flames and spread backwards toward the feeder. It soon became apparent that we were all products of that same deficient safety briefing as we scrambled to find the nearest fire-extinguishing equipment.

Stan began scaling the scorching hot dryer like King Kong. "Throw me the hose!" he instructed anyone within earshot. "And shut down the damn dryer!"

"Hose!" I repeated. "We're looking for a hose!"

In retrospect, I can see how foolish that must have looked, especially as we were working in an all-wood structure with gigantic two-story ovens, whose sole purpose it was to dry plywood core. Just then, someone made the mistake of unlocking the oven doors.

"Noooo!" Stan screamed. Everything seemed to proceed in slow motion from that point forward. At least, insofar as my film noir mind recalls such dramatic events.

When the fire met the oxygen-enriched air, an explosion jolted the doors and rocked the building. If not for the enormous safety latches that prevented the doors from blowing completely open, the force of the doors and the ensuing ball of flames would have killed everyone within a hundred-foot radius, which at this point meant approximately sixteen people. As it was, the flames that did escape gushed down the side of the dryer and blackened the burnished metal. Sawdust and just plain dust on top of the dryer ignited, making things rather hairy for Stan.

Chief finally grabbed the hose and tossed it like a lasso to Stan on top of the dryer. Stan wasted no time attacking the blaze at his feet. As he met the flames head-on, spraying through a ventilation shaft that was designed for such occurrences, the rest of us battled the blaze in the stacker.

Due to our delay in shutting down the dryer, wood was burning both in the stacker and atop the chain. By now, the whole mill was involved in dousing the inferno. Strangely enough, it was the drug crowd that offered the most support. How ironic, given that it was essentially drugs that started the fire in the first place.

When the fire was finally extinguished, I collapsed near a cart of wood along with Tari, the new kid and Chief, and observed that the next shift had already arrived and had been fighting the fire alongside us virtually the entire time. I guess I was so caught up in the excitement of the moment that I simply failed to notice.

It felt odd, if not a bit uncomfortable, hugging and congratulating all those employees who I had either built substantive cases against or would do so in the future. They were comrades in our united battle against the flames, not enemies. At that moment, I felt nothing but shame.

Against all they stood accused of, shouldn't saving the mill be factored in proportionately? On the other hand, wasn't it their criminal culpability that created the environment in which such iniquitous behavior, as demonstrated by Melba, could germinate and grow? It was hard in such situations to decide how far back to go in order to place blame.

That evening, when I was alone in a quiet room with my computer, I filled my report with laudable comments about my fellow co-workers and resident drug dealers, but lauded none more than Stan, whose heroism that evening had probably saved the mill.

Chapter 12

The following day, just before my shift began, Gordon called wanting to discuss my previous day's report.

"Had some excitement last night, I see." His tone seemed almost personable.

"You could call it that."

"Was Brenda on drugs, do you think?"

"Melba," I corrected. "Yeah, I believe so."

"Good. Good. Oh. About all that safety briefing stuff. . . . We know all about the problems in that area, so you don't haveta keep mentioning them."

"The building almost burned down, for God's sake. When am I supposed to mention safety issues?"

"When it's something we don't already know about."

"Pardon me for overreacting. It was the first fire I've seen there. And besides, how much could you or Boise know about all the problems I talked about?"

"It's not the fire. It's the safety briefing part. If the foreman isn't briefing people properly because he's on drugs or something, then fine. But don't suggest the company could have controlled it."

"But they could have. That's the point!"

"Why do you think you're there? To control it. That's why they're having you gather information. They wanna fix the problems."

"How they gonna do that without knowing what the problems are?"

"Just give that stuff directly to me before putting it in the reports, that's all. We don't wanna implicate the company that hired us. They'll make the necessary changes."

"You mean like they did with that machine that cut the guy's foot off. I gave them a simple twenty-dollar fix, and they have yet to implement it."

"There're other issues there besides safety. Let us worry about that. You just do your job."

"Nothing personal, Gordon, but it wasn't your ass almost crushed to death and then burned to death last night."

"I think you're exaggerating just a bit. Anyway . . ."

"Exaggerating! You think I'm exagg . . ." I stopped sharply, pausing to catch my breath and composure. "Okay, Gordon. Whatever you say. But I take what you're tellin' me is that I'm essentially on autopilot from here on out."

He came back sternly. "No, that's not at all what I'm sayin'. What I'm sayin' is that if you have anything to report that might even remotely implicate Boise in a lawsuit, speak to me first. That's all I'm sayin'. Why is that so difficult?"

"I would like to think that regardless of all the events I've put in my reports about rumored drug use by Stan, that you would place his actions last night in equal favor. If it weren't for him, there wouldn't be a mill. Ergo, no investigation."

"Well . . . ," he mumbled, implying disbelief. "We take everything into account at the end. But in the final analysis, it's Boise's call, not ours."

"You know, Gordon, you really shouldn't make the call on people like Stan sitting behind a desk five hundred miles away. He's got a chemical dependence, and he's made some real bad decisions with his life, but he's a dedicated employee and a hell of a lot better at his job than all the other dryer tenders combined."

"Dryer what?"

"Foremen."

"Don't get too caught up in all this, Ken."

"Excuse me for recognizing that what we do here affects people's lives and that it comes with a hell of alotta responsibility. And guilt, I might add. Of course, you don't know these people, so why would *you* give a shit?"

"*What*? You think you're the only investigator who's had a tough assignment?"

"No. Just the only one who's had a conscience about it."

"Well, maybe that's an area you need to work on."

"Well, at least that was honest. Better than I can say for the rest of the shit you've been feedin' me here today." I let out a huge sigh.

"While I gotcha on the phone . . . Take a look at that Tari. I think she's dirty."

"You mean sexually?"

"No, smart ass. Crank. I think you'll find there's a reason for her insight."

"You wanna elaborate on that?"

"I have it on good source she's a user."

"A source you can't share with your investigator," I said leadingly.

He didn't respond, so I followed with a sarcastic, somewhat accusatory tone. "You know, Gordon, you should really be careful with those smut films. I hear they can be very addictive."

"I'm sure I don't know what you're talking about. I have someone on the inside that . . ."

"Please. Spare me, already. No one's more inside than I am. And if I were you, I'd take down those bathroom cameras, ex post facto . . . or post haste . . . or whatever that phrase is."

"Why do you have to give me such a hard time on everything. We're not using any of this in court against anyone. Just take a closer look at her, okay?"

"Send me some pictures and I'll take a real close look at her."

"You're beginning to get on my last nerve."

"Fine, fine. I'll see what I can find. Later, Gordon."

"Wait! There's one other thing." His deportment became more congenial and conciliatory. "We have this person—you wouldn't know him, works for Wal-Mart—that claims he was on bereavement leave for a week, but his story seems a bit suspicious, you know what I mean? It just has an air about it. Anyhow, I was wondering . . . I mean, you're sorta good at figuring out this kinda stuff it seems. What would be the best way to go about determining whether he went to New York on bereavement leave or not?"

"What documentation has he shown his boss? To prove there even was a death."

"Well, that's it, you see. He's given her copies of funeral service junk, a travel itinerary, crap like that. No death certificate, though. That's what bugs me."

"Copies, huh? How 'bout a ticket. Anyone can get an itinerary or forge a funeral service record."

"He says it's in one of his suitcases and he has to wait till he unpacks. I think he's stalling."

"There's your answer. He's lying."

"What? Just like that? How can you know for sure from what I've told you?"

"You can't pack your ticket. You haveta show it to the flight attendant when you board. He's lying. Now the question is proving it."

"That's right," he thought out loud. "That's right, you can't pack your damn ticket! Fantastic! Now why can't all our conversations go this smoothly?"

"Because you spend too much time riposting instead of listening."

"So much for a good conversation. Thanks for the help, nevertheless."

"You still don't have your proof, you know."

"Don't need it. With this great detective work here, he'll spill his guts like a drunken gringo in a Tijuana flophouse. Good work."

"What if one of his family members really did die? I'd tread lightly here, Gordon. Really. I wouldn't go making that accusation unless I was absolutely sure. I mean, *absolutely* sure. That's a real sensitive one there. As well it should be, I might add."

"I'll take it under advisement. And thanks again."

*   *   *

I went to work that day with the nagging sense that the drug dealers were more principled than my own company. Still feeling the camaraderie of the prior evening, I was greeted with affectionate handshakes and back patting of the friendliest sort.

"Good job, yesterday," Sherry chirped with an insubstantial voice.

"Thanks. If you have time later this evening, I can give you the chilling details of what has become known in certain corridors of power as the Hell—ican Brief."

She smiled crookedly. "Well that was pretty obscure. Not your best effort. Pretty sad, actually. Anyway, the Rock n' Rodeo, saaay . . . midnight?"

"Midnight it is."

"You sure are a smooth one," Jim laughed. "Let's break together. I wanna discuss something."

"Hey!" Tari met us with a toothy grin on our way to the chain. "We've got all cake runs scheduled today. We'll be sweepin' as much as we're pullin'."

"Look out!" Paul hooted as he sped toward us on his Hyster.

We jumped out of the way, narrowly escaping certain injury. Jim retaliated by cursing at Paul loud enough to strain his voice, and Tari flipped him off. Just then, the Hyster skidded to a stop and proceeded to back toward us in a herky-jerky manner.

"You two better control your bitch," he warned.

I started toward him, my blood pressure boiling over. "What the fuck did you say, you fat, lush motherfucker!" Before I could mount the vehicle, he sped away, hoisting a middle finger in reprisal. "That little prick . . ." I was flabbergasted. "Does he really think I'm gonna let him get away with that?"

"Don't get so damn flustered. Screw him," Tari said, brushing some sawdust from her hair. "He's not worth getting booted over."

"Why is everyone so afraid of that fat ass?"

Jim offered, "He's got the company bent over. There's some sort of lawsuit pending."

"I thought they settled that."

He shook his head, his fat cheeks whooshing about, and quickly said, "Then it has something to do with the settlement, I think."

"Good," I smiled, throwing an arm around Jim's rounded shoulders and fat neck. "From now on, if I need the straight skinny, I'll know where to come." Releasing my grip, I became serious. "Fucker better sure as hell stay outta my damn way from now on, I tell ya." And I wasn't saying it simply for effect this time. It had become personal.

*   *   *

Unusual things started happening to all the stacks of wood I set up, and the fact that it started after I pissed off the Hyster driver was not lost on me. After being forced by the dryer tender—an "uncool" one—to leave the chain a couple times and conduct the humiliating task of restacking my pallets of wood, I had had just about enough for one evening.

The next time it happened, I rallied the troops, and we collectively petitioned the dryer tender and explained the situation. In a noncommittal, compromised and spineless decision, he instructed us to rebuild the stack; a task that implied to all who witnessed it that we were not very good at our jobs. And with these people, the last thing you ever wanted to do was prove yourself incapable of meeting the daily challenge of your assigned duty. Being good at this job was akin to machismo, even for women.

The one good outcome of the dryer tender's decision, I'd decided, was that Paul would not want to get off his comfortable seat again and actually work for a living. I was only partly correct.

About midway through what was essentially a cushy night, I found myself pulling perfectly symmetrical, slow-moving wood leisurely off the chain. The new guy, Matthew, a lanky, fair-skinned chap, turned out to be a very pleasant character. And good thing too, because he found himself having to play tête-à-tête tetherball with Tari and me practically all evening. He could pull a mean piece of wood, too, and that was certainly a plus.

One of the things I remember most about Matthew was the way he would tell depressing stories and inadvertently make them funny. Like the one he told us about him and his father hunting a deer impostor. According to Matthew, after a long day in the briar patch, where deer were as scarce as virgin interns in the Clinton White House, they headed for home with their tails between their legs—the hunters, not the deer. Traveling down the highway at 75 mph, Matthew's father spotted a big, seven-point buck a short distance off the side of the road. Not wanting to break the law, yet not wanting to pass up such a golden opportunity, they pulled off the road and did what hunters do. With bow and arrow in hand, the father drew back the bowstring, took aim and let one fly.

Now, I don't know a lot about archery, but I'm told that the pinging sound that the arrow made when it hit the deer's shoulder was not customary, nor were the fifteen law enforcement agents who sprang up from the tall grass a la the Viet Cong. What had me laughing hysterically, though, was the fact that an experienced hunter could see a stationary deer on the edge of the woods while traveling at 75 mph, have the motor skills and the vision to hit the deer with an arrow, yet not have the vision to see that the deer was made of metal nor the hunting savvy to know that a real deer probably would have noticed a person sneaking up on it in a big red truck. Oh, did I mention that his truck was cherry red? When I asked him why they didn't notice the dents where all the other arrows had struck the deer that day, he told me it so happens his father was the only hunter in a week to actually hit the target. Presumably, that is because any hunter dumb enough to shoot at a metal deer in the first place is probably drunk out of his gourd.

Anyhow, I was throwing "no lookers" into my cart while repeating, "I'm in the zone," when out of nowhere the cart behind me slammed against the back of my legs and pinned me to the moving chain. The splintered ends of the wood poked through my clothing and ruptured the outermost layers of skin. The blow also smashed my knee, which was already deteriorated from life, snapping off the top of the kneecap and dislodging a hunk of arthritic calcium the size of a quarter to float about— for the next five years. The only thing holding me up was the applied force of the cart.

"Damn!" I heard Paul shout. "Sorry 'bout that little buddy," he said incidentally before pulling away as if nothing had happened.

Matthew and Tari rushed to my side, and Stan, just moments later. "Don't move," Tari pleaded as I attempted to gain my feet.

"Are you high?" Stan cautiously inquired.

Tari reacted with incredulity, smacking Stan's shoulder with the back of her hand. "What kinda question's that?"

"If we need to call an ambulance, I wanna make sure he's not gonna get in trouble!"

"Well, are you?" he repeated.

"No, I'm fine. Help me up."

"Whatta you gonna do?" Tari evidently knew how stupid I could be in such circumstances.

I continued to seethe. "Stan? Can you keep the other dryer tender busy for a few minutes?"

"Jim?" he asked.

"Yeah, is that his name? Can you?"

"I'll try." He clapped his gloves together. "You gonna straighten that asshole out?"

"Hope to."

"Give me a few minutes. I'll take Jim up to the offices." He waved one of his gloves over his head in a swirling motion. "That'll give you plenty of time, I think."

"Ken," Tari pleaded, holding both of her hands tightly to my right wrist, "Forget about 'im. They haveta fire him for what he did this time. Right, Stan?"

"Unless they believe it's just another one of his dumb accidents," he responded.

"You don't get fired for committing multiple life-threatening accidents?" I asked of anyone who would answer.

Stan fielded the question: "If you did, he would've been out on his ass years ago."

"So if he rips his head off," Tari said of me, "Then fatso has enough clout around here to get 'im fired."

"Unless he's too frightened to retaliate," Stan conjectured. "Are you okay to stand?" he asked with genuine compassion, his hand already reaching beneath my arm.

"Yeah. We better get this chain movin' again. We don't want a repeat of last night."

After helping me to my feet, Stan trotted after Jim, stabbing his finger toward the elevated offices while still running away from us. I stretched out like an Olympic decathlete, pulling the occasional piece of wood that made its way to the end of the chain. Looking over at Tari, who was doing most of the work at the front of the chain, I couldn't help but feel her disappointment. Matthew, on the other hand, was grinning ear to ear and brushing his left nostril with an animated thumb like a boxer sparring for the press. I didn't need to look for Paul. Matthew's enthusiasm for a show-down told me that he would do that for me. Jerking his head over his left shoulder, Matthew signaled Paul's approach.

"Cover for me!" I exclaimed, tearing off after the speeding Hyster, the pain in my knee blocked by the natural analgesic known as rage. Just as he approached the Spreaders, I grabbed hold of the cage in an awkward and dangerous attempt at boarding the moving vehicle. Although my timing was impeccable for making an impression on a certain group of people, this was personal and had nothing to do with image building. It just so happens that the ancillary effect would be to elevate my rogue status and to give me greater credibility among my peers.

Gripping a vertical metal bar that anchored the cage to the Hyster, I attempted to pull myself aboard. My feet lifted off the ground and then returned to the concrete floor, skipping two or three times before rebounding. Gaining momentum, I tried again. My third attempt landed me firmly in the cockpit. And in the nick of time, I might add, because just as I hauled my torso into the cage I felt a large stack of palletized dogwood scrape against my ass.

Paul jammed on the brakes, launching me into the cockpit controls. I'm not sure if you've ever seen the operating controls of a Hyster, but trust me, you sure as hell don't want to slam into them at fifteen miles per hour any time soon. With protruding arms and large knobs, they inflict a special sort of punishment.

The next thing I knew, Paul yanked me off the torturous protuberances by my long, wavy hair—the last time I wore my hair that long—and flung me from the cockpit. Thrown halfway out of the vehicle, my arms dragged along the sawdust-laden floor as the Hyster began moving in reverse. Pushing off the floor with my fingertips, I recoiled into the cage, but not before my chin bounced off the metal runningboard and squirted blood in every direction. I kicked Paul behind the knees while I lay on my back. His legs buckled like a switchblade as he let out a scream of insanity. Bouncing from the floorboards, he attacked with crazed eyes and unbridled fists. The Hyster, now coasting, crashed anticlimactically into the platform of the perpetually spinning giant tablesaw.

Unable to take this attack, I resorted to the old fallback—never stop flailing. Frantically swinging back, I managed to extricate myself from the vehicle. I flew into a rage. "Let's go! Let's settle this!"

He gazed at me with a thousand-mile stare of exhaustion and then hastily made for the controls. "Oh, no you don't!" I grabbed him by the back of the head and jerked him from the safety of his cage.

Aided by a lazy eye, the deranged look returned to his face as he spun about and swatted at me like an epileptic baby on PCP. Ducking beneath the onslaught, I circled quickly and threw my arm around his throat in an attempt to choke his air off. The effect was not immediate, however, and provided him just enough time to push us backwards onto the saw's platform. The twelve-foot-high saw gave me reason for concern, especially as Paul, now on top of me, wiggled on his back, pushing us ever closer to spinning death.

"Didn't I just see this in a silent movie?" I said in an attempt to diffuse my own fear.

He stammered in a raspy voice. "Let . . . me . . . go!"

"One more inch," I cautioned, "and I'll snap your neck like a twig."

My threat fell on deaf ears as he wiggled closer and closer to our doom. When I began to feel the breeze of the spinning blade and smell the aroma of searing metal, I knew this had gone too far. Yanking his head to the side as though I were attempting to break his neck, I knew that he would turn in the opposite direction to resist. When he did, I rolled him the way of least resistance and scooted away from him in the opposite direction. Standing back from the platform, I was now surrounded by employees goading me on.

"Stay down!" I beseeched him. "Stay down!"

"Ahhhrrrr!" His shrill voice belied a bloated physique. Before I could ready myself, he planted a shoulder into my thorax and drove me backwards. Backpedaling like a defensive back in football, I abruptly fell on my behind, throwing my legs over my head—and him along with them—and, in one fell swoop, rolled myself on top of him. Several punches to his face not only modified his behavior but made me feel pretty rotten to boot. I guess I was getting a little too old and civilized for this sort of thing. Seeing this bully shielding his face and bawling his eyes out just didn't give me the same satisfaction and warm fuzzies it once did.

With everyone gathered about, mocking him, I pulled him up by his armpits and began assisting him toward the break room. When this sudden act of kindness was met with suspicious eyes, however, I placed my shoe on his back and pushed him to the ground. Reaching down, I ripped the work gloves from his belt loop and heaved them high atop the rafters. By pure dumb luck, they came to rest on the edge of a joist for all the mill to see. As unintended as it was, it came to be known as a symbol of the power that was growing within the company's underworld.

"Why the hell am I helping you?' I shouted. "You know where the cupcakes are! And fat boy? This is the last problem I have with you! Next time I won't be so philanthropic." As you might expect, I was feeling particularly good about myself by this point.

"Philanthraw . . . Philan what?" Steve said quizzically.

"Thropic. You know, *warm, giving*. Would it kill you to pick up a book once in a while?" I said facetiously to arousing, if not cathartic laughter.

I find it curious and even a bit disturbing that a person's sense of humor is often directly proportionate to how threatened his audience feels at the time of the joke. I would hear the word 'philanthropic' bastardized and misused ad nauseam for the next several months.

With my clothes torn and bloodied, and my body bruised and tattered, this day was hardly distinguishable from any other at that mill. I never had another problem with Paul again, and when I occasionally heard from good sources that he was involved in drugs, I let it slide, deciding he had paid enough penance for one investigation. And besides, I thought, all that I had written about him to this point should have been enough to put him on the unemployment line.

In hindsight, I suppose my guilt over what I had done had compromised my investigation with Paul. Don't misunderstand; it wasn't the physical pain that I had inflicted that caused my guilt, it was the humiliation. After all, physical pain eventually subsides.

Chapter 13

It was late August and blistering hot, and the shopping mall was hopping with golden-skinned girls with chiseled bodies. 'Twas the season for skimpy shorts and immodest navels. There is nothing quite like taut skin to broadcast a girl's innocence, just like the stretched necks of skyscraper-gazing tourists in the Big Apple broadcast that they are out-of-towners.

I went into a "nineties" kind of store and began feeling more like a real person again. "Can I help you?" a young girl in a vogue lime-green-and-black ensemble, asked.

"Actually, yes. I like this shirt, but is this the only color it comes in?"

"No, not at all. We have that in avocado, fuchsia, plum, salmon . . . ." I started to chuckle. "What?" She spoke with a puerile charm.

"Nothing. It just cracks me up, that's all. If you ask a man—*any* man—what color something is, he'll say one of the primary colors like blue, yellow or brown. But you ask a woman and she breaks them down into fruits, vegetables, fish, and . . . what the heck is fuchsia, by the way?"

"It's a color," she answered tenuously. "Pink."

"Pink. No wonder they call it fuchsia. To a guy, it's light red."

She giggled politely and then went on to sell me about a thousand dollars worth of fruits and vegetables.

From there, I made my way over to Macki, who was working in one of the mall's bookstores, and showed off my new wardrobe. After she provided me with some much-needed rejuvenation therapy, I drifted about the mall in search of some more simplicity and innocence. What I found, however, was banality, in all its pomp and circumstance. Somehow I thought a place like Medford would not be so commercially affected. Why I thought that, I have no idea. After all, it's not Albania. For that matter, Albania's not Albania.

"Ken!" I heard a male voice stab from the legions of shoppers. "Ken!"

The uneasy feeling the voice triggered told me that I probably didn't want to meet this person today. I responded by angling through the herd as if searching, hoping that I would elude the caller without alienating him as well.

The voice neared. "Ken, wait up!"

"Damn," I whispered. "Wrong way." Before I could retreat, the voice became manifest in the form of Caracas.

"Caracas." I appeared blithe. "What's up, dude?"

"Like what we've been seeing," he repeated twice, sounding more like a talent scout than a mill worker.

I responded with the appropriate level of paranoia. "You *following* me?"

"No, no, not at all." He extended his hands toward me. "We saw your Porsche in the parking lot when we drove by. Thought we'd come in and check you out."

His use of the phrase "No, not at all" told me he had been following me. People often inadvertently repeat phrases they've just heard, especially if they're concentrating on the conversation and if it lends itself to such repetition. He must have been in one of the dressing rooms when the sales girl spoke with me.

"Who's *we*? You gotta frog in your pocket?"

"Hey, Booch," another familiar voice spoke from behind me.

I turned partially to find Steve and the man I had called Cochise at the strip poker game at Caracas's house, standing only a few feet behind me. "Hey," I acknowledged benignly.

"We've got some business to discuss," Caracas said. "Got time?"

"A little. Wanna go outside?"

"Sounds good," Cochise stated, still breathing down my neck.

"What's your name, by the way?" I inquired.

His lips barely parted. "Devon."

"Nice to officially meet you, Cochise."

Once in the parking lot, we made our way to where I was parked. I was sure they wanted to sniff around my car on a day that I wasn't expecting to see them. Once there, they did just that, under the guise that they were impressed with the vehicle and wanted to "check it out."

Leaning against my vehicle, Steve explained what it was they wanted to discuss. "Heard you had an incident out at Table Rock."

"Your work?" I said.

"No, but we know whose it was. They didn't know you were cool. That's probably because the information came through your buddy, Keith. By the way, you fucking her?"

"Next question."

"Hey, man, just curious. Doesn't matter to me. The point is, they didn't know who you were, and they panicked."

"They pointed one of those laser dealies at us. Not what I'd call a threat."

"Unless it's connected to a gun," Devon interjected.

"Was it? Because if it was, it was taped to one. And if it was taped to one, what does that say about the type of guy you're dealing with?"

"The guy who fucked with you was not . . ." Steve tried to explain. "We weren't dealing with him. Not directly, anyway. It's complicated."

"So you're sayin' this crazy rumor about glue and blaze had something to do with that mess?" They stood silent and glanced back and forth at one another for several seconds. I broke the silence. "Oh, please, not the dramatic pause bullshit."

"Are you busy?" Devon said evenly.

"Why?"

"You wanna see the craziness?"

"Where we goin'?"

Another pause and then, "My place."

"I'll follow you. And boys . . . any signs of the crap I experienced on poker night and I'll kill every fuckin' one of you." They glanced at each other, smiled and walked away. They quickly boarded a big black truck that was parked just fifty feet away, and we were off. The fact that Caracas sat scrunched between the other two seemed to suggest that he was low man on the totem pole. And the fact that their vehicle was parked only fifty feet from mine in a parking lot as enormous as this one supported the supposition that they were indeed following me.

I contacted Bud via cell phone and apprised him of the situation, excluding the nonsense about the glue, of course. Let's face it, even if it were true, Bud would have hyperextended his pituitary just telling JACNET about it.

With Phil Collins's "In the Air Tonight" still somewhere back in my apartment, I put on the C & C Music Factory to alter my mood instead. I climbed into the appropriate personality befitting the occasion, and popped a bullet into the chamber of my gun, anticipating danger. "Everybody dance now!" thumped like an inner city anthem against complacency brought on by a relaxing day off. There *were* no days off in this business, just days when good music was needed more than other days.

As we left the main drag leading away from Medford and, for lack of a better word, cased a neighborhood, I forced myself to memorize the streets I was traveling on. Aware that we had crisscrossed some streets several times, I realized they were trying to make it as difficult as possible for me to retrace my steps. In some ways this made me a bit more comfortable, knowing that it was at least their intent to let me leave. There was always the possibility, though, that they were just plain stupid and that logic was never a factor in any of their decisions.

At the end of one of the streets was a small fenced-in yard that looked like it could use a gardener. Or a bulldozer. Steve pulled the truck alongside the chain-link fence, gritty dust roiling around it, and immediately shut down the engine. I performed a U-turn and parked on the opposite side of the street, leaving my car running.

Caracas stepped lightly over to me on the balls of his feet, avoiding the sound of his footfall on the road. "Try and be quiet," he advised. "Devon's wife doesn't want him involved in this stuff anymore."

I shut the car off and followed them. The gate jammed behind Caracas, so I hopped the fence.

"Watch your step," Devon said, appearing genuinely concerned. "Back here." He motioned with his head.

I stepped laterally as I passed by the side of the house leading to the rear, wanting to see the entire backyard before I crossed into it. The dealers sat down at a weathered picnic table and waited for me to join them. Devon toyed with a small rectangular piece of plywood.

"Come here," he said, motioning to me.

My steps were deliberate and my eyes keen. I sat down straddling the bench, keeping my back to the open field behind me. "Caracas?" Devon said while looking at me. "Go get the stuff."

"The stuff?" I inquired as Caracas headed for a small shack erected at the rear of the backyard.

"Don't worry."

"'I'm not. He comes back with anything made of metal and you sure as hell will be, though."

"You know," Steve said, "You sure as hell make a lot of threats."

"There they go, repeating my words again," I thought. "Stop pulling guns on me, pointing lasers at me and forcing me to do your lame ass drugs, and I'll change my demeanor."

"Ha!" Devon yelped. "I'm really starting to bond with this guy. You just wait and see what we got here." Caracas approached with a plastic bottle. "This's gonna blow your stockings off," Devon said, stoking the fire of anticipation with his words.

Caracas was also unusually animated. "You're gonna love this. You are," he insisted.

Devon rolled his eyes up from the piece of wood and glared at Caracas for a moment. "Sorry." Caracas apologized for taking so long.

"Where's the bucket?" Devon demanded, appearing agitated.

"Shit!" Caracas blurted as he dashed back into the shack. The naturalness of the conversation leading to Caracas's hasty departure made me suspicious that I was being duped by some crafty manipulators. I always tried to give the opposition more credit than they probably deserved just to remain on the safe side. If they were going to strike, now would certainly be the time.

As it turned out, they were either totally truthful or they simply did not deserve my complete respect, because Caracas did indeed return with a bucket. I must admit, however, I fully expected him to pull a gun out of that bucket.

Devon took the bucket and showed me its contents. "See," he said, "It's empty."

My hand continued to rest prudently on my gun beneath the table. "Doesn't look empty to me," I corrected him.

He turned the bucket in his hands to look inside. "Oh, yeah, the gloves," he said curiously before removing them. "Now it's empty."

"Promise me never to take this show on the road."

They were too focused for levity. Devon put the gloves on and placed the piece of wood inside the bucket. He then poured the mysterious liquid from the bottle into the bucket.

"Now what?" I asked.

"Now we wait," Steve answered, laying his head on the table between his arms.

"Someone's seen *way* too many movies," Devon offered lightly.

I attempted to strip away the tension I was sure we were all feeling. "You guys like movies?"

"You kidding?" Devon's candor about an activity that was not exactly befitting his macho image caught me off guard. "We go to 'em all the time, dude."

"Really? Whatta you prefer?"

"Everything, really. We go to alotta action flicks, but we like good comedies and other stuff, too."

"As opposed to bad comedies." I revisited his sense of humor.

"Good point." He smiled with an open mouth.

"Do you find a lot of that stuff realistic?" Caracas joined in. "We don't. Especially all the gun shit."

I wasn't sure if he was testing my knowledge of movies or guns. "You mean like bullets chasing people?"

"How do you mean?" Devon leaned forward.

I explained. "When the guy's running away, why don't they just shoot ahead of him and trail the bullets backwards. You could sweep 360 degrees in about two seconds with a MAC-10, and yet you always see these bullets chasing this guy who's crossing directly in front of the guy firing the machine gun. And the bullets are chasin' him for five fuckin' seconds. Please! Give me a break already!"

"That's true." Devon nodded his head profusely. "Good observation."

"Any kid with a squirt gun has already figured that one out," I added. "And how about the emptying of the clip bullshit to prove you're gun ain't loaded. How about the one in the chamber?"

"Don't remind me," Devon laughed.

"Oh, yeah," I said. "I almost forgot about that."

"Have you seen *Jurassic Park*?" Caracas grinned like a schoolboy.

"Are you kidding? The day it came out."

"Could you believe how realistic those dinosaurs looked?"

"Yeah, as if you had something to compare them to."

"Aaahh! No shit!" Devon teased. "It's like those idiots who say how much an actor looks like Jesus."

"Yeah," Steve added. "The same folks think all the Apostles were seated on the same side of the table. It doesn't dawn on them that Michelangelo probably didn't wanna paint the backs of six men."

Ignoring the harassment, Caracas continued to gush with praise. "I was freakin' out the whole movie. My popcorn was empty ten minutes into the picture."

"I don't know," I said. "The problem with Spielberg is that he won't kill a kid. Well, except in *Schindler's List*. But that was a true story. If he would just let a dinosaur bite the head off of one kid, I'd be on the edge of my seat for the next thirteen sequels."

"That's sick," Devon said, clutching his face in his hands.

"Whatta ya think is the corniest scene in movies?" Bones asked, still looking like a wide-eyed schoolboy. "I mean that ya see a lot in movies. Today? *I* think it's the whole saluting thing. You know, when someone salutes the hero at the end of the movie to show how respected and admired he is."

Devon said, "I hate the slow motion shit where you can only hear the guys breathing real loud like . . . in slow motion. Know what I'm sayin'?"

"Oh, man," I said. "I *hate* that. For me, though, it has to be the clapping. You know, first one guy starts clapping reeeal slow . . . and loud . . . and then everyone else joins in one at a time until the place erupts in applause. They generally throw a salute in there somewhere, too."

"Or how about . . ." Bones started.

Steve lifted his head slowly from the table. One of his eyebrows lifted. "It's working," he exclaimed.

A simmering sound emanated from the bucket and a powerful, phosphorus smell invaded the air. Within seconds, however, the smell and the sound dissipated. That is to say, *we* could no longer smell it. Fact is, the longer you smell something like that, the more difficult it is to detect it. "The sifter?" Devon said to Caracas with a small level of annoyance in his voice. "I'd kinda like to get this done before my wife comes out here."

"Relax," Caracas snapped back. "I'm not the hired help."

As Caracas slipped back into the shed, I realized they were nothing more than country yokels in smuggler's skin. Of course, if this dog-and-pony show were to actually produce crystal meth, then they could afford the rest of the smuggler's accoutrements and lifestyle as well. They'd still be country bumpkins, just richer ones.

Devon quickly poured the contents of the bucket into the strainer, seemingly not bothered that the liquid which passed through hit the table and blistered the paint. He then removed the wood from the bucket, tapped it lightly several times on the side of the strainer, and tossed the pieces on the ground. What remained in the strainer was a pasty, yellowish substance they claimed was crystal methamphetamine. Steve casually removed a small flask from his back pocket that was supposedly filled with tap water and tossed it to Devon. "Heads up," he said.

A quick splash over the contents of the strainer and a "Ta dahhh" from Devon signified that the process was complete. He held forth the goop for my examination.

"All I see is goop."

"Taste it."

"Are you nuts?"

"Okay, then. Take some with you and wait till it dries."

"Fine. Put it in some sort of container that doesn't melt."

"It's not gonna melt anything," Caracas insisted. "It's already stable."

"Fine. But I'm not. Put it in something glass. Or metal. Like this strainer. Except without the holes of course."

"And if you test it and it's crank? Then what? You in?" Devon pressed.

"In what?"

"Well . . ."

Steve interrupted. "The next big score."

"How big?"

"Big," Devon repeated.

"Thanks for clearing that up. What I mean is, how much are you gonna need from me?"

Devon volleyed looks between Steve and Caracas for a few moments. "Nothing yet?" he answered in the form of question.

"That's right," Caracas clarified. "We just want you to come along and see the operation."

"Now it's an operation?"

"Just come along and see," he encouraged.

"Why me?"

They looked at each other again. Caracas attempted an explanation. "It's a capital thing. You know, like the pool games we played. You and I put up the money and took all the profits." He thought for a moment. "And out of that profit we bought Tari beers all night. In exchange, she made all the runs to the bar."

"Who's Tari in this story?"

"Right now, we are. But we wanna get to be us. Well, you know, the pool players. Emphasis on 'players.'"

For some reason I actually understood what he was trying to say. "So this pick-up is already paid for?"

"Right."

"Then why do you need me?"

"We don't. I mean, not for this shipment. But we want you for the next one. Whenever that is. We just want you to see the operation so you can finance part of the next one, is what we're sayin'."

"What kinda financing we talking?"

"Depends." Devon stepped in.

"Upon what? Wait, forget that. How much is this one?"

"About ten million."

"*Excuse* me. You think I've got that kinda change? Sorry to disappoint ya fellas, but that ain't happening. My guy doesn't want . . ."

"No, you don't understand." Caracas delineated their proposal further. "What we want is to piggyback on a big shipment. We do all the transporting and take all the risk in exchange for our buyer's permission to take some off the top."

"How much?"

Steve put his two cents in, the most important two cents of all, "Ten kilos."

"I could probably swing that."

"Then you'll come?"

"When?"

"Tomorrow."

"Don't you guys work tomorrow?"

"I think we can swing a day off." Steve's response was met with rousing laughter.

"How silly of me," I said. "So how much you guys making from this little excursion?"

"Enough," Devon stated succinctly.

"How much?"

"Why?" he replied.

"Because I wanna know."

"Five a piece."

"And how many are there of you?"

"Counting you?"

"Am I getting paid?"

"No."

"Then, *not* counting me."

"Six," he responded with a mixture of apology and embarassment. All I could think was that if any of this were true, they were the biggest suckers I'd ever met. And if it were *all* true . . . my God. I quite literally didn't know what to think.

*   *   *

In order to keep my sanity, I called my parents (Dorothy and Ben) and my friend Mark Rizzo before going to bed that evening. As expected, they were the gravity boots I needed to stay grounded in normalcy: a planet far beyond the galaxy of Boise Cascade. I placed the alleged meth paste into an envelope and stuck it in my kitchen drawer.

After calling in my report, which omitted the ridiculous glue story, I typed on my book until about three the following morning.

Around 6:00 A.M. Caracas called to tell me that the trip was off. He was vague, but through the cluttered, evasive language I gathered it was me that was off, not the trip. Their trepidation about having me along actually had me believing there might be an inkling of truth to their tale. By this time I'd actually hoped it was true, because if it weren't, then these guys were adroit confidence men with extremely gifted minds. As you can imagine, the latter prospect was too much to stomach and far more frightening to contemplate.

Frustrated, and yet relieved, I called Macki to see what she had planned for the day. When she answered she sounded groggy and I realized it was only a few minutes after 6:00 A.M.

"I'm sorry, Macki," I apologized. "I forgot what time it was."

She sounded puzzled. "Ken?"

"Yeah. I'm sorry, Mack. I'll call you . . ."

"Ken!" She immediately perked up.

"Really, Mack. I'll call you back. I'm really sorry. I . . ."

"No, it's fine. I'm awake now."

Shortly into the conversation I received an incoming call. "Could you hold for a minute? I gotta . . . "

"Sure," she said gleefully.

"Hello?"

"Still me," Macki advised.

"Hello?"

"Hiiii," Tari greeted, in her distinct, drawn out manner.

"Can you hold for a second? I gotta get rid of this other caller."

"Uh-huhhh," she replied, breathy.

"Hello?"

"Didn't work," Tari advised.

I clicked again. "Hello?"

Macki seemed prepared for the disappointment. "Gotta go?"

"Yeah, I'm sorry. I'll call you later on. Is that okay?"

"Business?"

"Yup, sorry to say. Look, I'm really sorry, Mack, but I've gotta . . ."

"That's okay. You don't haveta explain. Call me later?"

"Yeah, that's what I'm sayin'. I'll call you this afternoon. We'll go to a movie or something."

"What's out?"

"Huh? Oh, I don't know. Check the paper. I really gotta go. I'll call you . . ."

"I know. You gotta go. 'Bye," she said ruefully and then abruptly hung up. Her displeasure was palpable. I could actually hear it in the way she hung up the phone.

I clicked back over to Tari. "Tari?"

"Hiiii. How are you?"

"Good, good. You work today?"

"Noooo," she replied, stretching another word in her trademark fashion. Although I could never faithfully recreate its essence in this medium—which probably says more about me as a writer than her as a seductress—all I can tell you is that it was personable, sultry and sensual, all at the same time. And, that was just her use of the word *no*. Just imagine how excited I would get when she trifled with a polysyllable. "You're off today, too, right?"

"Yeah, but I'm always off today. Tomorrow's our shared day, isn't it?"

"I took a vacation day," she explained.

The coincidence had me intrigued. "Any particular reason?"

"No. Just tired of that place, I guess. What are your . . . ?"

"Nothing now." I then decided to fish around. "My plans got canceled this morning."

"What were you gonna do? Because if you want I should go, I . . ."

"No, no. That's the point. I've got nothing planned now."

"Same here. I was going flying," she said parenthetically, "But the weather screwed that all up."

"Flying? You fly? I didn't know that."

"Oh, sure. I've been flying for years. You were in the Air Force, right?"

"Yeah . . ." I deliberated for a few moments. "You going with Keith?"

"Hell, no. He's scared shitless of flying. Just some friends. Why you ask?"

"Oh, nothing. Just curious." I changed subjects before she became suspicious. "So what d'you wanna do? Hiking?"

"Sure, that'd be fine. But I was kinda wanting to go into Ashland. They have some sorta festival thing going on this weekend, I think."

"Sounds . . ." I started to answer when a call came in. "Is that mine?"

"No, I think it's me. Can you . . . ?"

"Yeah, no problem. Go ahead."

Tari came back on about two minutes later. "Ken? Can I call you back?"

"Sure. If I'm not here, leave a message. Are we getting together this . . ."

"Yeah, I'll call you right back. Ba-bye." She hung up before I could respond. I've never understood why people say "bye-bye," but no one ever says "hi-hi."

*   *   *

When Gordon called seconds later, I provided him with many of the details surrounding this outrageous twist in the mill saga. He was not amused to say the least.

"Have you put this in any of the recent reports?"

"Don't you read them?"

"They show me them if something important happens."

"Then I guess I haven't."

"Good, then don't."

"Because?"

"Because they're jerking you around! If you bite, they'll never deal with you again. Drugs in glue . . . ? Are you *insane*?"

"I never said I believed it. I'm just saying . . ."

"Don't just say! They're checking you out for street smarts!"

"Going through a whole lotta trouble, wouldn'tcha say? Replete with a magic act that would make Zigfried and Roy envious, I might add. At the very least, it sounds like they're establishing my credibility for something big."

"They probably are. But not drugs in glue, I assure you."

"My trip to Crater Lake is not for a glue-and-pony show. It's for a shipment of drugs. I haven't in the least bit conveyed to them that I've bought into this whole glue thing. But it's certainly not unusual to make large-quantity buys in the middle of nowhere with the aid of airplanes. So my going along seems sorta natural, don'tcha think? And besides, they haven't tried to play me for a sucker by having me kick in any capital."

"Not without support. It's canceled for now, so stop worrying about it. But if they call you again on it . . ."

"Damn!" My call waiting flashed again. "Can you . . . ?"

"Yeah, sure. Go ahead."

"Yo."

"Still me."

"Son of a . . ." I grumbled in frustration. "Hello?"

My friend John Yearly was calling from California. "What's happenin'?"

"Hey! Can you hold? Let me shake this other caller."

As is customary with call waiting, I didn't wait for his consent. "Gordon?"

"Yeah?"

"It's business."

"Call me later on."

"Roger that." I then clicked back over. "John! What's goin' on?"

"Ever since you started working for Boise," he finished with a deadpan delivery, "My company can't get a decent ream of paper."

"That's probably why they call it getting reamed," began my rejoinder. "Anyhow, we don't make paper. We make plywood."

"Which would explain the knots in the bond. Did ya ever consider that the reason why they're the number one manufacturer of wood products is because their employees *are* on drugs?"

"Believe it or not, there's an element of truth to that."

"Work's that tough, huh?"

"It's insane."

"Speaking of insane," he segued in vintage John Yearly fashion, "How would you like to work in beautiful downtown Los Angeles?"

"I thought they weren't going to fill that position?"

"No, that's not what happened. They're just now getting around to doing it, that's all."

"I thought I came in third during that ridiculous eight-hour assessment."

"You did, but the other two guys have gotten jobs already."

"You may not have noticed, but I did too."

"No, I mean real jobs."

"A real job? Me? Can you imagine?"

"Had to happen sometime."

"I was actually down there a few months ago, you know. Downtown."

"Doin' what?"

"My job interview. There're alotta wackos down there. People talkin' to themselves, shouting at the world . . ."

"Now do you see how important music is?" John has always been a connoisseur of vintage rock music.

"You lost me."

"Same guy. Screaming at the world. But now he sings the words, instead. He's no longer a wacko, just a bad singer."

"With decaying clothes and bad hair."

"The point is," he attempted an explanation.

"Oh, goody, there's one of those, too."

"You know . . . ," he paused. "I just read a study that said if people tend to interrupt a lot and dominate conversations, they tend to die earlier than those who don't."

"Bullshit. If that were the case I'd be dead already."

"No argument here."

"So you mean if I stop interrupting people and become a regular Ann Landers, but still retain my hyperactive nature, I'll live longer?"

He tried to conceal his laughter. "No. And that's the point exactly."

"What the hell are you talking about? *You* on dope?"

"You don't have to be a straight-laced city employee to actually be one. Call yourself a personnel analyst but still be your animated self. Your title will be what a song is on the lips of a nut talking to himself in downtown Los Angeles."

"Sounds a bit contradictory, given the 'interrupting' study you were talking about earlier, but . . ."

"That might be true, so forget that part. Concentrate on my latest point. That's the brilliant one."

"Is someone offering me a job?"

"Olga said she'll be calling you sometime next week. I just wanted to give you a heads up. Are you interested?"

"I'm in the middle of a case up here. I can't just bail. Will it hold?"

"That's trivial bullshit. Whatta you care? You wanna be doin' that for the rest of your life?"

"Well, first of all, that's not the point. And secondly, my supervisor says that I'll be a case manager after my next case."

"Again, is that what you wanna be doing for the rest of your life?"

"No. But neither is what you do."

"It's a career. You should think of it in those terms. Is what you're doing *now* a career?"

"I don't think you're hearing me, here."

"I hear ya. I just think you're all caught up this 'I owe them something' crap. Do you think they'd give a fuck if you got dead tomorrow? And you're not even happy."

"What makes you say that?"

"Well, are you?"

"Partly. I mean, I like cleaning up these places so people have a decent place to work."

"So become a janitor."

"John, you wouldn't believe what drugs are doin' to the American work . . ."

"Spare me the apple pie and your jingoistic crapolo. Remind me what your book's about again?" His scathing comment referred to the fact that my first book, *CIA: Cocaine in America*, dealt with an ethically ambiguous CIA operation I was involved in.

"Ha, ha. Very funny."

"Okay, I'll grant you that getting drugs outta the workplace is a good thing, but is it worth the toll it's gonna take on your life? At least with this job you've got stability and a retirement plan, and you'll be helping the poor in the process. And if you ever plan on a family . . ."

"Okay, okay." He had worn me down. "Sold already. I see what you're sayin', and I appreciate it. I *really* do. But I gotta think about it a little before I just say yes. It's weird. I mean, I know what you're sayin' is right, but it's like, it's like this job is sorta the last vestige of youth I have. At least it seems that way, anyhow. I hate all the lying and manipulating, yet I love the game. Then again, I love winning the game, but I hate it when I've won. You know what I'm sayin'?"

"You don't haveta explain to me. Don't forget I did that crap for years."

"Yeah, I know. I'm just venting, I guess."

"So she should call you? Olga?"

"Absolutely," I said timidly. I thought for a few more seconds. "You're right. I mean, who am I kidding? I'd be crazy not to say yes, right? But I just wanna know it was my decision, not cajoling on your part."

"Don't interpret what I'm doing as cajoling. I'm just stating my opinion. You do what you want. I just think you'd be nuts not to at least consider a career before wasting any more of your life on what you're doing. Let's face it, a job that involves lying, manipulating, drinking to all hours, molesting women and selling drugs is not a career."

"Unless you count politics."

"Yeah, and the benefits are great, too, right? But seriously. Let me ask you this. Do you still eat a whole pan of brownies for dinner?"

"You catch me one time doin' that and I'm branded "bachelor" for life. You make it sound like I do it on a regular basis."

"See what I'm sayin'? That's not a real life."

"That's the problem with tryin' to reason with someone you've known for ten years."

"I think what you meant to say was, 'That's the problem with trying to *bullshit* someone who's known you for . . . I think it's been nine years, actually."

Before I could retort, another call came in. "Can you hold for a sec, John?"

I didn't wait for the answer and switched over. "Ken?" the caller said. "It's Caracas. We're on."

"When do you want me at the airport?"

"You're not going there. I'm downstairs in your parking lot. You'll go with me."

I preferred to drive myself, if for no other reason than it would give the police a place to begin looking if I disappeared. Just as that thought crossed my mind, in a most natural manner, John's advice struck home . . . like a sledgehammer. "No," I countered. "I'll follow you there."

"Suit yourself. And no weapons," Caracas demanded. "We pass through airport security on the way to our planes."

"Planes? As in plural?"

"You got it. Come on down."

We both hung up without saying good-bye. Before my phone hit the cradle, it rang again. "John!" I blurted.

"Forget about me?" he said.

"Yeah. Tell Olga to call me. I'm ready."

"One of your friends, I take it?"

"What else. It's one crazy story, I tell ya. Remind me to relate all the details sometime. I'm going to check it out right now."

"Years of experience tells me there's no such thing as a crazy story in that line of work. The crazier the story, the more likely it is that it's true. Be careful."

My first thought was, "John's sharing a tender moment? God, maybe this *is* serious."

"But as a precaution," he continued, "Go ahead and put a note in your car willing it to me. And don't forget to sign it. It's not valid if it's not signed."

"And then again," I thought, "Maybe not."

Not unlike every other case I had investigated, I would allow this case to steer itself and reveal its own unique nature. Maybe this was an elaborate ruse and maybe it wasn't, but one thing was for sure: I wasn't going to find out by sitting at home with my thumb up my stump. The trip to Crater Lake was on.

Chapter 15

I started to grab my Colt when I remembered Caracas's warning about airport security. I seized a can of soda from the refrigerator, where the stark supply of food had me gravitating ever closer toward that personnel analyst position in downtown Los Angeles, and drained the contents into the sink. I then attempted to cut open the bottom with a can opener. No dice. Now fraught with desperation and clumsy, I grabbed a butcher knife, stabbed the can and sawed halfway around the bottom. I bent back the aluminum, wrapped my derringer in a couple of paper towels to prevent rattling, and stuffed it inside. After folding the metal back into place, you could hardly tell the can had been defaced. Unless, of course, you looked at it from the bottom.

A stiff, blustery wind greeted me in the parking lot. The brisk, inclement air had the smell of impending rain. I found Caracas leaning against his Porsche 944 as if he were posing for *GQ*. "Did I get anything good today?" I called out.

"How do you mean?"

"My mail! I assume you've read it already?"

"No, not today," he answered candidly.

"I'll follow you!"

"Come here first!"

When I came alongside him, he flicked a cigarette onto the ground and said, still looking away, "I gotta frisk ya."

"For what?"

"For peace of mind."

"Go ahead, but I hope no one's looking out their window." I held my hands above my head as he quickly patted me down.

"Sorry 'bout that. Never can be too careful."

"Not a problem," I returned. "Now your turn." I proceeded to pat him down thoroughly.

*   *   *

We drove in tight formation, each trying to impress the other with our driving skills. Gusts of wind could be felt in the frame, jerking our cars toward the center divider like matchboxes. Inspired by the foreboding tenor of the drama that was unfolding, I rummaged once again for my perennial favorite, "In the Air Tonight," which, of course, I had inexplicably left in the CD case back at my place. I turned up the mood-altering album "Come Undone" by Duran Duran instead, and this was a fine surrogate under the circumstances. Anyone who thinks music has no effect on a person's mood and attitude should have been in my car that day.

The instant I exited my vehicle, Caracas queried, "You're not packing, right?"

"You said no guns."

"Good. We're ready to go then." His manner immediately became dictatorial. "You'll be staying in your plane."

"My plane? There's more than one?"

"Listen!" he chastised, showing me a side of himself I had not previously known. "I don't have time to explain this again. There are four to each plane. Two stay on board, and two jump."

"You bet your ass I'm stayin' in the plane."

"Stop interrupting!" He gripped his face in his hands for a moment. "After the jumpers reach their mark, one plane will land, and the other will hang around just long enough to see that the other plane gets back off the ground safely. After the cargo is loaded, that is. Once they're off, the guys that remain on the ground will go to another location and drive trucks back to Medford. After you land in Medford, call me on my pager. Here's the number."

He felt around in his pocket for the piece of paper with his phone number on it. "Leave the numbers 666 after your number so I know it's cool to come pick you up. Actually, you've got your car, don'tcha. Okay, so you'll follow me. Any questions?"

"A million, but if I'm stayin' in the air I guess it doesn't really matter."

"You may haveta land, you know?"

"Does my pilot know that?"

"Of course."

"Then I guess we're okay." Just as we were about to go through the metal detector, I snatched him by the back of the shirt. "How do I know what you're picking up is really what you say it is?"

"Just pray you don't haveta find out," he cautioned, shrugging my hand away. I took this to mean that if I verified the cargo it was only because I had to land, which would put me in harm's way.

"If I do," I declared, "I get paid. Understood?"

"Understood. We're parked in an area called the Jet Center. Just follow me."

I approached the metal detector casually, my coat slung across my shoulder and my left hand squeezing the aluminum soda can. Appearing fittingly ill prepared to "remove all metal objects" from my pockets, I placed the can in the tray and fumbled for my keys and spare change. Tossing the contents of my pockets onto the tray alongside the can, I passed through the detector completely unnoticed.

With the dexterity of a Las Vegas card dealer, I grabbed the can and trinkets as if they were a stack of chips and, through force of habit, routinely tilted the can to my lips. Luckily, no one was paying any attention to the bottom of the can.

Why airports continue to allow me to place my soda can on the tray is beyond me. Try it yourself sometime and you'll be astonished at the results. In fact, on more than one occasion I've placed a large McDonald's Diet Coke cup in that tray and waltzed through the terminal without it ever having been scrutinized for explosives. Do you know how much C4 can be stuffed into a large McDonald's soda cup? What if the terrorist says, "Super size it"? He'd have enough to take out a DC 10, I assure you.

Although they say flying is safer than taking a bath in your own home, whoever "they" are probably never considered the possibility that someone would be stupid enough to bathe with the likes of these malcontents.

"Explain why we don't wanna drive again." I half jested.

Caracas approached with his head angled to lessen the effects of the wind. With his eyes squinted, he grinned. "Don't worry 'bout it! We've flown in much worse!"

I elevated my voice to match the loudness of the wind. "Yeah, but have you landed in worse?"

"They always land! That's the easy part! Even the Hindenburg landed!"

"Great!"

I followed forthwith as he led me to one of the single-engine planes. "Tari." I was taken aback even though I had already concluded she was involved in this excursion in some unknown capacity. "What are you doin' here?"

She seemed equally disappointed. "I was gonna ask you the same thing."

"Caracas met me after work . . ."

Caracas interrupted. "Ken, you'll fly with Tari."

"I probably already know the answer to this question, but who's our pilot?"

"Ah-huh," he replied. "It's Tari!"

Much of my nervousness evaporated when he uttered her name. She was probably the only one I could trust at the mill. But I still wanted to know why she was so heavily involved with these lowlifes. Did she know what was about to go down?

There were eight of us in two planes. Of the eight, four would parachute out and rendezvous with the shipment. From there, they would hike to a remote landing strip and load the cargo onto the plane that landed. The mules would then return to Medford by vehicle. Our plane was there merely as a backup. The wind had picked up and the sky was darkening, and I, for one, had had just about enough thrills for one day.

* * *

Passing over Crater Lake was like a giant leap backwards in time, back to when God's finger first created this magnificent divot in the wilderness. I had never seen water so blue, nor is it likely I ever will again. At that instant, I wanted nothing more than to live by the shore of this oasis and fish to my heart's content. Within seconds of this fleeting reverie, my wish almost came true in the wake of a violent turbulent flow.

Tari's deft aviator skills were put to the test as she nosed the aircraft over, taking full advantage of the small plane's considerable flight envelope. The negative G forces sent blood gushing to our collective heads, affecting some more than others. Barely able to keep my balance, I reached frantically for the cockpit dash, fighting back the bile that had already crept into my throat. I clung to the dash like a stuffed suction cat to a station wagon's rear window, holding my breath with panicked anticipation. The two in back screamed with unabashed horror. All I kept thinking was, "They're the ones screaming, and we're the ones without parachutes." Reminding myself about the comparative dangers of my bathtub didn't make the experience any more palatable either.

The aircraft lifted on pockets of heated air and fell out from under us where the air was cooler. I would have been overcome with nausea had I not been distracted by an untenable fear.

"How we doing?" I tried to appear unruffled.

She was frank. "Not good."

"*Not good*, we should turn around, or *not good*, we're about to ditch?"

"Not good," she repeated.

"Okay." I exhaled. "I don't think I'm communicating here. *Not good . . .*"

"*Not good*, we should . . . Why are you here?!" She shook the yoke.

"Why am *I* here? Are you serious? Why the hell are you here? At least I've been up front with you about what I do. You, though . . . What the hell have you been?"

"Would you two shut the hell up and concentrate on flying this plane!" the male smuggler insisted.

"You're like a whiny-ass married couple," the woman opined. "You're both drug dealers! Okay? Get over it!"

"Who sounds like a whiny-ass married couple, now?" Tari retaliated, her gestures becoming more and more animated. "Oh, wait! You are a whiny-ass married couple. And *we weren't talking to you*! Now if you want me to slap this plane sideways and toss your lame asses out the door at two hundred feet, I will! So sit down and *shut the fuck up!*"

The woman, a tall Anglo with short, dark, lifeless hair and packed with muscles, rummaged through her satchel and removed a rather intimidating knife. "You were sayin', cunt?"

Attempting the same savoir faire as she had just displayed, I peeled back the bottom of my Coke can and sliced my finger wide open in the process. Rich crimson blood spurted across the exquisitely polished gun, lending art to an already melodramatic situation. "Give it to me," I said confidently, pointing the gun at her face while twisting in my seat for better comfort. "Handle first."

"How the hell'd you get that through security?" the man questioned, his gurgling voice frothy with saliva.

"I should ask her the same thing. Now put your tray tables up and place your seat backs in the full upright position. It's gonna be a bumpy ride."

Tari whispered, "Is that loaded?"

"Wouldn't do much good if it weren't. And besides, I'd never point an unloaded gun at anyone."

"You mean a loaded gun," she corrected. "Okay, everyone, buckle up! We're in for a bouncy ride!"

I continued with my original train of thought. "Don't ever point a weapon at someone if you don't intend to use it."

The aircraft yawed to the left and then unexpectedly banked hard to the right. Utter silence fell over the cabin as the wind slapped the plane in all directions. Tari grappled with the yoke, steering the craft on an ever-changing course of least resistance. A constant vortex of water flowing off the wing tip helped momentarily distract my focus from the horrendous danger we now faced.

As the turbulent air slammed the front of the aircraft like a squalling sea breaking over a rubber raft, Tari nosed the plane forward one last time and dropped below the hard ceiling to a height perilously unsuited for skydiving.

"We're too low," the woman screamed.

"If we drop you up there," I hollered, pointing out the top of the windscreen, "The wind'll tangle your chutes! You choose your poison!"

"What's our altitude?" she asked.

"We're bouncing between six hundred and seven hundred feet!" Tari explained. "You can't jump!"

"When you get over the target," the woman instructed, "Pull up to a thousand feet just long enough to get us out the door! Okay?"

"I'll try! But if I can't, the jump's off!"

"Good enough!"

* * *

With wings undulating, our aircraft sank into darkened plumes of gray, a hazy canopy that seemed to swell before us. With the other ship in the lead, we emerged from each thunder cloud in a new configuration, often close enough to read each other's identification number. Our collective gasps became increasingly intense each time we emerged from the clouds even closer than we had the time before.

My breathing became struggled, and a knot began to clench my throat. I had trouble filling my lungs with oxygen but couldn't understand why.

"You're hyperventilating," the man observed.

"No I'm not! I think there's some sort of gas leak in here, or something!"

"There's no gas leak. You're hyperventilating!" he repeated. "I've seen it a million times."

"Shut up with the 'hyperventilating,' already! Pussies like you hyperventilate," I retaliated. My head was becoming light, and a cold sweat crept into my shirt. I rubbed briskly at the dash with my head dropped between my arms and shouted, "Okay, I'm hyperventilating! What the hell do I do?"

"Just breathe in real deep and hold it for the count of two," Tari advised. "Good, good. Do it again." She waited. "Good, good. Now a couple more times without the holding part." She waited yet again. "Now keep breathing evenly and steadily." A few moments later she asked, "How you feelin'?"

"Better," I said quietly, humiliated.

"Good, 'cause we gotta small problem," she warned.

"Besides the obvious," I asked tentatively.

"I've lost instruments! Holy . . ."

"What instruments?"

"Navigational. Hell, all of 'em."

"How is that possible?"

"Shoddy maintenance? Electrical storm? Who knows. The point is, they're gone. All of 'em."

The woman in the rear exclaimed, "You don't need 'em! Just stick with the plane in front of us! Keep them in sight!"

"That's fine for now," Tari muttered, "But how 'bout on the way back?"

"Can you land without the glideslope?" I asked.

"In a storm? I don't know. But how 'bout just getting back to Medford? I don't know if I can do that."

"Don't you pilots," the man started, "don't you haveta, like, you know, be able to read stars and shit?"

"Hey, Copernicus," I said, attempting to point out the obvious, "Do you see any stars up there? If it was a clear day we wouldn't be having this problem, now would we?! Stupid shit."

"Get ready to go," the woman declared.

"Climb!" he insisted.

"Bullshit!" Tari replied. "It's now or never!"

To my astonishment, they dove headfirst into the rain-swept skies and quickly disappeared from sight. "Was that safe, what they just did?" I inquired. "Cause it didn't look safe."

She didn't respond, so I nudged her a bit. "Did you hear me?"

She reacted with anger. "This is not just a run-of-the-mill drug deal, you know?"

"Excuse me? Let me remove that plank from your eye!"

"What? What the hell's that s'posed to mean?"

"You're a hypocrite! That's what it's supposed to mean!"

She hinted at an excuse. "You have no idea why I'm here!" Just then, the aircraft performed an "uncommanded" roll to the right. Her subsequent scream told me that she did not intend for it to do that. When the plane rolled onto its back, I was sure we were dead.

Chapter 16

I . . . was . . . here," she groaned as she strained to pull the yoke counterclockwise, "to . . . protect . . . you!"

I was relieved to hear that she wasn't in this just for the money but disheartened somewhat to hear her say so in the past tense. Now I was sure we were goners.

"You better do something," I said, my voice steadily climbing. "Or we're *gonna eat it!*"

"I'm trying! I'm trying!" she grunted like a Russian weight lifter, pushing her feet hard against the floor and throwing her shoulder stiffly into the side window as she wrenched the yoke toward her body. At around two hundred feet off the deck, the aircraft began to right itself. With the tall pines stretching to meet us, we skimmed along the needles, too numb with fear to speak or even care. With a swig of air and a short lament, Tari lifted the aircraft slowly, mindful to keep us beneath the menacing thunderclouds.

"Now what?" I broke the silence.

"I'm not sure."

"Which direction do we want to go in from Crater Lake itself?"

"South by southeast. But it doesn't do us much good without some form of compass. Can you believe this piece of crap doesn't have a standard magnetic compass?"

"Is that unusual?"

"It's unheard of! I thought you were in the Air Force?" she questioned in a challenging tone.

"Hey, this is no time to argue. But to answer your question, our planes were a bit more sophisticated than this one."

"Come to think of it," her voice brewed with hope, "Why don't *you* fly? With your background, you'd do a better job than I would, probably."

I was visibly confounded by her implication. "What background?"

"The Air Force! Now c'mon, take the controls!"

"I was an aircraft maintenance officer, not a pilot. I could fix it if it crashed, but I can't prevent it from crashing."

"What? Everyone says you were a pilot."

"Hell, I must be one then," I said sarcastically. "Give me the stick."

"Very funny," she replied. "Do you know anything at all about flying?"

"Sounds to me like we need a navigator, not a pilot."

"You can navigate?" She became excited once again.

"Hell, no! I'm just sayin' that's what we need right now, that's all."

"We're gonna run outta fuel," she said despondently.

"Are we low?"

"No. At least I don't think so. But if we continue flying in the wrong direction, we'll never have enough to get back. We need to find a safe place to set down."

"How 'bout an airport?" I attempted to lighten the mood.

"Look for a field," she said gravely. "One large enough to set down in. Preferably a smooth one."

*   *   *

We bounced around for another ten minutes. The constant barrage of pelting rain and battering wind had made us weary and shell-shocked. We scoured the land in all directions, straining our eyes for anything resembling a sliver of flat, uncluttered land.

"There!" Tari thrust her finger into the windscreen.

"What?"

"Those fields!"

"Where?" Before she could respond, we passed directly over a multi-purpose playing field that had, among other things, a baseball diamond. "Yes! I see it!"

"We'll have to bank back around. It'll be tight, but I think we can make it! Hold on!"

As the plane banked hard left, I could hear its throaty motor sputtering away, something I was too scared to notice earlier. With my composure returning and my senses more reliable, a clear thought was allowed to invade my mind. A thought that my senses told me was relevant to our present situation. The problem, however, was that the thought had rushed through so quickly I hadn't time to remember it. As I racked my brain to bring the thought to the fore, I felt the plane begin its descent. When we tripped the treetops at the beginning of the ball fields, the thought flooded back in like gangbusters.

"Baseball field!" I exploded. "Pull up! Pull up!"

"What?! Are you serious?!"

"Pull up!" With that, my head snapped back in the seat and the plane narrowly missed the trees on the opposite side of the field. So close, in fact, that we would both later agreed there probably wasn't enough room to land after all.

"Oh, my God," she gasped. "Why did you do that?"

"The baseball field! They call left-handed pitchers south paws!"

"Because their . . . ," she leaned toward me.

I dove in midsentence ". . . pitching hand . . ."

We both finished the sentence simultaneously, "faces south!"

I added, "Does that help?"

"Yeah, I think? No, wait. How do we know that field is set up that way? Are they all the same?"

"Yeah. It's to ensure the batter isn't facing the setting sun."

"But he faces the rising sun, then."

"When's the last time you saw a baseball game begin at sunrise?"

"Oh, yeah," she thought for a moment. "That means we've been flying north of the drop zone for about twenty minutes, so . . . Yeah, okay. So that field . . . that was probably Klamath Falls. There's been some slipping . . . but I think I can at least get us to an area I recognize. Yeah, I think we can do this. Weather permitting and God willing, I think I can. Yeah, I think we're gonna be okay." She then declared, "South paw?! *Damn*, that was good!"

*   *   *

After about a half hour of restrained conversation, with neither of us wanting to fracture the unspoken truce that had grown out of our situational bonding, Tari snapped the treaty like a dry twig. "You know, I may be a money-grubbing, gold-digging bitch, but I draw the line somewhere."

"Don't give me that malarkey about doing this for me. You told me you were going flying before you had the first clue that I was coming along."

"Not true! Caracas told me about this thing last week, saying he was gonna ask you to tag along. When I heard you confirmed yesterday, I told 'im I'd help out."

"And he's not paying you a thing?"

"That's not the point. I didn't accept his offer until I knew you were going."

"And you're donating it all to charity. Yeah, yeah. Whatever, all right? I have my reasons too. Maybe not as altruistic as yours, but I have 'em."

"That five-thousand-dollar watch you're wearing says everything I need to know about your motivation," she said.

"If you think so little of me, then why are you here? Can you answer me that?!"

She stared solemnly into the canopy as clouds poured over and didn't respond. Breaking her concentration momentarily, she glanced down at the instrument panel and said sullenly, "Instruments are back on line."

"Great." My reaction was equally somber. "How far off course are we?"

"Not too. We'll make it."

A brief silence ensued. "If it's any consolation," I said, "I'm not getting paid a dime for any of this."

"You expect me to believe they roped you into this for nothing?"

"I don't expect shit. I expect you to land this bucket of bolts safely and then go marry a man you don't even love because his parents gave him a bunch of money to start his own business."

She let out an incredulous huff. "Where'd that come from?"

"Why should you be the only one allowed to criticize and judge?"

"Do you know how much drugs those losers will dump on Medford and the rest of Jackson County with what they got today? Do you? Do you care?"

"Do *I*? You're trying to tell me you've had no involvement in drugs? And besides, they're your friends, not mine!"

"Why? Because I'm civil to them? I hate them bastards! They only *think* I like 'em, and that keeps me safe."

"And how 'bout your boyfriend? He uses drugs."

"Not anymore. Except maybe the occasional joint."

"What is it you want me to say?"

"Doesn't matter, because you'd never mean it. Let's just forget about it, all right? You're right, we should go our separate ways when this is over."

As I struggled with how to respond, I realized that to say anything would just add more lies to the mountain of lies our relationship was buried beneath. I suppose I always knew that Tari and I weren't right for each other, but I'd always thought we'd be friends. I couldn't let the day end that way.

"What would you say," my lips were moving, but it was as though I had no control over what they were saying, "If I told you that I was here undercover? Called in by Boise to solve their drug problem. What would you say to that?"

She pretended to be suddenly interested in the plane's instrument panel. "Hmmm. The ILS isn't working. The glideslope is out. Huh. Everything else seems to be fine, though. Don't you find that rather odd?"

"Yeah." I went along with her. "Maybe it was intentional. They probably rigged it so we couldn't mark their drop zone."

"Because they know you're a narc?"

"Or you are."

"Why would they think that?"

"I don't know. Companies do send more than one agent in at a time, you know. They've been known to do that."

"But if you were an agent, you would know that."

"Not necessarily. Maybe you're here to check up on me."

"Yeah!" She snorted like a sow pig as a laugh crept into her voice. "And you failed miserably!"

"At least I'm not a drug dealer, though. Right?"

"You're serious about this?" She looked at me with a crooked smile.

"As a plane crash."

"Oh, my God," her breath fled. "Am I in trouble?"

"No. In fact, my boss . . ." I stopped myself midsentence. "Would you do me a favor before I go any further with this?"

"What?"

"Roll your sleeves up for me."

"What? Why? Is that where wires are worn these days?"

"No. Just do it for me, please."

"I can't."

"And why's that?" I said suspiciously.

"Look at these sleeves." She demonstrated how she could barely get her fingertips underneath the material around her hermetically sealed wrists. "They're not designed for that. Feel. Go ahead, feel." She attempted to roll them up. "See. I can't get them but a roll or two."

"Who wears a blouse like that on a drug run?"

"I don't like loose clothes around the cockpit. They get snagged on things. And besides, it's my first drug run."

I laughed. "That's good. Now, take it off."

"Take what off?"

"Your blouse."

"Excuse me?"

"You heard me. If you want me to explain everything, you'll take it off."

"I'm not wearing a damn wire! Frisk me if you want!"

"I don't wanna feel you. I wanna see you."

"I'm not wearing a bra."

"No bra. No wire. What's next?"

"No breasts! For you, that is."

"Well?"

"*Well,* what? You're shittin' me, right? You still want me to do it? Seriously?"

"More now than ever," I teased. "No, I'm just kidding. It has nothing to do with your breasts, I assure you."

"The moment a man says 'breast,' he forgets his own name. Whatever it is you're looking for, it'll all be forgotten when I remove my shirt. Notice I've been careful not to use the word 'blouse,' either. I've seen what that innocuous little word can do to you men, too. If I were a criminal, I'd rob banks naked. And when the cops would ask the tellers for a description, the men would describe my body perfectly, right down to my huge . . ." she paused, searching for the correct word, "areolas. But when asked to describe my face, they'd say, 'She had no head! Crazy bitch had no head!' Because they'd never look up."

"I'm sorry. You lost me after 'huge areolas.' You were saying?"

Tari was not amused. "Huh, that's hysterical. Finish your stupid story."

I remained reticent, resisting any affectation that might suggest my motives were anything but professional.

"You're not still wanting me to remove my blouse?"

I couldn't resist the humor. "Oh, my God, you said blouse."

She failed to see the humor once again. "Well, are you?"

"That's what I'm waiting for."

She stared straight ahead for several seconds. "Fine. Get your jollies." She rambled on and on the entire time it took her to unbutton her beige silk blouse and roll it inside out over her forearms.

"Give me your hands." I held her eyes with mine, never veering. She placed her hands out naturally, almost trusting. I slowly turned her palms out and looked quickly down at her forearms. "That's what I thought," I said with a calming voice. "No brand."

When I released her arms, she lunged toward me and hugged me. "Thank you."

"Who's flyin' the plane?" I said with a light chuckle.

"Thanks," she said, putting her shirt back on with little urgency.

"What were you saying about the instruments? They're working or something?"

"I think we already talked about that."

"Yeah, I suppose we have." My voice trailed off.

"You don't have to make small talk. I'm okay now. You were saying about this undercover stuff?" She tilted her eyes up at me inquisitively as she continued to button the bottom half of her blouse.

"Is that Medford up ahead?"

"Sure is. The undercover stuff . . . ?" she prodded.

"Yeah, well . . ."

"Have you been using me all this time? For information?"

"Not *all* this time. Only in the beginning. Not even then, really. I just knew you weren't one of them. I don't know why. I just did."

"When I think about it, you've asked me questions about drugs and stuff ever since we met. I mean, it's not like you stopped when we . . . Well, you know. Started kissing and junk."

"It's best not to think about it in too much detail. There's a fine line between being friendly with someone to get information and getting information from someone you just happen to be friendly with. Do you follow what I'm saying?"

"Did you tape any of these conver . . . God, you didn't tape us in the car that night?"

"I've never taped anything with us, I swear."

"So why you tellin' me all this? Is your investigation over?"

"No, not hardly. I wish it were over. It's really just getting started."

"Then why blow your cover with me?"

"I don't know. I guess I just couldn't stand to have you think that way of me. I'm not quite sure exactly."

"What if I told everyone? You really shouldn't tell people this."

"I haven't. Well, except for you, that is. And if you ratted me out, I'd just say you're making it up. But I'm not gonna haveta do that."

"No, you're not. But you couldn't have known that for sure. You still can't."

"Which shows you how much I trust you and how much I value your friendship."

She turned to me, a mildness coming over her face. Her lips drew slowly outward to form a perfect, tender smile. "What do you wanna know about that place [the mill]?"

"Nothing. Let's forget it exists for a while."

"Do you think they rigged this plane to crash?"

"I don't think they're smart enough. And besides, there're are much easier ways to do it. I think they were trying to see if I'd buy off on that whole drugs-in-the-glue shit, though. Still haven't figured out if it's true or not."

"Drugs in the what? The glue? You mean that rumor you told me that was so ridiculous?"

"Oh," I said. "You didn't know this was connected to that, I take it? Remind me to tell you about it sometime. It's a real doozie." For the remainder of the trip, we relaxed and shot the breeze.

"Airport," she announced softly.

"Well, I'll be damned. You did it, Tari. You really did it."

"It's not that hard when you have instruments."

"I'm sure there's a simple explanation for what happened. Regardless, don't let on that there was any sorta problem getting back. If they did have something to do with this, and I'm not sayin' they did, mind you, we wouldn't want them to think it worked or that we're suspicious of them or nothing. You know what I'm sayin'?"

"No, I agree. I would just really like to know what this was all about. The plane, the glue, the whole shebang."

"Me too." It then occurred to me that we never stuck around to see if the other group needed us to land. "If they ask," I instructed, "we couldn't rendezvous with them because we temporarily lost instruments and our visual on them. Be sure to say *temporarily*."

"I'll split the money with you when I get paid," she offered.

"No, you keep your mammary." We both laughed. "I mean money."

It was peculiar, but as I was leaving the airport that day I felt a strange loss. There was something very cozy and very secure about that aircraft, even in the midst of the storm's fury. It had made me feel isolated, set apart from all the madness of the mill. I would reflect fondly on that experience for the duration of my sentence there.

*   *   *

As I sat at my computer that evening, flipping between my book and my daily investigative report, I suddenly realized that my life hadn't changed a whole hell of a lot in the last ten years. The stories I found myself reflecting on and writing about were essentially the same stories I was presently living, only now the characters were poorer and had real jobs.

Sheets of tepid rain oscillated against a lonely window, washing away the filth of a long, dry season. As I labored at my writing, my weary eyes fought to see the words on the dirty screen, the filth of a decade not readily abated by a guilty heart and dripping face.

No longer able to stave off the fatigue, I laid my head between my folded arms and fell asleep at the table. A lethargic dreamscape soon poured forth. My thoughts slowly dissolved to a dreary factory on the outskirts of a blighted Midwestern town, where, on an ill-fated day, the innocuous tip of my baseball cap sent federal agents swarming around unsuspecting employees. With twitching cheeks and hollowed eyes, I searched inward, gazing despondently at the betrayal of those I had once called friends. One by one, employees were ambushed as they entered the building on a cool and dank morning.

The image of a young woman crept silently from the shadowed corners of my dream. Skulking agents, like spiders, exploded from the fringe, attacking the hazy figure. A flash of metal beneath her fatigued leather jacket attracted a pernicious hail of titanium-sleeved projectiles. Her coat dimpled with each impact, fusing to her skin, and billowed like a sail as the bullets exploded from the back, and she twisted violently as she fell to the cold concrete slab.

I peered into the recesses of my mind and viewed with great discomfort the deceived look that she wore so heavily. It was Tari, and she stared through me and those who hovered over her, her failing eyes falling upon a withered pair of work gloves dangling precariously from a dust-laden rafter high above our heads, her betrayer now revealed.

Calling myself out from my sleep, I awakened with a cold, clammy brow. The first thought that popped into my head was, "Are these the shadows of things to come or things that *could* be if I don't change?" After a hearty laugh, I crawled into bed knowing that nothing would change and that I would awaken tomorrow with the same objective. In the words of the Oakland Raiders' owner, Al Davis, "Just win, baby!"

Chapter 17

With my head at the foot of the bed and wondering if it had all been a bad dream, I awoke the following day to a nagging, pulsating, buzzing sound. After hurling my alarm clock across the room to the unforgiving cinderblock wall, I quickly realized it was not mine that was sounding. It was the neighbors'. It was 7:00 A.M., and it had been buzzing for at least fifteen minutes.

Stumbling to my door and then down the hall to the neighboring apartment, I pounded at the door as only a sleep-deprived maniac could. Before the elderly woman answering the door could ask what it was that I wanted, I vented my frustration over her total lack of respect and consideration for others. After she apologized profusely for not realizing that her son's heart monitor had gone off, explaining that she and her husband had grown accustomed to the alarm sounding whenever her son's heart had an arrhythmic beat, I slithered back down to my cave, feeling as you might expect.

About twenty minutes later, the phone rang. "Hello?" I said into the wrong end of the receiver. In an attempt to reverse it gracefully in my hand, I dropped it to the floor. "Wait a sec," I said from about five feet away before crawling over to pick it up. "Hello?"

"You alone?" Gordon asked.

"Sadly enough. No, wait. Let me check first," I said sarcastically. A second later I continued, "Nope. No one here."

If I didn't know better, I'd say he almost sounded sympathetic. "Place's really that small, huh?"

"You *got* that? I'm impressed."

"I read your report from last night."

"I called in a report?"

"You don't remember?"

"No. No, I don't. What'd it say? I hope nothing bad."

Maintaining a serious, almost grave tone, Gordon explained. "Why is it you think Boise might have some prejudicial hiring practices? Is it something you heard or just the fact that you haven't met any black people on your shift? Do you have any idea what the black/white ratio in Medford is?"

"That's alotta questions first thing in the morning."

"It's noon."

"It is? Damn." I collected my thoughts. "Well, first of all, there aren't any black people on my shift. It's not that I hadn't seen them. They're simply not there. And, insofar as the mill itself, I can't say for sure, but I've been told by several employees that the mill had a black employee working there at one time, but they chased him away. Notice I said 'a black man.' As in *one*."

"Well, that rumor's simply not true. Black people just don't apply to the mill. That's it, plain and simple. No big conspiracy."

"Maybe they don't apply for the same reason they don't apply to the KKK."

"*Now* Boise's the KKK?"

"I didn't say they were, but I bet they have a pretty active membership. The point is, it's not the *work* chasin' 'em away, it's the people."

"*How* do you know that?"

"Because I've spoken to a lot of these idiots that've said just that. They're proud of it. Not all of them, of course. Most of the employees here are good, hard-working people, but it only takes a handful to cause a problem. People are too afraid to stand up to these hillbillies."

"That's why *you're* there. That's it exactly. It's not hiring practices; it's unscrupulous employees who are chasing minorities away. And quite possibly the work itself."

Gordon had a bad habit of protecting the company at all cost. He steered this conversation as he steered all conversations, away from the company and toward the people we were investigating. No matter what I said, it would always get deflected away from those that hired us. Another one of those major conflict-of-interest problems.

"I'll buy half of what you just said because I lack evidence to the contrary. But I hope you're not suggesting that the grueling work is deterring black people from applying for jobs."

"I'm just raising possibilities. They're not applying; that's all I know."

"And I'm telling you why. *I'm* here. *You're* not. And management's gonna tell you whatever their lawyers tell 'em to tell you."

"All's I'm sayin' is it's possible, that's all. *Possible*. You do understand the word *possible*, don'tcha?"

"Gordon." I composed myself. "Like most conversations we have, this's goin' nowhere. Let's just . . ."

"I'm not arguing. I'm just telling you not to represent things conclusively when you don't have all the facts. The stuff you put in those reports becomes part of the permanent record. Just give us the facts."

"Except when it comes to employees stealing and using drugs. Then it's okay."

"No." His voice quickly trailed away. "Not then either. Anyhow, I'm sending another operative up there for a couple days to help you flush some of these Spreaders out into the open. Maybe we can even get to the bottom of that glue story you were telling me about a few days ago while we're at it."

I was relieved to hear him say "a few days ago," because that meant I hadn't written about the plane fiasco, yet. The other news, however, had me enraged. "Who?" I said, nearing the boiling point.

"Rick. He's good. He's done a lot of this stuff before."

"I've spoken to Rick. He's done about five cases, and none have involved drug buys. You send him up here and you might as well put a bulbous blue light on top of my car. The guy's a joke, Gordon. Everyone there knows it, too."

"Who you talkin' about? Who knows it? I don't know what the hell you're talkin' about half the time! The guy's got a track record. Where do you get off?"

"Juan, Glenn . . . Lots of people have told me about him. Hey, forget about it, all right? Damn. Send the son of a bitch. I don't give a fuck. And when they pop the lid on this thing, just remember we had this little talk."

"Glenn? Maybe that's why he's gone. And Juan? I can't believe . . ."

"Okay, 'nuff already. The only conversations I've had at K and S that have ever made any sense were with Glenn, Juan and Lydia. Hell, send her."

"Which Lydia?"

"In benefits."

"She's not an operative."

"No shit. I was being facetious. But I meant what I said about them being the only people there with a clue."

"I hope that doesn't include me?"

"No. You have a clue, but you also have an agenda. One that's not always practical where the rubber meets the road. Rick's a bad idea, Gordon. No matter what you think of me personally, ask yourself this: Could anyone else at K and S do what I've done in such a short period of time? And don't give me the political answer. I've heard that one already."

"I think you're too close to this. If it doesn't work out, what have we lost?"

"The case. Our lives. Trivial shit like that."

"Again with the histrionics? Rick's a smart guy. He won't hurt the case. He's a case manager for Chris' sakes."

I sighed in submission. "When's he coming?"

"He's on his way, actually. He'll call you when he arrives this evening. What time you off? Eleven?"

"Nice to know my opinion matters. Damn," I muttered. "Eleven-thirty. Tell 'im to call me at midnight. We'll go out tonight and meet with the appropriate people."

"Great. I'll tell him. I'll talk to you tomorrow."

"Thanks for the warning."

"It's gonna be fine. Relax."

*   *   *

After giving Rick all the particulars on what he could expect from these guys, we left his hotel and headed over to the bar. "Let's keep our goals simple," I said on the drive over. "All's we want is an invitation into their exclusive club, nothing more."

Each time I looked over at his callow puss, I had to fight back the burning compulsion to smack it. "I'm up here because I'm disappointed in the progress you've made in setting up my northwestern distribution," he said, as if it were true. "I wanna see firsthand what my money's being spent on."

"Okay, Tubs," I chuckled inadvertently. "This is not 'Miami Vice.' Is that a fake earring?"

"I don't know who it is you're referring to," he continued with the caricature. "But I'm your boss, Denton Isaac, biggest drug lord on the West fucking coast. And from now on, you'll address me with a little more respect."

"You've got Zig Zags (rolling papers) in your wallet and a hundred dollar bill rolled into a straw, don'tcha?"

"What the fuck is your problem exactly?" he snipped.

"Now, is this Denton or Rick I'm speaking to?" I asked in the tempered manner one uses to talk to an insane person.

"Do you even know how to be an undercover investigator? Maybe that's why Gordon sent me up here! To fix this shit you've gotten us into."

"Okay, it's Rick," I said in an ordinary manner before turning serious. "You don't walk into a situation like this with props and an AKA and expect them to swoon like junior high school cheerleaders. They'll see through that shit in a New York minute."

He finger combed his short, bristly hair as I spoke. "Is that a fake pinkie nail? Please tell me you just have poor hygiene."

"For your information, this's what people use. They cut into the packaging with 'em then they test the drugs. You need to start attending our training classes more regularly."

"First of all," I said gripping the steering wheel as though I were ringing out a wet towel, "No one scoops with a pinkie nail anymore. And even if they did, it wouldn't be a major trafficker and it wouldn't be *fake*." My voice continued to climb. "And the reason I don't attend those stupid, fucking classes is because I'm a thousand miles away and they're taught by morons like you!"

He interjected. "Who the hell do you think you're . . ."

"Shut up! I don't wanna hear another fuckin' word! If they see through this little charade of yours, *and they will*, you're on your own."

"You're off this case when I get back, if I have anything to do about it."

I backhanded him across the face. "Ahhhrr," he cried. "What the hell's wrong with you? I think you bloodied my damn lip!"

"At least now something about you is real. Oh. And don't ever threaten me again. I know where you live, and if I catch any flak over your little visit, I'll be sure to pay you a visit shortly thereafter."

"You're fuckin' nuts."

"Giving you more cause to worry," I said, turning the car into the Mutts parking lot.

Now parked, I swiveled in my seat to face him. "Okay, *Denton*. It doesn't matter any longer what I think of you or what you think of me. This is the real deal. From this point forward, our lives depend on one another. I'll carry my weight, and I expect you to carry yours."

I then looked him up and down and waved the back of my hand over his body as I spoke. "I just hope you know what you're doing with all this junk."

"Watch and learn," he said as he stepped from the car and sauntered toward the bar. "Watch and learn."

The door fell open to a smoke-filled room and the crack of pool balls, and the cackle of inebriated, scantily clad women set the appropriate ambiance. I acknowledged the bouncer with the obligatory gratuity, sliding a twenty to him when he shook my hand. Normally it was just a ten, but I was expecting trouble. I bulldozed my way through the crowd with Rick in tow, careful to violate every woman I could with my roaming eyes.

Steve, Devon, Caracas and the married couple from the plane sat with their backs to the bar and tracked our every step. "That's them at the bar just ahead," I mumbled to Rick.

"Got 'em." He began to sniffle profusely.

"Some more of that method acting?" I asked. "Or are you allergic to fun?"

"I know what I'm doin'," he insisted. "Just watch and learn."

"Devon," I greeted with an extended hand. "I want you guys to meet a friend of mine."

After introducing him to Devon, Steve and Caracas, I said to the other two, "I never did catch your names, by the way?"

"Tamara," she said, pointing the neck of her beer bottle into to her chest. "This is Larry."

"I heard you guys had some nav problems," Devon said with a grin.

"Nothing major. I was in the Air Force, don't forget. How'd the run go?"

"You trust him?" Caracas tapped the toe of his boot on Rick's leg.

Before I could answer, Rick dove in. "The question is, do *I* trust him? Whose money do think it is he's been throwing around up here? Now are we dealin' or just jerking each other off?"

"Hey," Devon slapped me on the chest and motioned me away. With his arm around my shoulder, we walked over to the pool tables. "What the fuck did you bring us here? Tell me you're not getting supplied your green by this faggot. Damn, dude, I can smell bacon from here. He's known us all of three seconds and he's talkin' deals?"

"He's not Five-O. He's just a little rich kid who wants to play with the big boys. I put up with all his wannabe shit because he's flushed with dead presidents. Just string him along, but don't tell him shit about anything that matters. Like yesterday, for instance."

"Don't worry, we won't," he laughed. "Do you know he's wearing a fake earring and fake tattoo?"

"I didn't notice the tattoo. Did you see the pinkie nail?"

"Fake too?"

"Like I said, 'wannabe.'"

"And that name—Denton? Sounds like some joke TV series I was watching last week." He then lampooned Rick with his own take on Rick's pseudonym. "Denton Isaac, a cop who doesn't play by the rules?"

I continued the satirizing. "They killed his wife. They've kidnapped his only child. They raped the family pet. But now he's mad . . . and out for revenge. And if he and his partner, Tyrone, don't kill each other first, they just might get to the bottom of this . . . before it's too late."

Devon laughed and took a swig of beer. "Hey." He seemed bewildered. "Where'd they go?"

"Well that can't be good," I said, worried.

Devon and I plowed through the crowd and went searching for them outside. To my surprise, Devon seemed genuinely concerned for Rick's welfare. "Shit! They should've waited for me to give the go ahead."

"Where would they take him?" I asked.

"Fuck!" he shouted, slapping his cowboy hat to his thigh and twisting about in circles.

"Should I be concerned?"

"Wait!" He turned both palms out in front of him. "Ssshhh. I think I hear something."

Just then, a piercing shriek split the evening solitude. "In back," I shouted.

Pebbles were exhausted from our soles like carbon monoxide from a 65 Nova. As we rounded the corner to the rear of the building, we saw Rick on his knees, his fingers interlaced behind his head and the beam of a flashlight illuminating his bloody and pulped face. The light became transient, caressing the side of the building and widening before it came to rest on our faces. With an arm folded across his eyes like Count Dracula to the morning sun, Devon yelled, "Turn that fucking thing off!"

"He's not a cop," Devon advised. "Why the hell didn't you guys wait for me?!"

"Too late," Steve said. "He's as much as admitted it already."

Blood dripped from the earring that now adorned his nose and a bloody hole marked the spot where it once dangled.

Devon seemed puzzled. "I thought it was a clip on?"

"It was," Caracas replied, "so we squeezed it before ripping it off. It works like the real thing now."

The hundred dollar bill was still tightly rolled in the shape of a straw, only now it was shoved way up into his nostril. The skin where the tattoo once drew across a negligible triceps muscle was now scattered among the many rocks it took to remove it.

"And that tattoo," Caracas became animated. "What a bitch that was to sand off."

"What the hell's wrong with you?" Devon asked, disturbed. "The guy's a little flaky, so you've gotta kick the shit out of him?"

"He's an investigator," Steve hollered.

A lump formed in my throat the size of a grapefruit. I could feel my skin become burning hot. He had spilled his guts, and we were both going to die, I just knew it.

"Tell 'em! Tell 'em," Steve demanded, laying a gun barrel to Rick's temple.

I interceded before Rick could give them the name and address of the company. "Was that before or after you beat the ever livin' shit out of him?"

"He says you're a PI, too. So I wouldn't get too witty."

"*He* did?" I said. "Then by all means, blow his fuckin' head off. I don't give a shit. Just let me get the hell outta here before you do it."

Steve turned his attention back to Rick. "Who do you work for?" His barrel quickly found its way into Rick's mouth.

"If you're gonna kill 'im, just do it!" I turned to say. "Don't torture the poor bastard. And take the damn gun out of his mouth so he can answer!"

I then spoke directly to Rick. "Give him a name! Make one up if you have to! The sooner you do, the sooner he gets this over with. Die with a little dignity, man."

Tamara shouted, "How do we know you're not an investigator, too?"

"You don't, bitch! And I wasn't talking to you!"

"Then you're not going anywhere!"

I turned slowly to face them, approximately fifty feet of nothingness separating us. "Go ahead. Make a play."

Steve then mumbled [to Tamara] loud enough for me to hear, "You don't wanna do that, trust me."

"Bullshit! What if he's an investigator, too?"

Devon then added, "Do you really think he's from the same planet as that moron? Do you?"

"What the hell you waiting for!" I taunted. "Oh, and guys, I wouldn't stand that close to her. I've seen bone fragments kill a person before." She placed her gun back in her boot.

"Rick," I said. "Let's go." I felt that I had them leaning back on their heels and decided this was the only opportunity we would have to get out of there alive. "Come on," I called with a marked sense of urgency.

Realizing that Rick would not move without encouragement, I walked over to his side, my right hand resting on my gun, and pulled him to his feet by the back of his hair. "Does anybody have a problem with this?" I said assertively. When no one objected, I said, "Good," and pulled Rick away.

"Wait!" Devon said sternly while circling to our front. "For our troubles," he said, snatching the hundred dollar bill from Rick's nose. "Drinks are on me," he declared.

* * *

The drive back to the hotel was somber. Once my heart returned to its normal rhythm, I thought hard about the repercussions this debacle would have on the entire case. The more I thought, the more I stewed. By the time we arrived at the hotel, I was steaming.

"Explain to me again about the pinkie nail." I wanted him to smart-off.

"You set me up," he simpered.

"Excuse me?"

"You heard me. You better start looking for a new . . ."

Before he could say "job," I slammed his head on the dashboard. Appearing to pull a tape recorder from my pants, I smashed it against his forehead again and again as I reprimanded him. "Do you see this? I taped the whole thing! Right up to and including the part where you gave up your cover! I think I may have even captured you pissing your pants! You breathe so much as a word of this and I'll send a copy to every investigator at K and S. Where do you think your credibility will be then? Huh?! Not a word! Not a *fucking word*! As far as Gordon knows, this was a complete success. You got it?!"

Naturally, I was bluffing. I would never be so brazen as to carry an actual tape recorder into a situation like that. But his conduct on this day told me he was too stupid to realize that. I had subtly removed the recorder from my door compartment just as we pulled up to the hotel.

"I've met monks with more street smarts than you. Get the hell outta my car. As it is, I probably'll never be able to get the stink out of it."

When the stakes got as high as this, there was no room for amateurs or wannabes. I just wanted to make sure he got that message. Better to hurt his delicate sensibilities now than to have to ship his remains home later.

I would later discover that in the short time Rick had to speak with Steve that evening, he had gone so far as to promise to pay this consortium of drug dealers an exorbitant remuneration on all future sales, provided Steve sold us a sample or two at the market rate. Simply put, he committed a flagrant infraction of the entrapment laws, which prohibit law enforcement officers from making offers so attractive that a person not already predisposed to commit a crime might be tempted to do so under the circumstances. Knowing that we would never have to make more than two sales with any given employee, Rick was not concerned with the future monetary implications of his empty promise.

Although we were not technically law enforcement, we were certainly a conduit of the legal system and therefore obliged to abide by its rules. Any deal I might strike with this group in the future would be tainted by this conversation if I didn't distance myself from it entirely.

Over the next couple weeks, I set my mind to building new relationships, such as with Shelly and Scott, in hopes that they would lead to more realistic enterprises. I would go slow and keep my sights low, I thought. But what I didn't realize, but probably should have, was that there was no such thing as laying low in a place with such high-profile criminals, especially when you were an investigator looking for crime. A series of unforeseen events would test my character like it had never been tested before, my CIA years notwithstanding. A stupendous caveat if I ever heard one.

Chapter 18

I was listening to my car stereo in the mill parking lot just before work one day when a large barn owl suddenly and unceremoniously dropped from the sky. I looked around to see if anyone else had seen this very strange sight, but it appeared no one had. Utterly flabbergasted by the episode, I got out of my car, leaving it running, and walked over to inspect the hapless creature. Picking up what looked like a divining rod, I poked at the carcass, flipping it onto its back. It was unscathed, yet dead as a doornail. I concluded that it must have had a heart attack or simply died of old age. When I set my lunch cooler in the break room just minutes later, I told several people of this extraordinary event. No one seemed too impressed. "Birds die," was the standard response. Unless, of course, you consider laughing to be a legitimate response. Who knows, maybe birds falling from the sky for no apparent reason is a common occurrence in Oregon.

About two hours into the shift, while busting my hump pulling a potpourri of wood off of Chain Six, I met an astonishingly friendly and considerate Hyster driver named George shortly after the chain inexplicably shut down. Well, compared to what I had just witnessed in the parking lot, *inexplicable* is probably too strong a word.

A slender, fairly attractive man, who I sensed was older than he appeared, stood casually at the front of the chain. Flipping wood with the debonair ease of Cary Grant, he worked his way toward me.

"You know where Scott is, right?" George said, having observed that I had been pulling all alone on the chain for quite some time now.

"On a very long break?"

"Selling guns in the parking lot. Give him time, he'll try ta sell you one."

"By 'guns,' you mean . . . ?"

"Name it. 30-06s, 30-30s, MAC-10s, 9 mms, twelve gauges, AR-15s, M-16s, whatever you want."

"So Mr. Clean ain't so clean after all," I commented.

"He's a redneck, know what I mean? You can't let this place get to ya," he rambled like a prisoner prepping the new convict on the block. "Try to remember this place operates 'round the clock. No one's gonna lose any sleep if you throw a piece of C grade into the A grade cart now and again. It's just a fucking job. You follow what I'm sayin'?"

"I hear ya. And thanks for the help, ahh . . .

"George. You're Ken, right?"

"Yeah, sure am. Well, George, my friend, as much as I hate to say it, I think we better turn this puppy back on."

"There ya go again," he said. "Takin' this shit way too serious."

"I just don't wanna repeat of the inferno on Four, that's all."

"I'm not sure that'd be such a bad thing," he said, pushing one of the full carts of wood out where he could get the forks under it. "This place's a petri dish for disease."

Before I could cull the full meaning behind what appeared to be a profoundly pejorative observation, he added, "Hold on, I'll turn it back on," and then climbed aboard his Hyster. With the precision of a surgeon, he pushed the actuating button with the corner of his right fork, and I was back in business.

With wood now stacked high above his vehicle, George pulled close to me and asked, "Whatta ya doin' tonight?"

"What'd you have in mind?"

"You know Shell and Donna?"

"Shelly? The cute one that works on that weird contraption up there?" I asked, pointing to the machine I had no name for.

"The Raymonds. Yeah. Some people call 'em the pluggers. That's her. Donna's the bigger dark-haired one who works the one next to her. They're comin' over tonight. Wanna join?"

The Raymond operators ran a unique machine that punched out knots in imperfect wood and filled them with unflawed pieces of football shaped wood, transforming flawed plywood into perfect Grade A plywood.

"Sure! Give me directions before you leave tonight!"

He acknowledged with a left-handed salute while raising the stack of wood to avoid a collision with a cart and sped away, all in one fluid motion.

*   *   *

When Scott returned after about an hour away from the chain, he explained his absence by saying that he thought the solo experience would be good for me. Without so much as a scrutinizing look, I turned and walked away, leaving him to pull alone.

"Where the fuck do you think you're going?"

"I heard there's a redneck selling guns in the parking lot!" I yelled loud enough for others to hear. "I'm gonna see if I can get me one of them there 'coon rifles!"

He became wild-eyed and belligerent. "Mutha fucker! Get your ass back here! You son of a . . ."

As his voice trailed off, I knew he was coming after me. There's just something about a fading voice that tells you they're stopping what they're doing and coming after you.

Just before I reached the Spreaders, Scott cut me off. "Get your ass back over there," he said, wheezing. "Right now!"

"Or?"

"Chief ain't here to protect your ass this time." His chest flexed in and out with each exaggerated breath.

"Jeez, and all this time I thought it was you he was protecting."

He thought about that for a moment and then warned me one last time, his face angled upward as he looked out the bottom of his eyes at me. "You goin' back or are we gonna get it on?"

Facing in the direction of Chain Six, I said blandly, "Your baby's on fire."

When he realized I was bluffing, he turned back around, only to find my fist buried in his esophagus. He crumbled like an melting iceberg and desperately gasped for air.

"Nope. Guess I was wrong. Must've been one of those mirages you always hear about," I said before realizing that my action now required me to go back and pull all alone again on Chain Six. "Damn it!" I screamed. As I stomped back to the chain, I shouted, "Little fucker pulled a Bill Cosby on me!"

Scott went home for the day, and I remained on Chain Six all alone for the rest of the evening. I suppose it was ironically apropos. When Phil finally broke me for lunch, I was five and a half pounds lighter.

The tuna fish tasted a bit pungent that night, but I chalked it up to bachelorhood. So what if it was a few days past its prime? It's not as if it had blue furry balls growing on it or anything.

Another hour or so had passed when I paid a visit to the bathroom. Now I've never been the most endowed person in the world, but something just didn't seem quite right this time. It was as if I was a perpetual member of the Polar Bear Club. It had virtually disappeared. I think Seinfeld calls it shrinkage.

Apparently I had become severely dehydrated, yet I had no other symptoms. Like thirst, for instance. It was not until I felt the sensation of choking that I fully appreciated the gravity of my situation. I was overdosing and it *really* sucked.

Clutching my throat, I staggered to the front of the chain to shut down the dryer. My arms had become as hard as rocks, and I could hardly walk because of the nausea and the struggle to breathe. George was the first to notice that I was having difficulties and quickly came to my side.

Leaping from his Hyster, he put his arm around me as I knelt to the floor. "What's the matter?" he said with his head ducked beneath mine and looking up at me.

"I don't know. I can't breathe. My throat. My blood pressure's through the roof."

"You do any crank today?"

Even on the verge of death, my first thought was, "Is everyone here a drug dealer?"

I answered, "Yeah." I hadn't, of course, but it occurred to me that I might have been drugged. I preferred everyone to think that I had taken the drugs voluntarily. If I was fortunate enough to live, the incident would pay great dividends.

"How much?"

"A lot. I think."

"Okay. We'll take care of you. It's gonna be all right. Just relax." He helped me onto the Hyster and hastily shuttled me to the First Aid Room.

"Damn!" he shouted as he tugged at the door. "It's locked."

George quickly radioed Stan and told him the nature of the emergency. Stan was there in no time flat. "Let's get him in here," Stan said, pushing back the door.

"Hey!" A voice blasted from inside the room as the door thrust open. Although my eyes were blurry, I could see that it was Jerry, one of the dryer tenders I rarely encountered during the normal course of my day. Jerry had a fifteen-year-old girl, a summer hire, bent over the table in the act of "consensual" sodomy.

"Out!" Stan demanded.

"Screw off!" Jerry retaliated, still inside the girl. "I mean it. Get the . . ."

"Get the fuck outta here!" George followed, pulling Jerry off the underage girl and shoving him out the door with his pants still wrapped around his ankles.

"You can pull your dress up . . . I mean, down, now," George said respectfully as he followed Stan's lead and kept his eyes above the girl's neckline. "We really need to get working on this guy."

"I'm sorry," she said with a trembling voice. "I'm so embar . . . I'm really . . ."

"I know," George said empathetically, "But we really need to . . . This guy really needs our help right now."

"Here." Stan shoved a drink of water in my face. "Drink it all and drink it quick."

Stan then said to George, "Get Phil. Tell 'im to go buy a case of beer and hurry his ass back. You better give him some money. You know Phil."

After seven huge cups of water, Stan encouraged a couple beers down my throat. The water was supposed to hydrate me and, in turn, lower my blood pressure, while the beer was intended to decrease my heart rate. I sensed it was a formula born out of experience.

When Caracas and Steve arrived on the scene, they immediately expressed concern over the advanced stage of my condition and collectively petitioned to get me to a hospital. It goes without saying that I no longer suspected that they had tried to kill me in that plane that day.

My breathing had become severely labored, and I could barely control my shivering. My recollection of the events of that day from that point forward emerges in snap shots only.

Before I knew it, the room was teeming with employees. Those I had once called enemies were fiercely battling for my life. Devon wrapped a thick wool blanket around my body and held me secure while the others monitored the constant flow of fluids that were being pumped into my body. I never knew it was possible for a person to drink so much.

"Slow down on the water," Caracas advised.

"If he can get it down," Steve countered, "he should drink it."

"No, he's right," George responded. "You can actually die from drinking too much water. We can slow his heart rate at this point with moderate doses of alcohol."

"Hey, Phil," Stan lashed out, "the beer's for Ken, ass wipe!"

"It's just freakin' me out," he muttered. "That's all."

"What the fuck did he say?" Stan asked of anyone who would answer. "Can never understand what that fucker's sayin'."

"I hear that," I said faintly. A tense laugh fluttered around the room.

*   *   *

When it appeared my condition was improving, George tried to lighten the conversation. "Did you guys hear what we saw when we brought Ken in here?"

"No. What?" Steve asked.

"Jerry. He had that cute, blond summer hire sprawled all across the table."

Before I could intercede in what I knew was about to become a debasing description of the young girl's attributes, George added, "A hundred bucks to the first person that kicks his ass all over the parking lot."

"I'll take your money," I said.

"In your condition?" Devon asked. "No way. I'll do it. Hell, I was gonna do it anyway."

"Boy," Caracas sighed. "It's times like this I wish you *were* a narc."

I laughed along with everyone else in the room, never feeling worse about what I did for a living. As a consolation, however, I took solace in the thought that, if not for their involvement in a myriad of illegal activities, all of these people could have, and probably would have, turned this sleaze bag over to the authorities. But then again, if I wasn't undercover, so would I. There was that plank again, rearing its ugly head.

But most of all, I was wracked with guilt over what it was I was doing to these guys. They had saved a mill, and now they had saved me.

"George?" Stan said.

"Yeah?"

"Why don't you take Booch home with you. Keep him awake until sunrise—without crystal."

"Good idea."

I sat up for the first time in several hours and looked around the room. "Who the hell's running the mill?"

"Jerry's so freaked out," Stan said, "He's making sure no one misses us. At least if he knows what's good for 'im."

"Devon?" I said with a parched throat.

"Yeah, what's up?"

"I want in on that morality therapy session with Jerry. Whatta ya say?"

"Sure. It'll hold."

"Thanks, bud."

I lay on George's couch all evening, and Shelly, who I discovered was a part-time EMS worker, tended to my every need. Once the "normal" conversation faded, I began to fade with it.

When I awakened the next evening and stepped outside George's home for what seemed like the first time, the peak of the sweltering summer was at hand. Mosquitoes patrolled the foul, swampy air of this rural community on the outskirts of town. The sun's rays flickered through what was once a dense forest, where sparsely plotted homes and narrowly paved streets melded discretely with a delicate ecosystem. Tightly wound roads, with their reduced visibility, further removed residents from the main-stream bustle of urban life.

When George drove me back to Boise to retrieve my car, we sat in the parking lot and talked about the personal family trials he had endured over the past few years. It was a sedate conversation about his divorce and how it led to his drug use. Although he was not attempting to excuse his behavior, the sordid details went a long way toward explaining it.

"You know," he said. "I'd really like to send that fucker to jail."

"Who?"

"Jerry. Who else."

"And you won't because . . . ?"

"Because you and your boys aren't gonna let me. Whatta ya think?"

"*My* boys? You mean *your* boys."

"They're not my boys. They didn't come there to save my life. They came to save yours and to protect their interests. An OD at the mill would bring a lot of unwanted attention. And the way I hear it, you're 'big money grip' to them."

"You seemed pretty chummy yourself, as I recall. And who did you think of first when there was a problem? Stan. Even though Shelly's the one with the EMS training."

"First of all, I'm not including Stan as one of the people I don't like . . ."

"Oh, now you don't even like them. Then why are you so damn friendly with them?"

"Because, if you haven't noticed, I got this little drug problem. And if I didn't involve them yesterday, you were screwed. The only thing that kept management away from that room was the fear they have of the people that were in it. Including you."

"So I must be one of those people you don't like?"

"No. You've never sold anything to anyone in the mill that I know of."

"You sound like those people who bitch about there being too many liquor stores in their neighborhood. Liquor stores go where there's a big demand for liquor. If Beverly Hills had a lot of alckies, there'd be a liquor store on every corner. If too many stores caused the problem, then they should put up a whole bunch of Christian bookstores in those areas. Maybe they'd end up with a bunch of people addicted to reading and treating their neighbors with respect and kindness."

"Yeah, right. They didn't prey on my situation?"

"Hey, pal, you're not the only one with a situation. I'm not sayin' they're not opportunists, but you share equally in your own Waterloo. You created the opportunity."

"Drug addiction's an illness, if you haven't heard."

"Then don't sit too close to me. I don't wanna catch it."

"Don't sit too close to that mill," he pointed through the windshield. "Or you probably will."

*   *   *

Our little talk swung the pendulum back against Caracas and company. Even though they had helped save my life, they were actively destroying lives at the same time. Not the least of which were their own.

George was one of the lucky ones in this investigation. He had the good fortune of saving the investigator's life before the investigator had a chance to drag his name through the proverbial mud. This very unselfish act would buy him one "get out of jail free and keep your job" pass.

You might ask, how equitable is this consideration, given the fact that others had already fallen victim to my daily reports prior to having the opportunity to assuage their misdeeds with acts of kindness and good-will? And I would probably answer, "In the world of drugs and deception, birds die."

Chapter 19

W hen I called Gordon the next day to explain my absence and to seek his advice concerning our resident statutory rapist, as you might expect, he was less than sympathetic. After insisting that it was not possible to get "high" from crystal methamphetamine in the manner I suggested (ingestion), he then claimed that my mental state at the time of the incident would hinder any attempt to prosecute Jerry for his actions. When I explained the glaring contradiction in his argument, he said that it would be my word against Jerry's and that we could not expect the others to corroborate my story, given the charges that would eventually be levied against them.

"So we give them immunity for their testimony," I said quite logically.

"Naaah. Boise won't go for that. And frankly, we're not gonna give up ten people for the price of one."

"First of all," I reacted. "There weren't ten witnesses; there were two. Unless you include the victim. And second, there's a hell of alotta difference between selling a few snippets of crank and raping a little girl."

"You have a rejoinder for everything I tell you," he said, frustrated. "Look, if you wanna know the truth, I don't consider fifteen below the age of consent, in most cases. If she brings charges, then by all means, testify. If your buddies wanna testify—great. But we're not gonna offer them the opportunity to start making demands for all their druggy cronies and lord knows what else."

I interrupted. "My buddies? Fifteen's the age of consent? Excuse me?"

"Wait," he barked. "Just hold on a second. Think of what it is we're trying to accomplish there. We gonna flush all that down the tubes to get one scumbag? If this guy's doin' *that* on company property, he's doin' other things, too. Find out what they are and nail him. You have the green light on this guy to do whatever's necessary to bring him down. Insofar as your witnesses are concerned, neither of them have sold you anything, anyhow. So what's their incentive to cooperate? We have no leverage."

"After what I saw yesterday, don't expect to get any on George."

"I don't know anything about that guy, but you sure as hell have reason to believe Devon's a player. And if George kept this whole thing hush-hush with you yesterday, you gotta ask yourself, 'why'? He must be a player too, don'tcha think?"

"I don't presume because someone wants to help a player, they're automatically players themselves. But I grant you, it's certainly worth investigating."

"Good. Hey, we agreed on something. Oh, and don't put anything in your reports about the drugging or the sex stuff, all right?"

"It would just end up on the cutting room floor if I did, so why bother? Will you at least promise to make the offer to either of these guys if we nail them for anything?"

"If we can make the offer as advertised. But if they demand any addendums, like including their pals in the deal, then all bets are off."

"Fair enough," I said. "Thanks, Gordon."

*   *   *

I had intended to do some grocery shopping before work, but a telephone call would modify my plans. "Hello?" I answered.

"Ken? It's me, Devon. Get to work a half-hour early today. Meet me at the far end of the parking lot, farthest from the mill. Know what I'm talkin' about?"

"Yeah. What's up?"

"I thought you wanted in on the ass kicking?"

"I do," I insisted, hoping that I could keep the behavior modification under control.

"Good. Then we'll see ya at 2:30. Later."

*   *   *

After much waffling, I decided not to call JACNET. I figured it was inevitable that I would have to hit the guy at least once. That just wouldn't go over well on video.

With the lyrics "Everybody was kung-fu fighting" blaring from my stereo, I drove hastily to the rear of the parking lot. Standing in a half-circle were all the pertinent people: Caracas, Steve, Devon, and surprisingly, Jerry. When my eyes made firm contact with Jerry's, I immediately lowered the volume on my extremely distasteful overture.

"Shit," I said under my breath as I approached on foot, my eyes fixed on the three sets of black leather biker gloves worn by my fellow would-be batterers.

"Glad you could make it," Caracas said sarcastically.

"Shut the fuck up, or you'll be next," I said, quickly establishing my rank.

"Where are your gloves?" Devon asked.

"I'll take what's coming to me if I haveta," Jerry interrupted, "But not from this guy. Who the fuck's he?"

After a hasty assessment of the situation, I reasoned that if I left this guy to suffer this indignity without me, there was a good chance he would not walk away from this parking lot. So, before he could mouth another word I hit him with an overhand right to the jaw, with just enough force to make him woozy for the rest of his punishment. Knowing what I do about beatings by multiple assailants, I was sure he would be better served if he couldn't feel the sting of every kick, knee and punch. I expected an immediate barrage of arms and legs to land on him, but instead, Devon knelt by his side and hoisted him gently to his feet.

"You know why you're here, Jerry. It's either this or a twenty-two behind the noggin. You chose this. I just want you to know that fucking little girls will getcha killed next time. No options. We're gonna break some fuckin' bones, and you're gonna take it and shut up. If you start screaming like a bitch, I'm gonna shoot ya and walk away. *With* me so far?"

"Ya." Jerry, who was a bit wobbly on his feet, began to sob softly.

"Okay," Devon said before turning to me. "You really should've wore gloves. You're gonna get your knuckles all cut up on this fuck."

When the attack began, I stepped back and watched as Jerry instinctively covered his face with his hands. Round house punches clobbered him from every direction. He fell to his knees, so they started to kick him.

I could hear the bones snap under the violent force of steel-toed shoes. Within seconds he was a rag doll, twisting and tossing in all directions. Blood splattered and splashed about, speckling the others' bodies like muddy stains on the clothes of children frolicking in rain puddles. They each took turns raising his leg and kicking him in the groin, until he began vomiting from the pain. With blood covering every square inch of his face, I stepped in to end the torture.

"Enough. Enough!" I pushed them back, shoving Steve and Caracas to the ground. They were exhausted and offered no resistance. It was not as I had expected. None of them appeared delighted in what they had done. It was as if they were punishing a child—a very bad child. They did it, but took no pleasure in it.

"Get his pants down," Devon said, depleted.

"What for?" I asked, already knowing the answer.

"Whatta you think? We're gonna show him what it's like to feel like you haveta do something you don't wanna. This thing in particular."

"No. I can't allow that."

"Who the fuck are you to allow anything?" He became angered, stepping closer to me.

"You've made your point. He won't be sticking it in any young girls for a while. You're done here. Let's just get the hell outta here before we get caught."

"For a while?" He threw his arms out toward me. "We aim to make him not wanna stick it in any young girls never again."

"By sticking your dicks in his ass?"

Devon pulled me aside and spoke in a lowered voice. "We're not gonna put our peckers in there. What kinda demented fucks do you think we are? We're gonna use this." He drew a dildo from his pocket. "And tell 'im it's our dicks. That's the other reason we wore the gloves."

"Well, that's a different thing altogether," I said. "I was actually beginning to think you were gonna do something demented."

"Devon," Steve hollered. "He's ready."

We turned to see that Jerry's pants were down around his ankles the way they were that night in the First Aid Room. Only now his rear was bruised and cut.

"Just shut the fuck up and wait," Devon castigated the other two. "Damn!"

"It's over, Devon. He's learned his lesson. He's learned. It's over. Reprisal's . . . It's over."

"Hey! That fuck gave it to a fifteen-year-old up the ass! You think she liked it?! That fuck's gonna feel what she felt! Now get outta my way unless you wanna join him."

Although I didn't want to chance him carrying out his threat, especially to save this sleaze bag, I felt it would be my only opportunity to refocus his anger.

"Are you threatening me, Cochise?"

"You don't have a problem with what this asshole did?"

"Apparently not as big a problem as you guys."

"That's 'cause you don't have kids. Now step aside."

"Hey, if this's about your kids, let's go get the asshole or assholes who . . ."

"Shut up!" He became enraged. "You don't talk about my kids! You don't! *You hear?!*"

"Fine. Whatever. I can see you have issues. But this matter here is settled. Go to work, Devon. Just go to work before I take your threat serious."

His eyes told me that I was in more trouble than it was probably worth. With a hand reaching into the back of his pants, he asked, rather ordinarily, "You gotta new backer?"

I responded apprehensively, completely caught off guard by the brusque change in his demeanor. "Huh? No. No, not yet. Why?"

"Get one. I think I'm ready to deal with you."

My response was shallow because my speech was filled with astonishment. "I'll letcha know."

"Good. Don't bring me a weasel this time."

"He had bank. Whatta ya want me to say?"

This whole financial backer thing that K and S drummed up was going to be the death of me. I could no longer make any sizable deal and say that it was my own money. This meant that they would always want to meet my backer. If I suddenly told Devon that I was awash with cash, he would become paranoid, and I would never buy from him or any of his friends again. I had to come up with a person who was savvy enough to persuade them and bad enough not to get a hundred dollar bill shoved up his nose, which meant that all K all S employees were out of the question. And then it hit me. Glenn!

As he walked away from me toward the mill, Devon shouted, "Hey! You owe me twenty bucks for a dildo!"

While grabbing my safety gear from the back of my car, I happened to catch a glimpse of Jerry as I peered over the canvas roof. He was on his back groaning and gurgling. I walked over and pulled him to a sitting position, leaning his back against a rusty car bumper.

His clothes had been rubbed smooth by the glancing blows and shined like silk that had been pressed with a hot iron. Blood and drool mixed to form strings of crimson pearls that collected about his now serrated neckline. A pebble, probably from a boot, was imbedded in his cheek. His nose was folded over to the point that only one nostril showed. With blood dripping into a pool so big that I could hear the droplets splash and see the ripples expand outward to the edge in perfect rings, I was afraid I had interceded too late. There was nothing left to do but pray.

"You're gonna be all right, Jerry," I told him. "From now on, though, ID them before you have 'em lift their skirts. It'll save ya both alotta pain in the long run. And if it happens again, I'll kill you myself. I swear I will."

At the time all this occurred, I was quite sure that this man got what he deserved. However, based upon the most recent nationwide poll concerning statutory rape, there seems to be a strong double standard regarding the punishment Americans feel is appropriate for men versus women. Specifically, the overwhelming consensus was that the female schoolteacher who raped that thirteen-year-old student had been punished enough by her pregnancy, the loss of her job and marriage, and the negative press, such that she should not be imprisoned. Reverse the genders and tell me that the age and special circumstances would not have landed a thirty-something man in prison for fifteen years. In fact, there wouldn't have been any discussion about it. No talk shows, no newspaper editorials, no discussion, period.

The message is clear. Somewhere deep down, men, and especially women, believe that women are the weaker sex. Not just in their ability to say 'no,' but in their ability to deal with the consequences of having 'yes' thrust upon them. Do I believe this? The answer is an emphatic "No!" But if society believes it, then who am I to question it? It just seems to me that if you want all the good that equality offers, you must also accept the bad, and more importantly, the responsibility.

The real kicker for me, however, occurred when I was recently asked to investigate an incident in Norfolk County, Massachusetts, wherein a thirty-something man who had never committed a sex-related offense before in his life was arrested for urinating in the woods. They called it "indecent exposure." A hundred homeless people do it every day outside my office in downtown Los Angeles, and they call it "urinating in public." The point is, the Massachusetts man was given a year of probation and made to attend group therapy for convicted sex offenders. Of course, he denied being a sex offender. The result: because he did not accept that as a condition of probation, he in effect refused what would have been an indeterminate sentence and was given six months in jail. So much for overcrowded jails and prisons. At least in Massachusetts. Are you listening, governor?

When I asked the head of probation—let's call him Mr. Sleazy—if a woman would receive the same punishment for exposing herself in public, he responded by insisting, "Women don't commit sex offenses." The Massachusetts man's immediate probation officer—let's call her Ms. Berg, as in *iceberg*—said, "All men are sexual predators, but it just so happens that only a small percentage of them ever get caught." What is worse, both officers implied that a financial contribution on my part would likely have expedited the man's release. If this is any indication of the mentality of our correctional system today, then I'm glad I no longer investigate suspected criminals for a living. I guess I'm simply out of step with this whole equality thing. Silly me, I thought the word *equality* was a derivation of the word *equal*. A woman masturbating in public wouldn't even get six months in jail and a year's probation. She'd get an adoring audience and enough cries of "You go, girl" to make Oprah Winfrey barf her guts out.

*   *   *

About 10:00 P.M. that evening, I had clean-up duty, and I swept my way over to Tari, who was all by her lonesome at the back end of the mill, where the noise and the heat were comparatively bearable. Pushing my broom across a tidy floor, I approached her platform under the guise of working in the area. The smile and drawn-out "Hi" that usually greeted me were missing. But for a brief acknowledgment, she hardly paid me any heed at all.

"Something I said?"

She didn't respond. She pretended to be immersed in the mindless task of pressing buttons on the automated grader.

"Hello?"

"Go away, you bully," she said.

"Bully?" I then caught myself. "Oh. You heard."

"I saw! How could you do that? Is that what they teach you? Is that in the private investigator's handbook?" She fought back her emotions.

"Keep it down, will ya. It's not what you . . ."

"What am I thinking?! Huh? What am I thinking?! You're mean! And you're not very nice! And . . . I trusted you!"

"Okay, let's calm down and talk about . . ."

"No! I won't calm down! I'll scream as loud as I please! Scream, scream, scream!"

"Tari?"

"You've used me."

"Tari?"

"You used me, Ken! You fuckin' used me!"

"Tari," I shouted. "Shut the hell up and listen for a friggin' moment! All right? It's not like that. They were gonna kick the crap outta that guy, regardless . . ."

"So you thought you'd join in? Sharpen your skills before they got too rusty? What'd he, not pay a drug debt or somethin'?"

"No." I stared hard into her eyes. "No. He raped a fifteen-year-old girl."

"What?" She was momentarily moved. "Bullshit. That's not true. I know Jerry. He wouldn't . . ."

"He did. You know that cute blond that works that cushy job in the center of the mill?"

"Yeah?"

"That's it. I mean, it appeared consensual but . . . Well, you know, to the degree it could. He wasn't forcing her or anything—physically."

"And those assholes . . . You're tryin' to tell me they're pissed off about it or something?"

"Surprised the fuck outta me, too. But that's what happened. I was just there to prevent them from killin' him."

"I saw you punch him. Is that how you prevent him from getting hurt? By punching him?"

"Only," I placed my hand out toward her to stop her from interrupting. "Only because he wanted me not to participate. I guess he didn't realize I was there to help."

"Gee, I wonder why. So you're sayin' he was there voluntarily? Is that . . . That doesn't make any . . ."

"It's one of those criminal code things or something. I know, it tripped me out, too. Anyway, he's alive, but ya won't see him around for a while. I don't think. But who knows around here."

Tari shook her head wildly. "I hate this shit! I just . . . It's so completely . . . It's so complicated and screwed up! What's wrong with these people? Ahhhh, I hate it! I do! I just hate every fuckin' bit of it!"

After she calmed, she grabbed me by the shirt and said, "Nail these bastards, Ken. Nail every last fucking one of 'em."

"Every last fucking one of 'em," I repeated softly.

Before I knew it, the palm of her hand was walloping me across the face. "No more swearing! Oh, God, I'm sorry. I'm sorry. No more swearing, though. From now on, no more swearing. I can't take this shit anymore. I want at least someone I know to be clean and good and . . . Oh, I'm so sorry. Did it hurt?"

"Fu . . . Fudge no." We both struggled to smile as we leaned into one another.

*   *   *

I called Glenn at home that evening. Glenn was definitely a late night kind of guy. After apprising him of my situation and recounting the details of the "Rick visit," he knew exactly what needed to be done.

"So I take it Gordo and Gino know nothing about this?" he asked.

"Whatta *you* think?"

"Then how do I get paid? I mean, my expenses, 'cause you know I'd do it for free."

"I'll pad the bill for a few days after you leave and bleed out the information we uncover over that same period. It'll just look like I gathered all the same facts during different after-hour meetings. Follow?"

"That's the way I'd do it. When do you need me?"

"No hurry. Just tell me when's convenient."

"How 'bout this weekend?"

"You really miss it, huh?"

A long silence ensued. "Ya, I do. I'll see ya there this weekend then?"

"This weekend it is. That's good. See ya, Glenn. And . . . and thanks."

* * *

By the time Glenn arrived on Saturday, he had already been up for twenty straight hours. Being the thoughtful person that he was, he decided to drive rather than fly and wound up saving me several hundred dollars in the process. As you know, if you don't give the airlines fourteen days' advance notice, you pay through the nose—never mind the fact that the planes are generally half empty all the time.

I met Glenn at the local Dairy Queen, where it seemed that all the Medford girls under the age of eighteen hung out at lunchtime. Glenn looked all dapper in his starched white shirt and thin black tie. The denim he wore looked fashionably worn, but never by a human. With black leather slip-on shoes that appeared as soft as butter, the look was complete.

"Whatta ya want?" I asked.

"Double Brazier with cheese, onion ring, diet."

After I ordered the exact same items, the cashier told me that my order came to ten dollars and three cents. How any two identical two orders could add up to an odd number was beyond me, but I didn't argue.

"I got it," Glenn advised, reaching deep into his pocket. He pulled out three pennies, slapped them on the counter and then grabbed the tray. "I'll get the condiments," he said. "Get us a table at the back."

I handed the woman the ten dollars and did as he asked. "You look sharp," I commented to him. "Quit drinking?"

"Is that what Gino or Gordo said happened to me? I drank myself out of a job?"

"Actually, it was Rick."

"Rick," he said with a grunt. "That shithead absconded with my job. Don't trust him, Ken. Whenever I would walk into a room unannounced and he was there, sure as shit he'd be bad-mouthing someone. Normally me. But I've heard him say shit about you, too, on occasion. That you're too unpredictable, too unprofessional, too rogue for management. Don't trust that S.O.B. He sees you as a threat." Without even stopping to take a breath, he added, "You think I look good, though?"

"Well, yeah. Except for that big ironed-in wrinkle on your chest, right there."

"You know, what is it about wrinkles? It takes two seconds to iron one in but twenty minutes to get one out."

*　*　*

After covering the many details of the investigation, including all the warts, I drove Glenn over to the mill and gave him the mini tour, which entailed a brief look inside. After seeing it firsthand, Glenn's only comment was, "My respect for you just went up a notch."

Glenn was kind of a legend at Krout and Schneider, so I couldn't resist asking him about some of the cases he handled during his storied career. The case that I think epitomizes Glenn best was the one where he spent the entire investigation at a Bank of America branch pushing a broom with his head bobbing and slinging like the Hunchback of Notre Dame and his speech slurred like the Elephant Man, all in an effort to convince drug dealers that he was a major "stoner." It worked, and Glenn took down the biggest drug dealers ever to grace the cover of a K and S "investigation summary report."

At around 8:00 P.M., Glenn and I left my apartment and headed over to the Red Lion Inn, where Caracas instructed us to meet him and the other dealers that evening. During the drive over, Glenn scanned the radio stations for anything country.

"What the hell are you looking for?" I asked. "You've already passed several good channels."

"Where are all the country stations?"

"In the country, where they belong," I said before studying his face for a reaction. "Oh, I forgot, you're a country fan, aren'tcha?"

"Yeah." He sounded genuinely bewildered. "I noticed all your presets are set to those acid rock, subliminal message, satanic stations."

"It's all pop music, for Pete's sakes. There aren't any hard rock channels there. Subliminal messages, my ass. Why is it people think you can be negatively influenced by evil subliminal messages but not positively influenced by good ones? They oughtta have songs with Christian lyrics repeated over and over beneath the main track. For no apparent reason, people like you start doing good deeds all over the country."

When Glenn finally locked onto a country station, he responded. "I'm sorry. Did you say something?"

"Ha, ha, very funny—oh, wait, there it is. Over there on the left." I directed his attention to the hotel. "Now I gotta remember how ta get over there from here. I always forget. I think I cross through this Taco Bell, here. Hold on," I cautioned as I veered hard across the flow of on-coming traffic.

Without so much as a gasp, Glenn said with a relaxed face, "That's the way I'd have done it. So why do you suppose they'd choose this place?"

"I don't know. Just promise me, Glenn, you won't go outside with them alone."

"Who you callin' Glenn? I don't know no Glenn! My name's Ganz! I'm here to check out my distribution problems!"

His mockery of Rick's abysmal thespian skills lightened the mood at just the right moment. We were still laughing as we entered the hotel lobby and nearly walked right into a sign that read: *Karaoke Every Saturday Night From 8:00 p.m. Until Closing.*

"Woooo! Yes sir-ree, Bob," Glenn hooted and danced about the lobby. "Yes! Let's party! Wooo, baby. Wooo, baby!"

"Lovely." My response was far more staid. "What in the world would these guys want with karaoke?" By then I was talking to myself, as Glenn was halfway down the staircase leading to the bar.

After all the formalities of introduction were complete, Glenn was wise enough and experienced enough not to initiate any business-related discussion. After dragging me on stage to sing a duet that I can hardly remember, Glenn led us back to a table charged with accusation and inquisition. Just as the eye of the storm began to swirl about Glenn, he politely excused himself from the table and took center stage, front. He whispered something in the DJ's ear and turned away from the TelePrompTer. It was clear that it would be a song he knew by heart.

When the music first began, I—and I assumed everyone else—recognized the tune. But it was not until the main lyric blasted from his lips that I knew precisely what the name of the song was.

Glenn, with his foot stomping irregularly and his body bent toward our table and shaking erratically and arrhythmically, began wailing "Secret . . . agent man! Secret . . . agent man!"

Looking around the room, it soon became apparent that there were many others with more than just a passing interest in the outcome of our meeting. I trolled with a predator's eye, wearing a blasé expression as I scanned the room for that one sign which indicated who was leading the pride. From across the floor I caught the genteel smile of a woman I'd never seen before. The fact that she was at a karaoke bar and seemed more interested in me than the singer led me to believe that she was an important piece of the Boise puzzle. With her focus still firmly on me, her hands came together in a graduately increasing pace until she was in full applause. The crowd immediately followed suit. We were in.

Chapter 20

When the song ended to an uproarious ovation, I got up from my seat and met Glenn halfway. "You got her?" he asked as we crossed.

"Got her," I affirmed.

"Good. I'm outta here."

I weaved my way between the tightly wedged tables, taking the most direct path to where she was seated. Her eyes never let me go, even as she spoke to the many bacchantic women seated next to her. I circled the large round table and smiled at all the upturned faces. When I made it to her side, I bent to her ear. "Would you like to sit at my table?" I looked to see if Glenn had actually left the bar. "Seems we've got a couple empty seats."

Still maintaining eye contact with me, she smacked the woman next to her on the shoulder and told her to make room. "Get lost," she said.

Not only did this indicate that she was in charge and lacked etiquette but that there was also no rhyme or reason to the positioning of people at her table. Generally there was a code or protocol for such things. She either lacked such a code, as seemed the case with Devon and company, or she was a fraud, which may have also been the case with Devon as well. Either way, it didn't matter. I sat at the table and played my hand.

"Mimi," she introduced herself by kissing me on the cheek. "Ken, correct?"

Everything about Mimi said "club girl." From her big, curly blond hair to her chic, revealing skirt, she looked like a facsimile of a real person, a glossy package with dull, blurry print and the insignia of the last man who touched her stamped across her forehead. At least, that's how she looked. Only time would tell if she would turn yellow and curl up around the edges.

"You know me from . . . ?" I nudged, suspecting that whoever she identified was likely the one in charge.

"Caracas. He talks about you all the time. I think you're his hero or something."

"Heroes just aren't what they used to be. But then again, neither are hero worshippers."

"He says you got a gun through airport security. Is that true?"

"If Caracas says it's true, I guess it's gotta be true."

"Pretty impressive. That was sure the shit about the plane, though, huh? Any trouble getting back?"

"No, not at all. The instruments came up before we even turned back."

"Oh." She attempted to mask her insight. "That's good. Glad to hear we didn't cause you any undue stress. Were you impressed with the operation?"

"They could've been retrieving deer manure for all I know. Hell, it was so damn stormy that day we couldn't see a damn thing on the ground for all the rain and clouds. So what the hell do I know?"

"I assure you, we don't spend that kinda dough on deer shit." She seemed a bit annoyed. "Here," she said, stuffing a wad of cash down my shirt pocket. "For your troubles. It was the best dung on the West Coast."

"If you want me for anything else, you know where to find me," I said, boldly kissing (biting) her on the lips and walking away. Her face turned beet red beneath four coats of makeup, concealing her embarrassment. As I made my way past Caracas's table, I leaned over and whispered in his ear, "You're the man. Make it happen."

Just as I made it to the staircase, Glenn slipped in behind me. Now I consider myself an extremely observant guy, but for the life of me I have no idea where he went the entire time I was carrying on with Mimi.

Glenn could always be counted on in tight situations. He was also the first to admit that he was probably the one who made it tight in the first place. But in my opinion, good investigators were supposed to make things tight. As any hunter will tell you, the real big game is generally not found in safe, wide open spaces. Ironically, Glenn was fired from K and S for his unreliability, which purportedly stemmed from a heavy dependence on alcohol. The truth of the matter is that he was the most dependable agent in the company.

"Here's your credit card bill," Glenn said, handing me the receipt and my USAA gold card (a card that signifies a person is or was a military officer). The amount of the bill added credence to the theory that he may have had just a teensy-weensy drinking problem.

"Good signature," I responded. "How did you . . . ? Oh, I almost forgot who I was talking to. 'Secret Agent Man'? Pretty ballsy. Where'd that come from?"

"Whatta ya mean?"

"Whatta ya mean, what do I mean? The secret agent stuff. That was great."

"Secret agent . . . ?" he thought aloud. "Oh, shit. I didn't even think of that. Holy cow! I thought it was 'Secret Asian Man'!" Glenn was such an expert at this game that I had no idea if he was pulling my chain. Glenn went on to explain that it's not what he sang that influenced them, it was how he sang it.

"Take the words *lamb* and *sheep*," he explained. "They're the same creature, but if ya wanna talk about sacrifice and charity, you talk *lamb*. If you wanna talk about followers and meekness, you talk *sheep*."

"But that goes to the words being spoken, not to how they were said, right?"

"*You* know what I mean."

"It was successful. That's all that matters."

Glenn and I parted company for the last time that evening, ending our relationship as it had started, with one of us employed and the other still searching. When I totaled the bill for that weekend it approximated the amount of money that Mimi had stuffed into my shirt pocket. It was sort of ironic, actually, that she bankrolled her own undoing.

* * *

I met Caracas in the mill parking lot the following Saturday and he asked me to go with him to some big shindig featuring some bygone country music star. It was called the Josephine County Fair and was held each year in a town called Grant's Pass. I accepted, even though I knew there weren't enough drugs on the Pacific seaboard to make the music palatable. But you would think that after five years of college in Kentucky it would have dawned on me that country music always translates to beautiful women. I'm not sure, but maybe that explains why it took me five years to graduate. Two hours later, an event occurred that would transform the puppet into the puppeteer.

Chapter 21

Like Paul Revere, a robust woman named Sam came charging up the stairs of the feeder on Chain Four declaring, "The nigger's back! The nigger's back! They rehired that nigger we chased out a ways back." In her mouth it sounded an awful lot like, "The British are coming! The British are coming!"

I wanted with every fiber of my body to backhand her across the face but opted instead to play it neutral. The timing just wasn't right. I needed to let things move along naturally and interfere only when and if it appeared the man was in danger. In the long run, I figured he was better off enduring their wrath now than in the future when I was no longer available to report it. It wasn't long, however, before I felt like the guy holding the camera while Rodney King was getting the snot kicked out of him. All the rationalization in the world wasn't going to make this poor bastard's experience any less repugnant. And in case you were wondering, the Zapruder position was the one my company advocated. Observe, document, film if possible, but don't influence. Unless, of course, you are manipulating someone into committing a crime. That, apparently, was acceptable.

I continued to hear rumblings from the chain, but was unable to see what was happening. Whenever there was a break in our action, Sam would leap to the ground and sprint to the dryer end. Upon her return, she would spread scurrilous rumors about the man's cowardice and lack of intelligence. Reasoning that I could not accurately report from my present position what had obviously become a very fluid situation, I left my post and traded places with Jim, who I knew would appreciate the break.

"How's it running?!" I asked Tari.

"Smooth! I appreciate the spacing!" She was referring to the sporadic flow of wood.

"It wasn't deliberate, I assure you! I just can't seem to get the knack for feeding. There are always these huge gaps and . . ."

"Have you heard?!"

"Heard what?!" I prayed that she wouldn't refer to the man as a nigger.

"See that black guy over there?!" She held a piece of wood with two hands and pointed it at the front of Chain Three.

"Uh huh."

"He used to work here! The asshole fucking with him was one of the ones that chased him away!"

With my concentration wholly on the black man, I continued to pull wood from the chain but paid no mind to the carts I was throwing it into. Three men, and I use the term *men* loosely, hovered around the physically fit black man, stabbing broomstick handles in his face as he attempted to pull wood from the front of Chain Three. One of those men, Scott, was in the middle of one of his patented ten-minute diatribes when it turned ugly.

"Tari?" I shouted. "Can you cover me?"

"Are you gonna be okay alone?"

"I won't be alone," I said, referring to the man being harassed.

Reaching beneath the conveyor, I pulled out one of the three brooms stored there, pretending to be preoccupied with pushing dust and wood chips into a pile, I sauntered over to the front of Chain Three.

"Excuse me," I said evenly to the black man, reaching my broom below the conveyor and pulling out a hunk of debris. I knelt down to do this, and as I looked up at him, I could see tears welling up in his eyes. He yanked the wood from the chain at an increasing tempo, creating a strobe effect for me as I observed his face through the stream of wood. It was not unlike temporarily freezing the motion of a fan blade by blinking in rapid succession or the effect you get when watching the wheels of a speeding car that appear to move backwards.

There is just something about a person bringing a grown man or woman to tears that gets me riled up. I rolled away from the dangerous flying wood, to all appearances completely disinterested in the affairs around me. After casually brushing myself off, I meandered over and shut off the dryer. For a brief moment, there was comparative silence. "Is there a problem?" Scott shouted in my direction.

I gripped the broom like a baseball bat and swung it against the dryer control panel. Three-quarters of the broom, including the brush, flew over the chain. The shaft that remained was blunt at one end and cutlery sharp at the other. In other words, it was perfect. Twirling the stick in my left hand, I advanced on them like Buford Pusser in a production of *West Side Story*. The combination of my anger, the company's stick and everyone's undivided attention had me swaggering like a constable with one step and strutting like a hoofer the next.

"What we got here," I said, standing shoulder to shoulder with the black man and slapping the stick in the palm of my hand, "Is a failure to communicate. Some men you just can't reach. So you get what we had here last week. Which is the way he wants it. Well, he gets it. I don't like it any more than you men." By the looks on their faces, I concluded that *Cool Hand Luke* probably wasn't part of their video collections.

The line was drawn. It was two against three, but I was still confident we would prevail. That confidence quickly eroded, however, under the weight of ten or so additions to their team. They seemed to come from nowhere and yet everywhere. From all locations except one, that is—the Spreaders.

A high-pitched yodel, for lack of a better word, similar to what you might expect to hear in the Middle East, suddenly rang out. It was Tari. Her tongue bounced around her mouth with stunning speed and definitude.

As if an ancient encrypted code had been cracked, a medley of Middle Eastern calls sprang up from the far corners of the mill. The first to join us were Chief and Rick, both of them yodeling with Tari. Machine after thunderous machine could be heard winding down as more and more people closed ranks in this civil war. Among the feeders and pullers there was no commonality. People who had worked side by side for years were polarized on this issue and willing to sever relationships over it. The Green End employees and the Spreaders were polarized, however, with Spreaders on our side and the Green Enders on the other. Those who chose not to participate, and there were many, did so for varied reasons. The most common was that they did not want to fight alongside drug dealers, or against them, depending upon the person.

With the likes of Linda, Paul and Scott staring me down and egging me on, my reasons for wanting to see this thing through to its natural, pugilistic fruition quickly mounted. A dull hollowness filled my ears like it often did when I departed the mill each evening. Only now it was in the middle of my shift. The tension grew proportionately as the crowd noise diminished. This inverse relationship was the antithesis of any mob mentality I had ever encountered. When the noise level reached nil, all hell was sure to break loose.

Just as I heard what appeared to be the last motor winding down, Stan threw down the gauntlet. "What the hell's happening?" he cried, exploding upon the scene. "You want this fucking place to burn to the ground?!"

"Don't worry," Tari advised. "We turned everything off. Including the dryers."

The veins in Stan's neck were about to burst. "Great! Then we'll be stacking wet wood all night! Do you know how much money that'll cost us? Now what in the shit is going on?! Will someone please tell me that?!"

Caracas, who was standing on the static conveyor, spoke up. "These rednecks are calling this guy nigger and shit, and won't let him do his damn job."

I don't know how, amid all the confusion, Caracas was able to figure out the origin of the confrontation, but I was elated that he knew and decided to come to the party anyhow. I was also pleasantly surprised that no one switched sides after hearing his explanation.

"I'll make this simple," Stan said staidly but firmly to the harassers, his futile attempt at self-restraint reddening his skin. "One more racial epithet from any of you *and you're fired*! You're fuckin' fired! You got that?! I'll do it myself! Now get your lazy asses back to work! Now!"

"I think they owe . . . ," I said to Stan, then leaned over to the black man. "What the hell's your name, by the way?"

"Doug," he offered, appearing extremely dazed. I guess if you're black and you live in southern Oregon, you have a name like Doug or Joe or Bill.

"I think they owe *Doug* here an apology."

"Get back to work, Ken," Stan warned, "or you'll be the first one out the door, I swear."

"Yeah, Kenny-koo," Linda said with a baneful sneer. "And while you're at it, why don'tcha take Barbie back to the doll house where you belong."

"What are you, twelve?" I asked.

"Oh, come on, Stan," Rick gibed. "Let us right-size the workforce for Boise." His comment was followed by a chorus of wood pounding on the chain and on the floor.

I could see Stan was being backed into a corner from which there was no further retreat and no escape. There would be a brawl, and there would definitely be firings. "Okay, everybody," I called out. "Move along! Nothing to see here! Okay, move along. Break it up, everybody. Move along." I then added, as I walked away. "I'll take care of the Three Musketeers on my own time."

As strange as this might sound, operatives were taught to do everything they could to keep criminally liable employees gainfully employed until the end of the case. There were two reasons for this. If you had nurtured a relationship with such employees and in the process gained their confidence, those employees would likely be the means by which you would establish relationships with other criminally culpable employees. The flip side was that any employee fired as a natural consequence of the company's daily operation—that is to say, an employee who would have been fired irrespective of our involvement—was not included in the overall head count at the end of the case. Translation: Krout and Schneider would lose money.

Bob Adams, for instance, was such a valuable resource for information that I felt it was incumbent upon me to go behind the scenes and salvage his job. After Bob missed several days of work while sitting in the drunk tank following his third DUI, Boise management acted judiciously and terminated his employment. When I discovered this, I used the K and S reporting system to inform management of the quandary I was in and to persuade them to rehire Bob. The fact is, Bob was providing me with delectable tidbits on a number of employees that proved extremely useful in my dealings with them, and it was imperative that I keep that information channel open.

Everyone gradually headed back to their stations, and the mill cycled back into high gear. Stan met me at Chain Four and apologized for threatening to fire me. "Not a problem," I said. "You did what ya had to do."

"Thanks." He turned to walk away and then abruptly stopped.

Looking at me from the corner of his eye, he added, "And thanks for not letting that thing get outta hand."

"If it were up to me, it would have. You're the reason it stopped. And what's up with the polysyllabic words? Epithet? Where'd that come from?"

Stan turned back toward me. "You liked that, huh? It was Larry (his boss), actually. All the dryer tenders were called in yesterday and briefed on Doug. They told us, 'any problems' we were to fire first and ask questions later."

"Then you should've fired them."

"And then what? Shut down the mill?"

"No, I guess you're right."

"Huh?" he said loudly. The noise returned to idyllic levels (for a mill), and natural speech had no place in an idyllic mill setting. "What?"

"Nothing! You're right!" Soon everyone was yelling once again in the mill. All was back to normal.

When I looked up from the chain at Tari, she smiled in a manner that could best be described as remorseful. There was a huge story behind that yodel, one that I probably didn't want to know entirely. The clamor of the mill drowned out the tension and the hatred, but I had already seen behind the veil of appearances and could no longer judge these people objectively. Up was no longer up exactly, and down not quite down. Given the choice, wouldn't you rather call as your friend a small-time drug dealer than a big-time hate monger? Apparently it wasn't my job to ensnare hate mongers, just small-time drug peddlers with a disdain for molesters and racists.

On the way out the door that evening, I asked Doug if he wanted to hang out with Caracas and me at the Josephine County Fair on Sunday. He accepted. I didn't tell Caracas, but based upon his support earlier that day, I figured it wouldn't be a problem.

When I visited Doug and his family at their apartment, he felt obliged to give me the grand tour. Although the decor had an English traditional accent, it was an eclectic montage of antediluvian furnishings and passé art ranged along the walls in no perceptible pattern. Although the apartment was quite large, the amenities choked the space like weeds, taking up every square inch that wasn't a regular thoroughfare.

His wife was a demure woman with cheeks I wanted to kiss every time I laid eyes on her. Her plump, dimpled smile shaved ten years off her age and said more about who she was than anything she could say herself. She was articulate and polite, but it was the former that had me questioning what her husband was doing working at a mill. Two intelligent people could do better than to have one staying at home with the kids and the other busting his ass in an insane asylum like that.

"Good-looking kids," I said.

"Thanks," Doug's wife, Kim, responded. "What do you say?" she then said to her two children—a boy and girl.

"Thank you," they both answered in shy, timid voices.

"Don't thank me. Thank your parents." I perceived their lack of comprehension, so I added, "You're very welcome."

"So," Doug started. "You ready to go?"

"Sure. It was nice to meet . . ."

Kim shuffled toward me before I could finish; a nervous twitch was in her voice and in her manner. With hands raised to her front, she said, "So you . . . you . . . my husband says . . . Doug says you're goin' to a concert?"

My eyes and head shifted back and forth between the two, sensing that there had been tension over Doug's decision to go with us. "Uhhh. Is everything okay here? 'Cause I don't wanna . . ."

"Yeah," she replied. "I just . . . I . . . I heard about what happened at the mill and . . ."

"Honey?" Doug pleaded as he shuffled the kids off to the kitchen. "He doesn't need to hear that."

"No, no, it's fine. You should've told her about that crap."

"Everything's gonna be fine." He took her affectionately by the arms and spoke more softly. "It's okay, baby. It is. Those guys were in the minority. Ken's my friend. Caracas too. Okay? Okay, baby? I won't go if you don't want me to. Really, it's no big."

Kim stepped slightly to one side of Doug and directed her response to me. "Ken? I know you're not one of the guys who treated my Doug badly. I'm just . . . You . . . We've gotta family here and . . . I just want him to be okay. I want us to be happy. I'm not doing a very good job explaining . . ."

"You're doing fine. And I completely know where you're coming from here. That's not to say I can relate to what Doug went through that day, 'cause I can't. Unlike Doug, every time I've been the minority in what people would call the wrong place at the wrong time—and the wrong color—I've been treated good. I don't know, maybe that's why I feel I can't relate. I don't know. The point I'm trying to make, and not doing a very good job of it, I might add, is that you have a right to be concerned. People can attribute prejudice to ignorance, but you and I both know that's a crock. If you educate a racist, he's just a well-read racist. Some people are just selfish, cowardly bastards, and that's what we have at the mill to some degree. I don't know. I don't know what I'm tryin' to say either. I guess I feel a strange need to apologize on behalf of the white race because of those idiots."

"It's amazing how often I feel the same way," she offered with a telling smile. She then grabbed Doug's shirt and buttoned one of the buttons and patted him on the chest. "Go have a good time, sweetie."

"Are you sure?"

She looked at me and smiled. "Yeah, I'm sure."

I suddenly felt a huge responsibility that I hadn't felt when I walked into this place. All I could think was, "Please God, don't let him die on my watch." Then I felt guilty for having thought such a thing. Sometimes it just doesn't pay to get overly analytical in this business.

*   *   *

My car was barely in Caracas's driveway when he came storming out. "Where have you been?" Upon seeing Doug, he switched gears. "Hey, dude. You coming?"

"Yeah, if that's okay."

"Sure, why the hell wouldn't it be." His question was rhetorical be-cause, not unlike me, he had no idea what it must have been like to have to ask such a question.

Caracas tossed a bag in the back of my car (the top was down) and asked me to pop the hood. Doug got out of the car for what I knew was his discomfort with what would be the seating arrangement. With my hood open and the three of us standing at the front of the car, Caracas removed a gun from the back of his pants (in a belt holster) and laid it in the trunk. I asked what I already knew Doug wanted to ask. "What's that for?"

"You never know."

"Well, if 'you never know' occurs, what the hell good's it gonna do us locked up here in the trunk?"

"You gonna let me put it up front?"

I dropped the hood with the gun still inside. "Good point," I said. "Let's go."

Doug stood indecisively outside the car as Caracas moved around him. Before I could tell Caracas to get in the back, he pulled the seat forward and did what was right. As I studied Doug's face for a moment, I under-stood that sometimes it's best to get in the back seat in life even if your legs are longer than the legs of the person sitting up front. In this case, it was probably a toss-up. It's not that I think people should be obliged to pay a debt they never owed, but they should *want* to pay a portion of it, regardless. Societal changes happen in small, individual increments, not through legislation, and certainly not all at once.

"So where to?" I asked.

"The five, north," Caracas directed. "I wanna stop on the way at this really cool army surplus store and pick up some fatigues. It's on the way."

"Sure. I'm easy."

We were barely on our way when Caracas asked me to stop at a bar called Maxis so he could play some video poker. We drank the obligatory beer and were on our way. With additional stops at the Iris Club in Ashland (to the south) and the Library Club in Grant's Pass, we were several dollars poorer and a few beers south of sobriety.

"Are you okay to drive?" Doug appeared worried.

"If not," Caracas leaned into the cockpit and put out a feeler to Doug. "I can set him up."

"How do mean?"

"How do you think?"

"Ohhh. Gotcha." Doug's tone didn't seem totally disagreeable.

"Need a boost, Booch?" Caracas leaned into the front compartment once again.

"No, thanks. I may ask ya to drive later on, though."

He then broadsided me in the way only Caracas could. "Saw your car at that drug test place on Royal Avenue on Friday. What's up? Boise give ya a hard time 'bout the other night?"

I had gone to the clinic on a directive from K and S shortly after the overdosing incident, not for health reasons, but to cover the company's gigantic ass in the event someone later accused me of having participated in the crimes for which I was sent to investigate. The fact that the test was administered two days later and that I used a drug flushing kit, enabled me to avoid detection. The problem now, however, was explaining it.

I responded almost without thought. "I'm getting a life insurance policy and they require a complete blood work-up."

"Didn't they require a drug profile?"

I had already seen that question coming. Nevertheless, he surprised me once again by using a word like 'profile.' Who knows, maybe if you're a regular drug user that's a word you run into a lot. "Tari gave me a flush kit," I said. "And besides, I'm not a drug addict like yourself."

"I don't do it as much as you might think." He became defensive, but his manner remained congenial.

"Good thing."

"In case either of you care," Doug joined in. "I don't do anything that doesn't come from a clear mountain spring."

"We *don't* care," I teased. "But now that you broached the subject, I didn't know Colt 45 came from the mountains?"

"It doesn't," Caracas added. "It comes from . . . Darn! I was tryin' to come up with something funny there."

Doug said, "You shoulda said 'I didn't know your wife came from a clear mountain spring.'" He spun about in his seat to see if Caracas was as slow as I was. "Get it? Don't 'do anything' that doesn't come from a clear mountain spring?"

"You talk about your wife that way, dude?" I said earnestly, crimping my eyebrows for effect.

Caracas caught on quickly, and we held our composure as long as we could, which was about ten seconds. "Now who's slow?" Caracas said, grinning.

"Slow down," Caracas shouted. "It should be right around here somewhere. Damn. I know it's here somewhere. Wait. Turn up there." He pointed over Doug's shoulder. I turned, but it soon became apparent that we were lost. With no structures higher than three stories, it was like driving through the back lot of Universal Studios.

"I know it's here," he continued to mumble.

"Let's get directions," Doug advised. "Pull over and I'll ask this guy up here."

"If it's all the same with you," I said, downshifting into second gear, "I'd rather take my chances with someone that lives here, like that woman over there on roller blades pushing the stroller."

"What makes you so sure . . . ?" Doug began to question.

I interrupted, "Because that guy is putting money in the meter."

"So?" Caracas said. "Maybe he lives too far away to walk. It doesn't mean he's not from around here."

"It's Sunday. Sign back there said free parking on Sundays and on any days after 6:00 P.M. A local would know that. Hell, anyone with a clue would know that."

"So why this woman?" Doug asked as we pulled alongside her.

"Those three-wheel jogging strollers don't collapse or fold up. You can't fit one in a car." I then directed my words to the woman. "Excuse me. Excuse me? Miss? Miss?"

Doug rejoined, "She could've drove a truck."

"Yes?" The woman responded.

"We're looking for an army surplus . . ."

"You just passed it about a block back. Just turn around here and hang a right at the next street. It'll be on your left about two blocks down."

"Thank you! Cute baby, by the way."

"Thank you. And good luck."

"She still could've been driving a truck," Caracas said.

"Yeah. She could have," I said with a gloating smile.

*   *   *

Rummaging through the surplus store was semieducational in terms of military history, but wholly didactic in its approach to all things militaristic. Having served in the armed forces for six years, I have an entirely different view of war and killing in general than most people. The taking of life is sometimes necessary to preserve freedom or to rebuke aggression, but should never be viewed as glorious, or worse, perfunctory. The fact is, most of the men who groped the apparel and rolfed the trade weapons were pseudomercenaries with countless stories about battles they never fought.

Caracas purchased several pairs of camouflage fatigues, a pair of green, steel-toed jungle boots, a grenade case, a canteen and a hunting knife big enough to skin a grizzly bear. Doug bought himself a pair of green fatigues, the kind that didn't need to be tucked into boots, and I walked out empty-handed. "Taking this 'no taxation without representation' thing a bit literal, aren't we, Caracas?" I said as we trooped back into the car.

"Just work shit. Except the knife."

"You're wearing those boots to work this time of the year?"

"Why not?"

"Because it's six thousand degrees."

"So I don't wear the boots," he explained. "What's the difference?"

"Then you got the wrong kind of fatigues. They look stupid unless they're tied and tucked in. You do realize that, don'tcha?" I suspected he got camouflage for his little escapades in the woods, but I wasn't positive.

His voice exhibited frustration. "So I wear the damned boots. It won't kill me."

Not wanting to show my hand, I quickly changed the subject. "That was a buncha shit you got at the mill last week, huh." I glanced over at Doug to prompt a response.

He laughed for a moment. "Yeah, boy. That was something all right. I thought they were gonna lynch my black ass right then and there. I never did thank you guys for all the help, did I?"

"I think a beer sometimes says that which mere words can't," Caracas quipped as he reached around the seat and gripped Doug by the shoulders.

"Next one's on me, then," Doug proclaimed.

*   *   *

We arrived at the fair a few minutes later. As expected, there were miles of trucks lined up tightly along a muddy trail of mutilated grass. Large grandstands and tall chain-link fences, smothered in advertisements, obscured our view of the happenings. We sloshed our way to the meandering line at the main entrance and shuffled languidly toward the gate with the rest of the drunken herd.

The gaggle in front of us, six guys and as many women, were becoming as loud as they were obnoxious, and I sensed there would be trouble. As their gutter humor teetered precariously on racist, I cleared my throat and politely asked that they respect their present company.

"What the fuck's your problemo?" one of the drunker ones asked.

"The racist stuff," I said. "Could ya please tone it down just a notch."

"Hey, don't worry about it," Doug said softly. "It's no big deal."

"Yeah, asshole." The drunk poked his cowboy hat toward me. "It's no big deal. Just ask the nigger, if you don't believe me." His friends apparently thought he had crossed the line and immediately chastised him for his transgression.

"No, man!" he yelled back at them as he stumbled sideways. "We weren't joking about blacks. That's my fucking point. Asshole's jumping our shit for nothin'! I was saying *spic*, not *nigger*, and he butted his head in!"

"Whatever, dude. Just tone it down. That's all I'm asking."

After the group collectively apologized, the drunk turned on me. Apparently, I wasn't country enough for him. "Where the fuck's your cowboy hat, dickhead?"

I glanced down at his wide leather belt and oversized buckle and noticed his name inscribed on it. "So, Jim," I asked, "Why do all you country boys wear belts with your names inscribed on them? Get too drunk to remember it?"

Even in his inebriated state he could detect the antagonism in my sarcasm. "So you city folk know who's kicking your punk ass." His friends all laughed—more tense than anything else.

"Really," I retorted. "I thought it was so truck drivers knew who they were fucking."

He lunged at me a couple times, only to fall flat on his face in the gooey mud. His friends apologized profusely and kept him at bay.

"Why do you let that shit get to you?" Doug asked as we walked through the gate and parted company with the drunken idiot.

"I think the *real* question is, why don't you?" Caracas said.

"Guys like that . . . I don't know, look at that shit. He had as much a problem with Ken not being cowboy enough as he had with me not being light enough. What's the point?"

"That's a good point," I said, changing the direction of the conversation. "They gotta sell cowboy hats here, right?"

"Oh, sure," Caracas replied. "And while we're at it, let's see if they sell lighter skin, too."

"Exactly," Doug said.

"Exactly what?" I asked.

"What Caracas is trying to say is that I can't change the color of my skin, so I've learned to deal with it."

"That's not what I was saying. I was just kiddin' around. And I don't think you should adapt to idiots like that. You should demand they adapt to you. Guys like that only need 9 millimeters of persuasion."

"How am I supposed to do that?"

"You mean shoot 'im?" Caracas asked.

"No, you moron. Make them adapt to me? How do I do that?"

"Hell if I know. I'm not the one who's had thirty years to think about it."

"You see, I don't put it in that perspective," Doug said, turning sideways to avoid oncoming traffic. "It would be no different if one of you tried to fit into an all-black community or an all-black workplace. The only difference is that you guys outnumber us. Blacks wouldn't treat whites any better than whites treat us if we outnumbered you. If you don't believe me, move to Nigeria."

"I'm not so sure," I said. "I was stranded in black communities many times when I used to travel cross-country a bunch and never once had a problem. In fact, they've always been friendly and helpful to me. I can't say the same for all white communities, though. I can't tell ya how many times I've had fights there. Hell, I've never even had a fight with a black guy before."

"Exactly," Doug agreed.

"There he goes again with that 'exactly' stuff," Caracas responded.

"No, no." Doug stopped to face us, his hands forcefully accenting everything he said. "My point is that most bad things that happen to people are done by their own race. Look at gang violence. Hell, look at slavery. Who do you think sold the slaves to the whites in the first place? You don't think whitey came stormin' into Africa and just started loading boats, do ya? The only reason Europeans bought black slaves to begin with is because white slaves couldn't hack it. They weren't hardy enough and went belly-up on them. It was an economic thing, plain and simple. African tribes were trading in slaves long before Europeans showed up. You won a battle, you took slaves. That's just the way it was. Shit, in places like Ghana, it still is. Little girls are sent into slavery for the sins of their relatives. And it's actually worse. The priests keep the tradition alive so they can continue to rape ten-year-old girls. . . ."

Caracas spoke over him. "Gotta love a place that steeped in tradition."

Doug didn't skip a beat. "And in Uganda, rebels have been forcing young children to fight the government and kill innocent people for years."

"Young children? You mean as opposed to old children?" I said. "And Gaza? I thought that was in Israel?"

"It is," Caracas replied. "It's a big strip club."

"I said Ghana, not Gaza. And it's the Gaza strip, not the Gaza strip club."

"I was joking for Chris' sakes. I know where Ghana is. It's on the West Bank, I mean, coast."

"Anyhow, the point I'm trying to make is . . . well, when you think about it, it's almost egotistical for white people to suggest they ever controlled the fate of the African people."

"You mean whitey?" I teased.

"Exactly. Who do you think freed the slaves? Slaves don't free slaves. Apparently there were good white people even when slavery was the comon practice. And that's what I believe. I believe there are more good white and black people than bad people, but the bad ones get most of the press.

Take the incident at the mill the other day, for instance. A few . . ."

"A little more than a few," I interjected.

"Whatever. But you catch my meaning. A few assholes can make that place look pretty ugly for a guy like me if I let it get to me."

"I'll give ya this," I said. "You're a better man than me."

"Exactly."

*   *   *

Doug's neoteric political views managed to strip away the tension that I was not even aware existed between us. Bouncing from sausage booth to beer booth to pretzel booth and then back to the beer booth, we took fully of the country fare experience and shared a great deal of ourselves and our beliefs. It wasn't until many hours had passed that I realized Doug had been treated kindly and in an unremarkably ordinary way by all the other fairgoers throughout the day. Had it not been for his earlier observations, the only thing I would have taken from that day was the memory of a drunken racist. Instead, I can reflect back on a day spent laughing and discovering with two friends—yes, *friends*.

"Do you know why God didn't make women like men?" Doug asked in a groggy stupor as we sat in my car in Caracas's driveway and stared up at the night sky.

"You mean physically," Caracas asked.

"No, no. I mean, like, physically. Like sex. Why he didn't make them want it as much as us."

"You mean physically," I said.

"Yeah. Like physically want to do it with the ladies."

"By the time I get the answer," Caracas said, "I'll be too old to get it up."

Doug stuck his leg out the window and rendered his theory. "Because there would be sex everywhere, all the time. Who would be left to say 'no'? You'd go into the grocery store, and there would be people having sex right there on the floor or in the vegetable section. At the gas station it'd be, like, 'Hey, I'm filling it up. Wanna have sex while we pump?' or something like that. It'd be in the street, in the office . . ."

"Okay, we get it already," I said.

"He's got a point, you know," Caracas added.

"Nothing a good hat wouldn't cover," I followed.

Caracas looked at his watch. "You must have a real understanding wife."

"Yeah," Doug said with a contented sigh. And then reality shook him good. "Holy shit! I forgot to call!"

Before I could turn the key in the ignition, the smell of sawdust invaded my nasal passages and a tightness gripped my neck. The weekend was over.

Chapter 23

It was not until Monday morning, while standing half-naked in my kitchen, that I realized I hadn't accomplished a single thing with regard to Caracas, and Mimi's instruction to work through him from now on. Frustrated over that realization, I pounded on the countertop and jarred loose the knob of one of the kitchen drawers. In the course of replacing the knob I noticed something quite disturbing, something that literally sent chills up my spine and made the hair on my arms stand at attention. The bag of yellow paste that I had placed in the drawer weeks earlier looked remarkably like crystal methamphetamine powder now.

Lacking the immediate ability to test it legally or even the inclination to try, I removed a tiny amount from the bag—just enough to cover the tip of my finger—and snorted it. Suffice it to say that it passed the Ken Bucchi litmus test. I placed the remainder back in the drawer and went to work at the mill. It was at least another week before I got around to screwing that knob in.

I was uncommonly euphoric throughout the day, and it was not until George brought it to my attention that I realized my mood had been artificially induced. I'm ashamed to say that there were many moments during that investigation when I reflected on that day and wondered whether I would be better off with a snootful. Although I never succumbed to the temptation, I certainly understood why some people did, and in retrospect, I think that understanding served me well. The difference between me and those who did succumb was that I was humble enough to admit my weaknesses and informed enough to recognize that what started out as want would soon become need and that what felt like euphoria would soon become depression.

I pulled wood that evening like a man with tree sap in his veins. And in this microcosmic planet called Boise Cascade, that made me king of the mill. Standing at the front of Chain Three pulling eight-foot strips, I dismissed the normal rotations, and with the aid of chemicals and accolades, snapped pine against the back of the cart in perfect cadence. When the cheering subsided, I tipped my cap and dragged my sweat-drenched body to the rear of the chain.

"That was unbelievable," a huge man—both in circumference and in height—with gray, receded hair and tape-mended gloves said while shaking his head back and forth. "Howda ya do that?"

"It was a fluke! Sometimes I just get in a zone!" Pulling some of his wood as we crossed, I asked, "What's your name, by the way? I've seen you around, but we've never actually . . ."

"Jim! But there're alotta Jims so just call me Tank like everyone else."

"Tank? Where'd they get that one?!" I said sarcastically. "All right! Good luck, Panzer."

"Pansy?" he roared.

"No! Panzer! As in 'German Panzer'!"

"Oh, yeah! I thought I was gonna haveta throw you." I knew my limits, and he was clearly well beyond them, so I smiled and raised my hands as if to surrender. "This's premature gray!" he said by way of explanation. The only problem is, I hadn't asked.

"Maybe when it came in ten years ago!"

He quaked with laugher. "I like that! It is, though! I'm only thirty-five!"

I was about to say that no one could get that heavy in just thirty-five years, but better judgment and self-preservation restrained my comedic impulse. Good thing, too, because he was the type of guy who would pull a hundred pounds of wood off the chain with one hand just to avoid the fast, repetitive motion needed to pull it off one sheet at a time.

Instead, I followed with something more lighthearted. "You're stretching this inane conversation just to keep from having to pull the entire cart yourself, aren't ya?" As I mentioned, I was pulling his wood the entire time we spoke.

"Those are some real nice shoes," he said facetiously to keep me talking . . . and pulling. "Where'd ya get 'em?"

"You should worry more about your gloves than the damned shoes, dude! Don'tcha think it's time for a new pair?"

"Not at eight bucks a pop! That's like workin' an hour a day for nothin'! No sir-ree, not me!" Because the company had been reimbursing me for my gloves each time they blew a gasket, I hadn't considered the net impact of having to replace them two or three times a week, sometimes more. I also wasn't making twelve measly dollars an hour like the rest of these poor slobs. What made matters even worse was that Pullers tore gloves at a rate five times that of Feeders and Spreaders, yet were given no special dispensation.

I was about to suggest the possibility of supplementing his income, but it was a bug that I just didn't want to put in anyone's ear any more. And besides, his foreboding presence didn't exactly scream speed freak, if you know what I mean.

I swear it couldn't have been more than two minutes later that I heard Tank scream "Sliver!" The six-inch sliver that pierced the web between his thumb and index finger was still attached to the eight-foot strip. It was so thick that it bore the full weight of the bigger piece of wood without snapping. With at least three inches of wood showing on the business end of the splinter, there would be no comfortable method of extracting it.

"Get 'im to the First Aid Room," instructed Stan, who was always on the scene before any other dryer tender.

"I think this's above your local sliver remover's pay grade, Stan," I said.

"No," Tank quickly intervened on his own behalf. "That'll be fine, Stan."

Stan's motivations were transparent. First, he didn't want to involve the company's insurance carrier because incidents such as this reflected negatively on all the dryer tenders' safety record. Second, he could never be too sure who was on drugs at any given time. You see, at Boise, if you got into an accident requiring outside medical attention, you could and probably would be required to take a drug test. This policy worked in Boise's favor, given that so many people were on drugs and therefore were extremely reluctant to seek formal medical attention. Ergo, no insurance claim.

No matter how grave, incidents that didn't require immediate professional medical attention did not count against middle management's safety record and did not place an employee in jeopardy of being drug tested. Consequently, this practice tacitly encouraged such dangerous behavior.

The reason Tank refused medical attention was entirely different. It was machismo, pure and simple. The more pain you endured, the more respect you received and the more privileges you were extended.

"Gotta separate the strip," Phil mumbled, his head joining the circle of heads huddled over Tank. And then it happened. A hand—an anonymous hand—reached through the ring of heads from above and extended toward Tank, the center of the palm rich with rose-colored powder. "Go ahead. Snort it," several voices galvanized as one.

"It'll help with the pain," Phil advised.

"Yeah?" Tank asked with a naive grimace. Someone *accidentally* bumped the plank and that was enough encouragement for Tank—he snorted the meth. His fate was sealed, at least insofar as this incident was concerned. If he went to the hospital now, he would be fired for drug use, and if he ever wanted to sue . . . well, you get the picture.

"Hold him," Stan instructed, then proceeded to separate the sliver from the plank. "Let's go amd get 'im to the First Aid Room!"

"How ya feelin'?" I asked as we guided him onto the couch in the First Aid Room.

"Not as bad as you would think. That stuff you gave me really works."

"I didn't . . . ," I started to correct him. "Good. Good to hear it."

"Now the fun part," Stan moaned begrudgingly. "Where the hell's Tom?" Tom was the gentleman who removed the sliver from my arm after the accident when I first began working there.

"We're gonna haveta do it without him," said Caracas, who had just arrived with his clan. "Here." He pushed through the pack. "Let me handle it."

Caracas poured alcohol directly over the wound—with predictable results. Tank yowled like a coyote in heat. "Have him bite down on a piece of wood for God's sakes. I'm tired of listening to him." Devon's tone was as sympathetic as his words.

"Well, get me something then," Caracas shouted. "Don't just stand there!"

I took a turn at venting my frustration while I assisted the others in restraining Tank. "You're tellin' me we can't find a piece of wood quicker than this in a fucking plywood mill?"

Devon reached through the circle of hands as if to help control Tank's thrashing and snapped the sliver through his hand. "Here," he said. "Have 'im bite down on this." He pressed the bloody hunk of wood into Tank's screaming mouth. "Can we please go now?"

Tank's cheeks expanded and contracted with strained regularity; torrents of air were expelled from his nose and mouth as he fought bravely to gain his composure.

"Give 'im a bump," Stan directed Phil.

"I only have . . . ," Phil began to gripe.

"Bump 'im," Steve barked.

Phil dabbed some powder that he kept in a small vial into the palm of his hand and placed it under Tank's nose. Tank did what his body demanded and snorted it like a pig.

After bandaging him up, Stan gave Tank two new pairs of gloves and strongly admonished him not to use tape on them ever again. With the assistance of the additional "bump" of crystal methamphetamine and testosterone—always a dangerous mix—Tank was back to work in less than two hours.

The following day, after reporting on the complex safety and legal issues surrounding Boise's safety policies, which included the mill compelling employees to purchase their own safety gloves and Boise's treatment of serious injuries, Gordon responded with his usual rhetoric about liability and reporting procedures, and the appropriateness of the information included therein. In other words, he didn't like me biting the hand that fed him.

The only good thing about drug dealers is that they occasionally interrupt asinine conversations like the one I was having with Gordon. In this case, it was Devon, and he was ready to deal—finally. This would keep Gordon off my back for a while because he wanted nothing more than to nail a Spreader. No pun intended. Spreaders were such a tight-knit corps that if you got just one of them in the interview room the flood gates would burst open. At least that is what Gordon had been claiming right along.

Chapter 24

Standing in the park on a damp, drizzly afternoon waiting for Devon's truck to appear, I felt an uneasy sense of déjà vu. It wasn't the park or the presence of JACNET, or even the dismal weather conditions that sparked this uneasiness, but rather the sense of a pending betrayal. I staved off these counterproductive feelings by rationalizing that if I didn't make a second deal with him, the most that could happen was that he would eventually lose his job. A small price to pay for the quantities he wanted to sell.

This would also buy me enough time with K and S to devote more effort to altering the tragic destinies of people like Doug and Caracas, while still not placing Devon in jeopardy of incarceration. I felt like a fly in a *Far Side* comic strip looking down at his new baby boy saying, "Don'tcha just wish they could stay maggots forever?" I guess what I'm trying to say is that in a mill brimming with morally bankrupt people, these two seemed almost cute and cuddly by comparison. I would also have more time now to ensnare—some might say entrap—flies like Linda, Scott, Jerry and Paul in my web. This may not have been a morally bankrupt strategy, but it sure as hell taxed my credit line.

"Finally," I said in relief and to alert JACNET that Devon had arrived. He drove cautiously down the graded lot, indecorously surveying the area for any indications of trouble. His jacked-up black truck faced the rainswept field, parked parallel with mine about five spaces away. He sat and watched for at least two minutes, carefully studying the cars parked on the opposite side of the field where it so happened JACNET was positioned. The distance and the lighting were such that you couldn't determine whether someone was actually sitting in a vehicle unless they made a sudden movement. He looked endlessly for such a movement.

When he finally got out of his vehicle, we met halfway, his back coincidentally to JACNET's position. "Yours or mine?" he asked.

"Doesn't matter. Mine'd be fine." As soon as the words left my mouth JACNET flashed their headlights. I knew that it meant they wanted me to conduct business in his vehicle, but I had no idea why.

"What the hell was that?" he asked, startled.

Because his back was still toward JACNET, I was sure he hadn't seen the flash. "What?"

"Your eyes. I saw headlights." He turned about and then quickly back to me. "Who's out there?"

"Like a million people drivin' around with their brights on. Don't wig out on me now."

"That wasn't a person drivin'. That was someone flashing. And you were looking straight at them."

Just then, as we were both looking back toward the parking lot, a car hit a speed bump and its lights, due to the temporary change in trajectory, appeared to brighten. "There ya go," I said. "Was it something like that?"

"Hmmm. Yeah . . . I suppose." He thought for a moment. "Whose car?"

I knew that he was a bit more paranoid than when he arrived, so I said "mine," believing that he would do the opposite. "No, no, no. We'll take care of this over here," he insisted, as he led me hastily to his truck. Once inside, he forewent the obligatory spiel about me being a standard narc and dove headlong into a much more creative and colorful portrait of me. "You were in the Air Force?"

"News flash . . . no shit."

"Yeah, well, I think you forgot to mention that you were in the OSI while you were in there. That's what everyone's been sayin'."

"Sure. That's exactly what happened. Then I came up here to Boise Cascade to catch a bunch of minor leaguers like yourself. Can we please skip the paranoid fuck-tango just this one time and get this thing over with so I can get back to the station and have the lab test this shit you call pure."

He gazed at me without blinking for a minute and then raised his eyebrows. "Slipped up, huh?"

"Yeah, that's what I did. You caught me. You wanna do this or not? I don't have time for this shit, I really don't."

"Say you weren't in the OSI and that you're not a cop. Say it."

"It." I stared back at him for a moment. "I'm not a cop, and I was never in the OSI. Happy?"

"And that you're not working for the cops."

"Oh, my fucking . . ." I exhaled exuberantly. "And I'm not working for the cops. And if you ask me another fucking question I'm gonna hand this money to the first person that walks by. Don't call my bluff on this one, Cochise." I thought for a second. "You know, you kill me. What if I were in the OSI or the DEA or whatever the fuck you think I'm in? You know how much shit I'd have on you already? You're gonna start getting cautious on me now? You sons of bitches get dumber and dumber all the time."

"Fuck you, all right! I've never been caught because I don't make stupid mistakes! Got it?"

"Yeah, yeah. Whatever. You wanna do this or not?"

"Let me see the cash."

"Here it is. Count it. All five grand of it. In fact, let me count it. I don't want any other paranoid confusion later on." I proceeded to count the money out loud. "Now let me see the meth."

"Eighty-six the 'paranoid' crap, all right. You can never be too careful."

"Careful? *What* careful? What do you know about me *now* that you didn't know before you came here? *What*? I answer 'no' to a couple questions about being a cop? Who's gonna say, 'yeah, I'm a cop?' You know, if you're gonna do this for a living, learn the craft. It's embarrassing. You give the rest of us dealers a bad name."

"I learned what I needed to learn. I could tell by your reaction that you're not a pig. And it doesn't matter anyhow; you can't bust me if you say you're not a cop. It's entrapment. And don't talk to me about earning a living. I'm making a much better living than you with this shit. I *heard* where you live."

Not only was he given to fits of marked stupidity, as in his futile attempt to taint the arrest by invoking that urban legend about law enforcement agents having to disclose their true identity when challenged to do so, but he was also such a raving egotist that he took the bait and admitted he was more than just a recreational dealer.

"It's called low profile; you should take a lesson."

He turned and looked at my car. "Yeah, that's reeeeeal low profile."

"It is," I explained. "In the physical sense it's very low profile. Only a Lamborghini or Vector are lower." His expression told me that he didn't catch the humor. "It's low to the ground? Profile? Anyway, you do things your way, and I'll do things mine."

"I get the joke. It just ain't funny, that's all." Without explanation, he then leaned across me and opened the glove box, removing a large flathead screwdriver. With his left hand guiding the driver head, he pried at the speedometer until it popped loose. He then unscrewed the face and passed the partially disassembled instrument under my nose. Although the contents were still sealed in a plastic baggy, the peanut-butter-colored powder was powerful enough to cause a burning sensation in my sinuses. I knew that this was the best stuff I had bought to date.

"So you never intended to make the deal in my car?"

"Not so stupid after all, huh?"

Unlike many of the others I dealt with, with Devon it was all business. In fact, he never even bothered to threaten me. On the way back to my rendezvous with JACNET, I racked my brain trying to come up with a logical explanation for why anyone would conduct an illegal transaction with a person they already believed to be a narc. I came up with two explanations; either I was a brilliant investigator or he, and everyone else at the mill, was incredibly desperate. I settled on the only rationale that made sense.

*   *   *

"Sorry about the lights," Joe apologized as I got into the back seat of his Ford Taurus in the Fred Meyer's parking lot.

"Yeah, what the hell was that all about? Why'd you want me to make the deal in his vehicle? Better photo op?"

Mike explained. "If his vehicle is used in the commission of the sale, it's subject to confiscation. Talk about a strong motivation to roll on your friends. Did you get a good look at his wheels? It's worth some real bread, and he sure as hell ain't gonna part with it lightly."

"Ohhh, yeah, that's right. I forgot about that. That goes for Phil and Shannon too, I take it?"

"Sure, Shannon, but forget Phil. It would cost us more to tow it than it's worth. But it's the same for a lot of 'em. Including Jim and Rick. Always try to do the deal in their vehicle. We probably should've told you that in the beginning, I suppose."

"Does that go for illegal gun sales, too?"

"You got a gun dealer?" Joe asked, titillated.

"I think so. I'll call you in a couple days when I have more details. We're just now becoming buddies."

"Well," Joe said, "Everyone should have at least one arms dealer in their Rolodex."

Chapter 25

Over the next few weeks I couldn't help but notice that Tank seemed more spry, less physically encumbered by his bulk than usual. Something was different about him, and I was afraid I knew just what it was. Sadly enough, one serendipitous turn toward the seductive powder could mar an individual's entire future. When Tank broke out into song while hurling sheets of wood against the back of his cart, I was sure he was neck deep in treacherous, shark-infested waters. With Phil as his lifeguard, it was only a matter of time before he was thrown a bucket of chum in place of a life preserver.

Tank's obvious financial distress meant that Phil was probably giving him free samples, just enough to peak his cravings. Once Tank began to pay for his high, Phil would slowly increase the purity to initiate the early stages of addiction. He would then taper off the purity to encourage Tank to buy more and more. When the purity was eventually increased again, Tank, who was now accustomed to snorting a certain amount each day, would maintain that level and, as a result, become a junkie. It was a formula that was probably hatched back when man first deceived man.

Throughout the day I was a distant and inactive listener to those who attempted conversation. I deliberated endlessly over whether or not to intercede or simply allow things to take their natural course. But because my mere presence in the mill had, by its very nature, infected the natural order of things, I decided to meddle.

I monitored Tank's every move, even when he went to the bathroom. I knew that I could not let him out of my sight, even for a moment, if I was to confront him or his supplier at an opportune moment. I also knew, sadly enough, that I would need the help of my fellow drug dealers if I was to make any meaningful headway in averting Tank's inevitable downfall.

With Tari and Jim helping me coordinate my breaks with Tank's, I was able to keep close tabs on him throughout the evening. The trouble started when I tried to perform a one-man intervention.

I followed Phil and Tank out to the parking lot during lunch. Observing from a safe distance, I watched as they climbed into Phil's ratty pickup truck. The glow of a cigarette suggested that they intended to be a while. I snuck up from behind the vehicle until I was close enough to hear them chattering. Phil was explaining to Tank that he could no longer afford to give him the drugs for free. He might just as well have been saying, "This is stage two of your slide into chemical dependency, chum."

With the element of surprise on my side, not to mention sobriety, I ripped open Phil's door and snatched the gun from beneath his seat. I took a glancing blow to the side of the head from his left shoe but was none the worse for wear. Massaging my temple aggressively, I stepped back and ordered them out of the vehicle.

"What are you doing?" Phil exploded.

"Oh, God." Tank sniveled like a man caught peeping in a window. "We're under arrest."

"Bullshit. He's not a cop. He's ripping us off."

"Out of the car," I said in a controlled voice. "Come over on this side, Tank."

"What the hell you doing, man? Everyone knows I snort it as fast as I get it. Whatta you expect to get here?"

"Shut up." I motioned Tank closer to where Phil and I were standing by flicking Phil's gun in a circular motion. "Come here. Over here, damn it!"

"Hey. I'm broke, too, guy. This is like . . . I mean, I don't do this sorta thing . . . I just started . . ."

"Yeah, yeah. I know. Pay attention! Look at Phil," I said succinctly. "He's a loser, and he's tryin' to make you a loser, too, just so he can feed his habit. You don't wanna end up like this, Panzer. Believe me, you don't."

"Did you call me 'pansy'?" he said pathetically, attempting to regain his dignity with some ill-advised levity. "Remember?" he laughed disingenuously.

"You're not gonna get another deal in this mill, ever . . ." Phil's voice trailed off into inaudible clutter.

I dropped the safety and pressed the barrel to his temple. "I'm sorry. I didn't catch all that."

Phil closed his eyes tightly and twisted his head downward. "You're fuckin' up, dude."

"That's right, Phil. The newspapers'll say I fucked up and that traces of methamphetamine were found in the victim's body during an autopsy. So shut the fuck up!"

"That's it, man. I'm done. I swear. No more. Oh, shit . . ." Tank began to sob out loud.

"What the fuck are you doing?" a bewildered-looking Phil said to Tank.

"What you should've done before you became such a fucking lowlife."

"Yeah, right," Phil said. "I'm such a lowlife; that's why you've bought from me. Yeah, right. I'm the loser."

I smiled revealingly before offering, "You sure as hell are." It was my way of telling him that he was going to prison but at the same time not providing him any evidence to use against me. I could tell instantly that it found its target.

"Leave him alone," I commanded harshly.

"Well, well, well." He took on a sudden air of confidence. "Try tellin' them what ya just told me." Phil flipped his head a couple times to signify the approach of the cavalry.

"What's goin' on?" Devon inquired.

I responded flippantly. "It's a private matter, Sergeant O'Roark."

"Not if it's on our turf, it's not. Now I repeat, what's the problem?"

"I think you said 'what's going on' the first time, but my response is still the same . . . take Captain Binghamton and Corporal Klinger back to the fort. You know the way, don't you? A right at the rock that looks like a bear and a left at the bear that looks like a rock."

"Don't tell me where the fuck to go," his voice climbed. "Now what *the fuck* you doin' sticking your nose in Phil's *business*?"

"It's not Phil's business; it's mine. And if he . . . and for that matter, *you* . . . don't get the fuck offa my turf real quick like, I'm gonna . . ."

"What are ya gonna do? Huh! What?"

"He's a . . ." Phil started to accuse, prompting me to pistolwhip him a couple times before firing a shot at Devon's feet. It ricocheted off somebody's van and lodged in the side of a truck.

"I don't think you hear so well," I said with clenched teeth. "Am I gonna haveta give you a limp?"

Caracas slapped Devon upside the left ear and confirmed once and for all the pecking order of these pseudonihilists. "Get outta here," he told Devon. "You, too, Steve." He then motioned me aside. "Why ya interfering with this penny-ante shit?"

"If we're in this for the big bucks, then we don't need the Phils of this world. I just don't want Tank ending up like Phil, that's all. Tank's a friend of mine."

"No. I agree, but this nickel and dime stuff here keeps Phil happy and, well, you know . . . out of our hair."

"Until he gets caught."

"Hey, cops aren't allowed on private property without permission or a warrant and such. What's the harm if it keeps Phil from fucking things up by getting in trouble off site? Do you agree?"

"To a point. The problem with that line of reasoning is that if you allow him to create a whole crop of little *Phil*istines, you've multiplied the problem. *You* agree?"

"I can see that. So let's talk about it." He gently reached out and laid his hand on the gun. "Why don'tcha empty it and give it back to the little prick."

Although he was being as gracious and diplomatic as Boutros Boutros-Ghali, the condescending nature of his tone made me feel like his arm was around my shoulder the entire time. I emptied the weapon, then tossed it far into the brush that bordered the parking lot where we stood. "Fetch, bitch," I said to Phil.

"Phil," Caracas said as we walked away. "Tank's off limits, bro."

"Good. Now let's talk about your cohort's attitu . . . ," I started.

"Wait a sec," he interrupted as he turned around. "Hey, Tank!" Tank responded with a pathetic quiver. "You're on the wagon!" Leaving Tank alone with his fear and humiliation, Caracas and I strolled back to the mill. The matter-of-fact manner in which the situation was dealt with had apparently conveyed the criminal hierarchy well enough to Tank to preclude any future response on his part. He not only stopped using drugs from that day forward, but he also thanked Caracas and me for helping him kick the habit. Not that I wouldn't mind taking all the credit for his sobriety, but the fact is, I later discovered that it was mostly the result of intervention by Chief and his church. Chief and Tank? Wouldn't you like to have them on your church football team?

As Caracas and I neared the entrance to the mill, he began telling me a story about how he once controlled a situation similar to the one I just found myself in. The problem was, however, he told it in such a way that the people gathered outside the mill on break probably had no idea he was recounting a story as opposed to reprimanding me. I'm sure you've encountered this in your own life, when the person telling the story practically whispers the part where he says something like, "So I tell this guy," and then about bursts your eardrums when he describes what it is he actually told the guy. Of course, my brilliant technique for dealing with the situation was to practically shout responses like, "You really said that to *him*?" You're probably wondering why I mention this. I guess it's to illustrate not only the uncomfortable, subservient role I temporarilly had to play but also the constant battle the operative is forced to wage in order to keep his or her reputation and status intact.

Back in the break room, Caracas, Steve, Devon and I discussed the ground rules for all future parking lot transactions. Throughout the conversation, Caracas repeatedly spun a quarter on the table that divided us. With little more than an occasional glance to see where it was located on the table, he consistently stopped the coin in mid-revolution, still rigidly on its edge. He was cooler than a Canadian cucumber.

I was pleased to hear that no one conducted regular business in the parking lot unless they received advance permission from this cadre, specifically, Caracas. That included, surprisingly enough, people they weren't particularly fond of like Scott, Linda and Shannon. I was not pleased to hear, however, that most of these permissions were blanket approvals, which is why Phil was allowed to create new junkies like Tank any time his own addiction necessitated it.

"What is he, your brother?" Devon said derisively.

"If he was," I said before leaning across the table at him, "You'd be bleeding with Phil in that parking lot, not sitting in here pretending to be Don Corleone."

"You wanna take this outside?"

"Okay, okay." Caracas interceded. "Enough with the testosterone, already. Come on, guys. Let's just hash this whole thing out like civilized human beings. Ken? You don't want Tank wigged out like Phil. Then I propose you buy Phil's nickel-and-dime shit when he's desperate. Whatta ya say?"

"Fair enough," I conceded. "And Devon? If I ever decide to waltz with you in the parking lot, I won't be asking you for your dance card."

Steve jumped in with some tension-relieving humor before Devon was forced to bump or fold. "Jeeze, did someone turn on 'Nick at Night'? I feel like I'm in a James Cagney movie here."

Caracas said in his best Cagney imitation, "Yoooou dirty mill rat. Yoooou did it to my sister; now I'm gonna do it to yoooou, you seeeee."

Devon withdrew in a manner that allowed him to save face. "Hey. It's just business, man. You need to stop getting so damned involved."

"Aaaah, that's all right." Caracas remained partially in character. "I think you're right about this one, Booooch. Fuck Phil. Fuck him. I'm not sure 'bout youse guys, but I don't want another strung-out dope head on my conscience, you seeee." His words carried with them a sense of genuine moral conviction. Then he concluded, "If he gives us any trouble, we off him, you seeee." So much for my powers of discernment.

*   *   *

As minor as the events of that afternoon were, they were significant enough for me to determine once and for all (sound familiar?) what I needed to do with regard to who went to jail, who lost their job and who walked away scot-free. Although that may sound grandiose, the fact remains that if you have a UCI at your workplace, he or she has the ability to steer most people's fate.

I would one day conduct an investigation at Rockwell International in Newport Beach, California, however, and I discovered that I was merely the conductor, with the power to give tickets and summarily remove passengers from the train, but it was K and S, and ultimately the host company, that drove the engine and decided which track to take. During that case, I caught a number of people involved in inappropriate behavior such as drug dealing and theft, including the head of Rockwell's security, who also happened to know the exact nature of my employment with the company, but Rockwell fired employees on a purely discretionary basis.

One of the employees who was spared was an upper-level manager. In my supervisor's words, "He's making a lot of money for the company. They can't afford to lose him." By comparison, they fired a woman nicknamed "Flipper" simply because she made a lot of waves at the company. Although there was a lot of hearsay evidence against her, there were no concrete facts. To this day, I am haunted by what happened to her. She was a hard-working, dedicated employee who just happened to have a bad habit. A habit, I might add, that had not crossed over from her private life into the workplace.

Without the assistance of foresight, I forged ahead undaunted, believing that I could make right that which I couldn't. I was aware that Boise did not have the resources to fund an interminable investigation, so I set my sights on bagging some of the heavy hitters like Devon and the married couple, fleshing out the boat glue affair, and simply reporting on the smaller dealers who conducted regular business on the premises. This way I could trade up for the souls of people like Tari and George by offering up the Devons of the world and trade down with the sheer volume of names and information I could furnish on the Scotts of the world. Throw in a floating lab, a gunrunner, an auxiliary cop and a woman who claims to turn glue into speed, and you've got a conductor who can drive a train from the caboose.

I ordered some high-resolution cameras to be placed in certain key areas of the parking lot and began taking my lunch breaks in my vehicle. By taking copious notes and supplying supportive video, I was able to throw Boise about fifteen bones. More importantly, it bought me time and earned me much-needed bargaining chips. Whenever Gordon pressed me on taking my relationships with George and Tari to the next level, I pursued one of the people caught on camera and consummated a minor drug deal with them.

Everyone seemed to follow this pattern, except one. Consequently, it was with this person that I probably committed my most unethical act, an action that a number of veteran operatives later told me was as common as bogus entries in reports.

It began quite innocently with Gordon's constant pestering about Tari. Not wanting to deal with his perpetual nagging, yet wanting to use the valuable information she was supplying, I began attributing her statements to a known drug dealer. The drug dealer was Linda, and it so happened that she was slick enough to conduct most of her drug deals during the course of the workday. With a dependable group of users on her weekly distribution list, she would subtly pass them drugs at work and collect the money at a later date. Of course, the later date sometimes turned out to be advanced payment on the next deal as well. If my eyes were cameras, we still wouldn't have had enough evidence to fire her.

I tracked her weekly drops and dredged up as much information on her and her patrons as possible through my own network of dealers, liars and thieves—Tari notwithstanding. I then assured her a seat at the interview table by taking a gram of the crystal methamphetamine from my kitchen drawer—the crank that had allegedly been separated from the glue—and claimed that she had stuffed it in my pocket during work. I knew that she could not be prosecuted or fired for such an unsubstantiated claim but that she *would* be interviewed. She was definitely a drug dealer, so the way I saw it, if she blinked during her interview, she would be an unemployed drug dealer. It was also a way of getting JACNET to test the suspect crystal without having to divulge how I came to possess it.

When I met up with Joe in the Fred Meyer's parking lot that evening, he tested a pinch of the drugs while sitting there in his vehicle, just as he had so many times before.

"Wow," he said breathlessly. "It doesn't get any purer than this. Find out where she gets it. This stuff's primo. No, correct that. There's primo and then there's this. The lab boys are gonna have a field day with this one."

If only you could have seen my face at that very instant. It must have changed color as often as a chameleon on a plaid jacket. I was at first amazed that the substance even passed for the genuine article. Although I knew it had elements of speed in it, having already tested it myself, I had no idea that it would bear out molecularly and to such a degree of purity. I was also concerned that I could no longer connect these drugs to the whole glue affair. Sure, I had some left in the drawer, but its chemical fingerprint would match it to the crystal I had just given Joe. But most importantly, I was miffed at myself for having made Linda out to be a bigger player than she probably was. I wanted her to pay with her job if her confessions warranted it, but not because of the fear and hysteria this JACNET report would generate at the Boise Cascade corporate office.

And by the way, not that it matters a whole hill of beans, but it so happens that a very reliable source disclosed to me a few weeks earlier that Linda was the one who placed the Mickey Finn in my sandwich that evening. The sweet taste of revenge didn't banish the bitter taste of tainted tuna like I thought it would, though. Oh, well. As they say in Medford, birds die.

*   *   *

I was running down the home stretch, and the interview list had ballooned to about forty employees, excluding big Rick, that is, since he had tendered his resignation just a few weeks earlier. In corporate investigation terms, he didn't count when assessing the overall impact of the investigation. Believe it or not, I was strongly encouraged by K and S to persuade him to stay on even though he represented no credible resource for information relevant to the case. In other words, it was like cutting a death row inmate down from his noose and then executing him a few minutes later. If he died on the rope, it was a suicide; if he died in the chair, it was points toward reelection for the D.A. and the governor.

My plan to tie up the many loose ends into a tightly woven knot in the waning moments of the investigation was tangled at best. I would first go through George to buy a weapon from Scott. This would fulfill my promise to JACNET and make both K and S and myself happy in the process. I would then make a second deal with Devon, which would not only ensure his prosecution but represent a major score for all parties involved. When the many ancillary players rolled on one another and the head count was tallied, it would be a boon for K and S and most assuredly be reflected in my bonus. Finally, I would attempt to get Jim to grease the path to the supposed floating lab operated by the wrecking company owner. This was probably a pipe dream, but it represented the closest thing to a coup de grace I could imagine.

The discord between Scott and me had run so deep, however, that I had no expectation of salvaging anything remotely resembling an actual business relationship before the case wrapped. The key was to find the source of his weapons by tracing the serial number (if it wasn't filed down) of one of them back to its last recorded owner; for instance, a legal owner who sold a gun to a licensed pawnshop that later reported the gun stolen. If the pawnshop were involved in the scam, Scott would immediately roll over on them. The pawnshop in turn would claim that Scott stole the gun from them. Either way, the D.A. wins and so do we. Based on the volume and continuous flow of weapons through his trunk, however, I presumed that he wasn't stealing the guns. I was only half right.

Chapter 26

George reluctantly agreed to purchase a weapon from Scott on my behalf, but not without considerable probing as to why I wanted it specifically from him. After explaining that I needed a distinctive weapon—a fully automatic MAC-10 with a two-inch barrel and an abridged stock—and that I had it on good faith that Scott was plugged in with all the right people, he acquiesced.

The price of the gun was a cool two grand—more than I was willing to shell out on my own, but the price of the weapon nonetheless. I had George offer Scott five hundred dollars up front with a guarantee of two thousand more within thirty days of delivery. Scott agreed.

After giving George very specific instructions not to conduct the transaction in the Boise Cascade parking lot, I sat in my car one day during my lunch break and watched as Scott lifted a MAC-10 from the trunk of his car, which was located in the far corner of the parking lot, and showed it to George. Realizing that once George doled out the cash on closed-circuit TV his employment was all but terminated, I moved into action, intent on scuttling the deal.

Without so much as a cursory inspection of the weapon, George reached for his wallet, which raised a red flag of overeagerness. The deal would quickly turn ugly if I did not intervene.

"George," I called out from a considerable distance. "Would ya at least check to see if it's plastic for God's sakes?"

Scott hoisted the MAC-10 to his shoulder and then calmly reached into a green canvas bag and removed a large banana clip. I slid my gun out discreetly, not at all comfortable with my present surroundings, especially because of the bullet-fest that might ensue. Raising my weapon slowly in Scott's direction as I scanned my surroundings for onlookers, I said assertively, "I wouldn't!"

"I knew you were a cop, you fucking pig!"

"I'm not a cop, dick breath. I'm just not partial to having machine-gun-toting mill workers accusing me of bein' one." I smiled and scratched my upper lip. "The good news, though, is that you probably wouldn't be loading a clip into a gun that wasn't real. Huh?"

"This gun's for you?"

"Would you've sold it to me if I'd asked?" I took the gun from his hand and laid it in the trunk. "Well?"

"Drop the fucking gun," said a voice creeping up from behind me.

"Hey," Scott yelled. "It's cool. He's not a cop." His voice then lowered considerably. "Come on, man. Someone's gonna . . . See, look. People are noticing, man. Getcha ass over here and chill."

"Just put the gun away, then," the man said.

I tucked it away in my pants and hung my shirt over the top. "Hey, Mike," George greeted him in an ordinary manner, not frazzled in the least by his presence.

"George," he acknowledged. "Who's your friend?"

"Ken? Mike. Mike? Ken."

"Yeah, I heard of you," he said, rancorous. "Let's go, Scott. It's begin-ning to smell a lot like pork around here." The only thing I remember about Mike's appearance was a rather fresh scar that stood out on his right shoulder, consistent with the superficial gash a bullet might cause. The fact that his cropped sleeves were inappropriate for the weather drew my attention to it that much more. Likely the intended outcome.

"How 'bout my gun?" I persisted.

"I'll get back to you."

"Then there's the little matter about the cash. . . ."

"Oh, yeah," Scott said before wadding up the money and hurling it in my face.

"How's that neck of yours, by the way," I shouted as they began to fade from view.

*   *   *

The deal was dead on arrival the moment it began in the parking lot, but I had what I thought I'd been looking for, and what I believed would interest JACNET far more than some small time gunrunner. The individual watching over the deal had been guarding these weapons like a mother guarding her cubs. He was definitely the source. The only question now was who the hell was he?

"So, who the hell was he?"

"Mike," George answered.

"Yeah, I gathered that. Who's Mike?"

"He's a lathe operator at the Boise mill in White City."

"Really?"

"Well, that's how I know him. He's a cop, too. Well, an auxiliary cop, actually."

"What's that?"

"He's an aux . . ."

"Yeah, I heard what you said. I'm not deaf." My mind began to reel, replaying all that had just transpired.

"Don't worry about it. He's cool."

"He's cool? Yeah, that's good. We tried to buy a stolen gun from a cop."

"It's not stolen," he assured me. "He gets them from the evidence room long after they've been used in trial. No one's gonna miss those guns. And even if they did, they'd be traced back to the police. Big shit."

"Big shit? It'll be a real big shit when he gets caught and rats us all out!"

"He's not gonna . . ."

"Arrrr, forget about it, all right?" I pretended to be frustrated, throwing my arms up and walking away. Obviously I was not worried about Mike plea bargaining his way into community service somewhere down the road. What concerned me was that he now possessed my fingerprints and would likely run an FBI check on them. That concerned me quite a bit, actually. Especially as I recalled that an auxiliary cop had been linked to this whole glue/drug business, too. And that scar wasn't helping matters, either.

Before I could respond to that little problem, however, I had to retrieve a very incriminating piece of videotape. To be certain, this undercover corporate investigation work was becoming less direct and rather circuitous and devious. If I wanted things to happen my way, I needed to act and act quickly.

I received an unexpected visit from Gordon the following morning that redefined the word *quickly* for me. Calling me from the Red Lion Inn, apparently the only hotel in town, he asked that I join him and Bud for breakfast. After informing me that the case would wind down over the next few weeks, he showed me the elements that K and S felt were necessary for this to constitute a successful investigation. In addition to his favorite targets, whose cases were all but sewn up, except possibly Devon, there were some new ones. He began with the Green End of the mill; specifically, with an unassuming fellow named Joshua.

"Seen this guy before?" Gordon asked, thumping his finger on a photograph he had placed before me on the table.

"Yeah. Nice guy, actually. Why? You know something about him?"

He slid another photo across the table. This one was a bit more compromising. It was a black-and-white shot of Joshua in a bathroom stall taken from overhead. "See what he's doin' there?"

"Yeah, takin' a dump." I looked up at Gordon. "Just kidding. No, ahhh, he's shooting something in his leg there. Sure, I see it. Doesn't mean anything, though. We have no idea what's in the needle."

"Who gives a shit. He's shooting something illegal. That's all that matters."

"Is he diabetic?"

Bud looked over at Gordon, and Gordon stared blankly at me. "Well?" I nudged.

"Well, what?" Gordon reacted. "I assure you he's not injecting insulin in the bathroom. It's either heroin or speed. Or some hodgepodge concoction. Whatta they call it . . . a soup or something like that?"

"He's a pretty big boy. Maybe it's steroids."

I could see the wind vanish from his sail. "And are they legal?" he said. "No."

"Far cry from heroin, though. With so little time left in the investigation, do we really wanna spend time on crap like this?"

"Doesn't matter. Even if it is steroids, it'll open up the Green End during interviews. If he gives us names, who knows where that might lead. It's a numbers game, and the way I see it, you have nothing on Green End employees, correct?"

"I have nothing on upper management either, but we're not trumping up charges on any of them in hopes of getting someone to roll."

"If we had one of 'em sticking a needle in his arm, we would."

"Put a camera in the executive bathrooms and you might."

"Look, I'm not gonna argue with you this time. Just look into it, okay?"

"Is that all?"

"I want ya to get me something on Tari and George, too. Just something that enables us to talk with them. I think we have enough already, but I'd like a little something more substantial."

"Far as I can tell, they're both clean. You know something I don't?"

"Meaning?"

"Am I mistaken, or did you just say you probably had enough already to interview the both of them?"

"*You* gave us the information. They may be clean, but they sure know a hell of a lot about what goes on in that place. It'll be interesting to talk with them."

"If that's gonna be your criteria, hell, why not interview the entire shift. Interview me. Hell, interview the whole fuckin' mill for that matter."

"Why do you give a hoot?"

"Because I don't pollute?"

"What?"

"You're the boss, Gordon. I'm gonna do what you want, regardless. As long as it's legal. So don't get your ovaries in an uproar. I'm just tryin' to give you information you may not have considered, instead of sitting here like a yes-man."

"A 'yes' every now and then wouldn't hurt." He tilted his head sideways and looked over at Bud. "Now I can't remember where the hell I was."

Bud finally spoke. "I think we need to talk about Caracas."

"That's right, Caracas. What can we get from him in the next few weeks?"

"We don't really need him to sell me anything if I get Devon. Devon's the number one guy in that ring, anyway. But if I were you, I'd interview Caracas and offer him a walk if he gives up other Spreaders. Talk to him about the rapist, too. With his testimony and the ones we pick up as a result, we should be able to fire that child-molesting prick. Same goes for George. He'd give ya Jerry. I'm sure of it."

"You really think Caracas'll give us other Spreaders like Steve and that married couple there . . . the bosses? Tamara and Larry, I believe."

"And the rapist," I said enthusiastically in response to his detached expression. "Let's not forget about him."

"Right, right. Okay. Let's approach it that way. Unless he offers to sell you something, of course."

"How 'bout Scott?" I said.

"What about him? We don't have anything on him yet. We had something on tape recently that looked like a real score, but the tape went tits up on us."

"You interview the right people, and you've got him for a major charge of harassment for what he did to Doug that day."

"Oh, yeah, right." It was obvious that he had no intention of charging Scott with this disgusting offense. The legal implications for Boise and the fact that the firm didn't get points for such finds were probably at work in his less-than-spirited response.

*　*　*

The first chance I got that day I rushed over to where Tari was seated at the automatic stacker to the rear of the mill. As I hemmed and hawed in my pitiful attempt to explain the trouble I had inadvertently got her into, she dropped a bombshell.

"I'm quitting."

"What? The job? Why?"

"I'm gonna marry Keith, and we're gonna start our own excavation business."

"Just like that," I reacted, forgetting what it was I had set out to tell her. "What about us?"

"There never was an 'us.' You have your investigation, and when it's over, so will we . . . be."

"What?"

"Admit it, you've used me, mostly. You never wanted a relationship with me."

"Where'd that come from? I thought we worked all that out."

"When? When have you ever tried to date me like a real . . . well, you know . . . dating thing?"

"It's had nothing to do with the investigation, and it's had everything to do with your relationship. And this confirms it. You've never let go of this guy, and it's obvious you love him. But don't lay that guilt trip on me. If you were totally free, then, yeah, I'd've dated you. But you never were. But I thought we could at least be friends."

"Like I'm ever gonna see you again. When your case is over, you're hittin' the bricks. I'll never see you again. Come on, admit it. You're gone after this, and you're never comin' back."

"No, not if you get married. I don't think Keith-baby would approve. And I can't say as I'd blame him. Is it what you want, though? Marriage? With him?"

She thought for a moment. "Yeah," she said with a smile and a hint of revelation. At that moment, while studying her face fiercely, I finally believed she loved him, and I was actually quite pleased.

"Bye, Tari. Be happy." We hugged for what seemed an eternity and then parted. I never laid eyes on her again.

In retrospect, it turned out for the best for all parties involved. Unless you count K and S's interests, that is. Tari would never suffer the indignity of a Krout and Schneider postinvestigation interrogation—I mean interview—and Keith would get what he earned.

With one innocent person spared the uncertainty of an interview, I took my broom in hand and swept my way across the mill to Chain Six, pretending to myself that I could simply sweep aside my thoughts and feelings for Tari. I couldn't.

"Yo!" I called to George, who was dashing about on his Hyster.

George immediately spun around and barreled toward me. "Hey, what's up? You look a little funny. Everything okay?"

"What are ya doin' this eve . . ."

"Booch," Stan hollered from a ways away, "Where the hell you been?! I need you to help break Three! We're fifteen minutes behind schedule over there!"

"I'll meet ya in the parking lot after work," George advised.

"Sounds good, I'll . . ."

Stan's voice swelled with impatience. "Let's go, damn it!"

"Could ya grab Caracas for me, and tell 'im I need to talk to him?"

"Sure thing. Later, dude," George said while speeding away and tipping his cap to Stan.

*   *   *

Caracas sent a Spreader over to break me for lunch, something that was almost unheard of at the mill. Spreaders were simply too narcissistic to subjugate themselves in service to bottom feeders like us. To them, we were just above Feeders and right below pollywogs on the biological food chain.

Although I had called the meeting, it was as though he had summoned me. He was holding court in the break room when I arrived. "Guys." He motioned for several employees to leave. "Excuse us, please. We have *real* business to discuss here."

When the break room cleared, except for some employees huddled in the corner who appeared not to know better, I asked Caracas to adjourn with me to a more private location.

"Worried about those people? Don't. They won't have a clue what you're talking about. What are we talking about, by the way?"

"I got some cash I need to spend. You think we can get something going with Devon?"

"Hey, the ruse is over,"

My heart sank. "How's that?"

"You know *I'm* the man, not Devon. I'll getcha whatcha need. Whatta ya need?"

I did my best to conceal my sense of relief. For a moment, I thought he was going to tell me that Mike ran my prints and had discovered my true identity. "I need at least five ounces, but I don't need it from you."

"What's the difference?"

"The difference is that if something goes wrong with this small-time shit I'm doin' with him, the people I work for can still lay down some big scores with you. All's I'm doin' right now is demonstrating to my people your ability to come through with quality shit on short notice. Once I've established that, you and I will strike up something with your wrecking yard buddy and that Mimi chick."

"That's where she gets it," he said ordinarily. "Why not get that goin' now?"

"Let's do it, but I'm still gonna need a few ounces from Devon, baby, ASAP."

"I'll have 'em melt a board."

I grinned. "Ahhh, I still have my doubts about all that stuff, I tell ya."

"You shouldn't. Haven't you tested the crank that came from that piece of wood yet?"

"The hand is quicker than the eye."

"Thomas, Thomas. So full of doubt. I'll set up a meeting with Mr. Green, and we'll see what we can do about filling your stocking for Christmas."

"Mr. Green? Who's Mr. Green?"

His delay in answering suggested he had spoken out of school. "It's a pseudonym. An alias, kind of. He provided us with that shipment that rainy afternoon."

"And Mimi?"

"She . . . Well, she sorta makes sure we get the quality glue we need to fill our customer's orders. That's why we need Mr. Green for *your* little order. I assume you have no need for a dinghy. I gather you can transport safely already or you wouldn't be here, correct?"

"Yeah." I paused. "I'm just tryin' to figure out what you just said. Pseudonym? You've been screwing around with that thesaurus again, haven't ya? You're gonna sprain your tongue one of these days if you're not careful."

"I was gonna say nom de plume, but you kinda caught me off guard there."

In an effort to catch him off guard again, I added, "Green? Owner of Emerald Wrecking, I presume?"

He fought for control of his grin. "Yeah, did I say . . . ?"

"No. I've dealt with other people around here that use him. He's got the lab that floats. At least that's how the urban legend goes."

"If you're paying top dollar, he'll probably do business with you. He'll wanna meet first, I would imagine. You up for it?"

"Set it up. But it can't go down until I've filled my immediate need. The ounces from Devon?"

"Yeah, sure. I don't quite get it, but sure, we can do that first."

I was reasonably sure that it was safe to demand this odd strategy with Caracas because he knew that I had already consummated a deal with Devon and that it hadn't led to his arrest. I was counting heavily on his not knowing the two-deal rule governing indictments.

*   *   *

Under the guise that a high-level source within Boise management had confided in me that there was a narc among us, I briefed George on what to do if he were ever called in for questioning. First and foremost, I told him that I was informed that if a person admitted himself into a detoxification clinic prior to being accused of an offense, they were given immunity from any disciplinary action. Providing they weren't caught for dealing drugs, of course. This was not only accurate information about the rules of engagement but represented the only hope he had for saving his life. At least in my humble opinion. Funny thing about these rules of engagement. Those affected by them generally don't learn about them until it's too late. It's the UCI equivalent of the *Animal House* "Double Secret Probation" clause.

I then told him that cooperation would be generously rewarded and that all of us who witnessed Jerry rape that young girl, for instance, should use that information as a bargaining chip.

George appeared visibly distraught, almost numb. "What are you gonna do?"

"I'm not sure. I have less ties here than you. No family. I don't own anything here but my car. I don't know. Maybe I'll move on to greener pastures."

"Maybe I will too."

"You're gonna be fine. Just do what I'm telling you."

"Why . . . why'd this guy in management tell you all this?"

I placed two fingers to my nose and sniffed. "Of course," he reacted. "What's *he* gonna do?"

"Are you kidding? Those guys never get in trouble. He's only telling me so I don't rat him out."

"I should've been buyin' from you. I probably wouldn't be in any trouble right now."

"I told ya before, I don't sell directly to anyone here at the mill. He and I have another arrangement entirely."

"Yeah, what's that?"

"It's a whole boat dinghy–drugs thing. It's complicated."

"You mean with the glue?"

Another successful fishing expedition. "You know about it?"

"I thought you would've known that. Aren't you working with Caracas on this? He didn't tell ya I knew about all that?" He observed the puzzled look on my face. "Hmmm. I guess not. That's strange."

"Emerald Wrecking, right?"

"You asking or telling?" he said.

"Well, I haven't been formally introduced yet. I've met Mimi, though. Lovely gal. I did a run for them over Crater Lake."

"So I heard. I don't know all the details of how things work, and frankly I don't wanna. But if you're asking me about Mimi and Green, there's not much I can tell you. Green cooks it, and Mimi packages and distributes it. Why Crater Lake when he cooks on the ocean is way above my pay grade. And how it all works—the glue, the boats—I haven't the first clue. You probably know more than I do, I bet."

"Why you know about any of this is what I wanna know. I mean, why would anyone tell *you?*"

"Where do you think the profits from the sale of my first home went? It's wrapped up in this whole mess."

"I thought your wife took you to the cleaner's."

"Not the dry cleaner's. She emptied the checking and savings accounts, but I got the net on the house sale. It's kinda hard to run with the house sale profits."

I shook my head with confusion and shrugged off the many questions I had banging about my head. "What . . . ? Have they paid you back?"

"It's just started. They haven't made the first boats yet."

"And you have *how* much invested?"

"Eighty."

"Eighty?" I gasped. "Do you even know if it works?"

"No," he said sarcastically. "I'm goin' on a hunch. Of course, I know it'll work! They demonstrated it for me. Several times. It works all right. Purest shit I ever had."

"Are they lookin' for me to invest?"

"Why the hell'd you think they tell you so much? Of course. You're gonna, aren'tcha?"

"That's why they chose a rainy day," I mumbled to myself.

"How's that?"

"How many people have invested in this whole thing? That you know of, anyhow?"

"I don't know. Maybe ten . . . that I know of."

"Eighty apiece?"

"I don't know. It varies. Why?"

"When'd you first hear about this glue stuff?"

"Ummm. I guess it was about January or February. Why, what's the matter?" His voice had a sinking feel to it. "My money's gone, isn't it?"

"No, it's not that. It's . . ." my voice faded as I attempted to conceal my insight. As I replayed all the events of the case, I started to realize that this could have been a ruse from the beginning. A sleight-of-hand trick that formed the cornerstone of an elaborate scam.

The con began before my arrival, so I was sure that it had nothing to do with me. But why would they pull a scam that would eventually blow up in their collective faces? Sure, no one could go to the police when they didn't recoup their investment, but they certainly could band together and take matters into their own hands, especially because they knew who all the other investors were. At least it appeared that George knew. I was long on questions and embarrassingly short on answers . . . and time.

"No, it's not," he said. "It's all gone. I know it. Caracas said the only thing that would screw this deal up is if we lost our jobs. Well, if they lost their jobs and weren't able to make the boats . . ."

"No, I'm sure everything's okay. Look, I gotta take care of some things. Just relax and don't worry about it. I'll take care of things. I promise."

George ran his hands through his hair several times and rocked forward to press his head against the steering wheel. He was on the brink of a complete mental and emotional breakdown, and I was powerless to do anything about it. I might as well have been saying, "There, there, now. There, there."

"If there's an investigation goin' on, I'm ruined . . . and there's nothing you or anyone else can do about it now."

"I've got some things to take care of. I'll call ya tomorrow, okay?"

"Sure. Whatever."

"Just give it time. It won't look so bleak." Or in other words, *there, there, now. There, there*.

"See ya."

"You know," I started, not knowing where I was going. "I was talking to this . . ."

Just then, Shelly threw open the back door to George's car and dove into the back seat. "Hey, guys. Where we goin'?"

"I don't know. George's a little bummed."

"I'm fine. Finish your story." He seemed almost desperate for me to make a point that would help him cope.

"Yeah," I said, hoping to come up with something that made sense. "As I was saying, I was talking to this Japanese girl one time and, I don't know, I guess we were talkin' about babies or something. Anyway, I was tellin' her how proud my brother was that his baby's first words were "Da da." And then I asked her what Japanese babies first words were. She thought for a moment and said, "Da da or papa.""

"I don't . . . what?" George responded with confusion. "What were we . . . How's that relate to my situation?!"

Shelly said, "I don't even know your situation, and I'm tryin' to make sense of what he just said."

"My point is that babies just naturally say "Da da" because it's the easiest or the most natural thing to say. It has no significance. Yet my brother, like all first dads, I guess, was attaching all this significance to it. Like any situation, if you place it in perspective, it's not that significant. Certainly not worth killing yourself over."

"What!" Shelly gasped. "You're thinking of committing . . ."

"No!" George snapped. "What the hell ya tellin' her shit like that for?"

"I didn't mean to say . . . I was just makin' a point. And not a very sharp one, I might add."

"Well," George said, "It actually wasn't all that dull, either. Thanks. I mean, for tryin' at least." A tight, twitchy smile creased his face. "You really were tap dancing there, weren'tcha?"

"No, that actually happened. I dated this Japanese girl back in college. Her name was Barbi, actually. I think that's why I dumped her. Can you imagine a lifetime of 'Hey, Ken. Where's Barbi?'"

"And then there's the language thing." Shelly's demeanor suggested sincerity.

"You're kidding me, right?" I didn't wait for a response. "She spoke English. She was an American. I met her in college."

"Thank God," George said. "It's not the most romantic language, that's for sure. You haveta admit, though, it's a pretty good killing language." He then went on to give his rendition of *Romeo and Juliet* as performed by Japanese actors. It did sound like they were killing each other.

"I don't know. She could be mighty sexy at times."

"That's all you guys ever think about," Shelly said playfully as she leaned into the front seat, her elbows resting on the seatbacks. "It's true. I heard a man thinks about sex once every fifteen seconds."

"I'm sorry," George said. "What were you sayin'?"

"Oh, that's a bunch of horse pucky," I said. "Watch, I'll show you." I pretended to meditate. "No, wait. Give me another chance." Another pause. "Oh, wait. Let me try again. No, no, wait. Wait, I can do this. . . . I swear." Another ten seconds passed. "Okay, how was that? Did I make it?"

"Huh," Shelly asked. "I'm sorry. What'd you say? I was preoccupied with my shopping."

George and I said simultaneously, "What?"

"If I have to explain it, it ain't funny."

George responded with a dull tone. "I have a funny feelin' that even if you explained it, it wouldn't be all that funny. And based on my ex's shopping habits, I don't think I wantcha to, either."

"And on that depressing note," I said, "Whatta ya say we go shoot some pool? Suddenly it seems I have some free time on my hands."

"I'm not depressed, actually. Believe it or not, that stupid thing you said earlier is starting to make some sense to me. I mean, what's the worst that can happen? It's not the end of the world, is it?"

"Sounds like too quick a recovery to me," I said. "Just give it time. All of it. The wife, the job, the money . . . all of it. That's all I was tryin' to say. None of it will destroy you. Believe it or not, my next suggestion was actually gonna be church. . . . Well, God, anyhow." I studied them both for a reaction, knowing that I probably just gave the farm away with regard to my true identity.

"That's not so crazy, really," George said. "Let's go shoot some pool and talk about it."

We did, and for the first time during this dreary investigation, I felt that I had made a real difference.

Although the temperature had fallen well below what any sensible person would consider optimum convertible conditions, when I left George and Shelly, I dropped the top, popped in Leo Sayer's "When I Need Love" and went cruising about town. As I ruminated over the loss of a relationship that never really was, Sayer took me back to a much sweeter time in my life, a time when "love" only applied to family, friends and puppy dogs and could only be truly experienced, at least the romantic variety, vicariously through songs like this one.

That night convinced me that the repeat button on the CD player should come with a giant disclaimer: "This option may enhance or distort memories of lost relationships. Please consult your physician if use of this button persists." Long about the time Mr. Sayer hit his fifteenth straight saxophone solo and, dare I say, his hundredth "I just hold out my hand," I was reflecting fondly on the last words ever spoken between Tari and me. My recollection, which admittedly may have been a bit distorted by RBS, or repeat button syndrome, was that our parting dialogue went something like this: "Here's looking at you, kid." For which I believe her response was, "Frankly, my dear, I don't give a damn." I've had a healthy respect for the repeat button and Leo Sayer's "When I Need Love" ever since.

Chapter 27

After quickly laying waste to the Joshua issue by purchasing a couple vials of steroids from him, I delved heavily back into the Boise riddle: "Was there crystal in them there barrels of glue?"

I went to the Hideaway Club one night when I wasn't working and waited for the steady flow of Boise employees to stream through. With my eyes peeled for Caracas and Devon, I politely greeted anyone that smelled like lumber or had the overall countenance of petrified wood. Three hours and three beers later, at exactly midnight, they walked in together . . . and they were looking for me. When they saw me perched on my stool, they looked into my eyes, and I saw what they must have seen. Let's just say it has wings and leave it at that.

They sat on either side of me at the bar, and without preamble Caracas said, "Can you get a quarter million?"

"Sounds a bit steep for a few ounces."

"I'm serious," he said. "Green and Mimi gave the green light to cut you in. On the entire operation. You'll get back ten times that."

"I suppose that's better than a Mimi light," I quipped. "But again, I need the five ounces from Devon first."

"What are you, *nuts*? That's chump change. I'm offering you the whole ball of wax here."

"Wax from your fucking ear. You're not offering *me* shit. My boy needs to test the consistency of your product before he takes a chance like that.

It's his call. If you can't come through on that in a timely manner, how's he gonna trust you with a quarter mill?"

"You've seen the qual . . ."

"Look," I said harshly. "You're not hearing me here! You've heard the conditions! If I don't get the ounces by the end of the week, all bets are off. Dig?"

"I'll get it for ya," Devon said. "Just say when."

"Day after tomorrow! Same place. Call me that morning with the time. I work that day, so make it morning."

"Okay, okay." Caracas seemed distressed. "Wait here a second. I wanna make some calls. Just wait here, okay? Here." He tossed a wad of cash onto the bar. "Just relax and have a couple drinks."

I peeled off a hundred-dollar bill from the top, believing much smaller bills lay beneath the rind. I was wrong. All told, there was over two thousand dollars of succulent pulp. If he had tossed me that grubstake a couple days earlier, I would simply have thought him flush with money and carefree about dispensing with it. I knew better now. Like everything else in this elaborate machination, this was a prop, and as such demanded a particular response. Letting my conscience be my guide, I bought a couple drinks, tipped big and stuffed the rest in my pocket.

"Let's go," Caracas blurted the moment he returned to the bar.

"Go where?"

Devon answered, "To meet Green, right?"

"To meet Green," Caracas confirmed.

"Wa . . . wa . . . wait," I stammered, unclenching Caracas's fingers from my triceps. "Were you hearing me back there? I want the sample first."

"And you'll get it," Caracas assured. "But I want you to meet Green and go over our offer in advance so we don't haveta waste any more fuckin' time after you give the ounces to your boy. See what I'm sayin'?"

I thought for a second and then agreed to the request. "I'll follow you. Where we goin'?"

"Emerald Wrecking."

*   *   *

I drove into the wrecking yard at such a slow rate of speed that I could hear the pebbles grind beneath my tires and the exhaust rat-a-tat-tat behind my head. A scrawny white man pulled back a chain-link fence, and we crept our way past. As I shut the car down, I placed the stick in reverse just in case I needed to make a hasty getaway. I followed Caracas and Devon into the structure, where the only light available crawled out from beneath a weathered wooden door.

After Caracas knocked out a ridiculous code on the door, the door fell open. Mimi was there along with a man I presumed was the infamous Mr. Green. Plastered all over the walls were posters of scantily clad women toting monkey wrenches and paint buffers, bent stiff-legged over a wide assortment of vintage automobiles. Something in the way Mimi accosted me with a French kiss the moment I stepped into the room told me that she was probably not offended by Green's rather pedestrian taste in art. Mimi withdrew her lips slowly and then introduced me to Mr. Green. "A handshake will do," I said.

When he shook my hand I detected a roughness that suggested the wrecking business was more than just a facade. Twisting in his fingers what appeared to be a fake mustache, he presented his proposition. "Boise's about to get a very large order of dinghies that it needs to fill. We can increase that order if we come up with the capital in time to fill it."

"I'm afraid you have me at a loss. Caracas hasn't explained all the details of this operation. At least not enough for me to explain it to my people, and certainly not enough to get them to fork over so gratuitously. What exactly are we talking? The crystal goes in the glue. The order comes in for X amount of dinghies. The special glue is used. The boats go out and are then distributed to the customers who will in turn break down the glue and extract the drugs? Is that it, basically?"

"Generally, yes."

I leaned my head back. "How do you control waste, and how do you ensure that the correct glue is used on each order?"

"Good questions. As you can see, everyone on this Spreader team— Steve, Devon, Caracas—is involved. They won't let any glue go to waste. We don't care if the dinghy floats. You follow? The Rustler on that shift is also involved. He's the one who picks the glue." He looked about the room and then flipped his hands out to his sides. "Anything else?"

"Plenty. In fact, the most obvious question of all: Why go through so much trouble? Why not just sell it *as is* like the rest of the free world?"

"Distribution," he said mildly. "We plan to ship throughout the country. We've got orders from all corners of the U.S. As you may or may not know, it's a federal offense once you cross your own state border. You know, interstate commerce laws. With this method, the only risk we run is getting it to Medford and then into the glue."

"Besides cooking it."

"Well, yeah. But *I* assumed all that risk already. And the way I do it, not really much risk at that."

"Yeah, I heard that urban legend already."

"But it's irrelevant. That's all been done already. When these dinghies go out of that mill, no one will be the wiser. *You've* seen it. Did that piece of wood look strange to you before they broke it down and extracted the crystal?"

"I gotta admit, it didn't. But answer me this, how do you get it into the Boise glue? And more importantly, what's the formula for getting it out again later on?"

"Now come on." He unfolded his arms across the table and bobbed his hands like an Italian grandmother prompting a child to eat. "Would ya respect me if I told ya all that? Some things gotta remain a secret, otherwise you and your backers could cut us out like an unborn fetus at a pro-choice rally in a Watts coat hanger factory. Not that I don't trust you, but I gotta keep good business sense about me."

"Bottom line, how much are we talking here?"

"For you? Profit?" He waited briefly for my acknowledgment. "Ten-fold. Maybe eight. But good either way."

"That's *guaranteed*?"

He spoke through his laughter. "I'm tellin' ya, for most of these guys it's an Horatio Alger story. From ditches to riches to bitches."

"And then back to ditches," Mimi said.

"Yeah," Green agreed. "So you should probably leave out the bitches part. And like I tell all of 'em, you be patient and play it cool, and if we don't all get arrested, we all get rich. Filthy rich! Down right pornographic!"

"Arrested?" I thought. "Arrested? Why would he tell everyone that? George mentioned that, too, in fact."

And then it occurred to me. If the Spreaders got arrested or fired before they were able to pull off this crazy scheme, none of the investors could expect to get paid off. Is it possible they knew about the investigation at the mill in advance of my arrival?

"Oh, no, wait," I thought. "George said the scam began back in

January, and I didn't get here until spring. And why would they involve me if they already knew about the investigation? They wouldn't want to take a chance on me figuring out their scam, would they? They would probably want to get fired for something small, too, which explains why they've been dealing in such small quantities with so many different people."

And then it struck me. "The investigators before me arrived about the same time this scam began," I thought. "Is it possible they got wind of the investigation but didn't know who the investigator was? Given that the two prior investigators lost their jobs somewhere along the way probably means these guys didn't know for certain who the investigator was. Maybe they do think I'm a player. Maybe that's why they were dragging things out. Could it be they were just waiting for someone to catch them? That would also explain why Devon was so willing to sell me ounces. After all, that's a pretty serious offense. He couldn't possibly think I was the narc. He and the rest of 'em weren't wanting to spend any more time in jail than they had to. The offenses they'd be willing to get fired or arrested for were surely minor ones. Just enough trouble to get taken out of a position to be able to carry out this hare-brained con. I was probably just another coincidental mark to them who just happened to come along while they were waiting to get fired or arrested. Or both."

"Could these guys be that smart? Then again, what's the alternative? That they mix glue and crystal and sell it in boats? Pleeease." I was getting dizzy with the possibilities.

"I'll make it happen," I said, extending my hand to shake. "I'll need to bring him those ounces as a show of good faith."

"Agreed." He turned his head sideways and stared into my eyes. "You feelin' all right? You look a bit peaked."

"No, I'm fine." My speech was brisk and gravelly. "Just haven't eaten in a while, that's all."

"Well, go get some rest," Green said. "Nothing's worth killing yourself over."

Chapter 28

It was the following day, just three hours before I was scheduled to go to work, when the dreaded phone began to ring. "Ken," I said before letting out a great big yawn.

"Yeah, it's Joe. Can you talk?"

"Sure. It's refreshing to hear someone ask me that first."

"Your people pretty careless, I take it?"

"You haveta ask? So what's up?"

"The D.A.'s wrapping things up. I guess we don't get Devon after all, huh?"

"Why? Why she ending it all of a sudden-like?"

"Oh, I guess that was probably my fault. I think I mentioned that you guys were winding down your investigation here real soon. She says she wants to make sure all the T's are crossed before you go. We've gotta grand jury convening day after tomorrow. Our final report has to be on her desk this afternoon. Translation—we're outta time, buddy."

"So Devon walks, and a pissload of Spreaders along with him?"

"Unless you can get a deal set up within the next hour or so."

"Are you offering?"

"Well, I wasn't, but . . . Do you really think you can do that? 'Cause if ya can, Mike and I might be able to throw together a report in time to meet our deadline."

"Might? Because it's a lot of effort for 'might.'"

"No, we can do it. We can do it. Is that the direction we're . . . "

"I'll call ya," I said and abruptly hung up.

I called Devon, and when I wasn't able to reach him, I immediately phoned Caracas. It was the beginning of the cold season and apparently the hunting season as well. And that is exactly where I was told Devon could be found at the time my call came through. Using the greatest sense of urgency I could marshal, I implored Caracas to act quickly, insisting that an impending meeting with my supplier was pushing the time clock ahead.

With the impression I made earlier that my investment in the dinghies hinged upon the proven consistency and surety of their crystal pipeline, Caracas was propelled into action. Paging Devon in the thicket would not have been a big deal had Devon the foresight to place his pager on 'vibrate' before leaving the house that morning. But he didn't, and I'm told that the page arrived at the most inopportune moment imaginable.

With a cell phone ever at the ready, Devon was able to make timely contact with Caracas and beat a path post haste to the same park where we had conducted business earlier. With one stop along the way, that is: to pick up a package from Mimi. A package that would be his undoing.

I didn't have much time to talk to JACNET before they sent me into the park that day, so I performed a one-way conversation with them via my body-wire while I stood in the frigid air. "I didn't have time to tell you earlier," I said, wrapping my arms tightly around my chest and smacking my shoulders to keep warm. "But Devon's supplier, Mimi, gets her meth from a guy named Green. He owns Emerald Wrecking. We talked about him before. Anyway, he cooks on the ocean. He's got a boat. Run his name through whatever licensing agency he had to go through to make his boat legal, and you'll find out where his slip is located. Or at least where he stores it. He's probably named it after the color green, I'm guessing. You might wanna keep close tabs on Devon today when he leaves. He didn't have any time to prepare for this deal, so he'll probably meet up with Caracas or Mimi right after the buy."

I then spoke to myself. "Where the hell is he? I'm freezin' my cannolies off out here."

A half-hour had passed since the time scheduled for our meeting, and still there was no Devon. The flash of headlights across the park told me we were running out of time. "A few more minutes, guys. He'll be here, I know it."

Fifteen more minutes evaporated, and still no Devon. The flashing lights now smacked of impatience. "Five more minutes. That's all I'm . . . Wait, is that his truck winding through the . . . Yeah, that's it! We're on, guys."

When Devon asked that we conduct business in my car, I had no qualms, because I knew our previous transaction had already earmarked his vehicle for confiscation. He carried with him a boom box that pounded out the popular rap flavor of the month as we moved with little exigency to my vehicle. I was wearing the "hat wire" that day and feeling a bit self-conscious. This time it was my decision, however. I knew the deal would go down in a vehicle and didn't want any of the dialogue getting lost in all that good old Pittsburgh steel that lay below the windshield. After all, we had but one shot at this guy.

First things first, I needed him to quell the radio so JACNET could hear our conversation. "You wanna turn that racket down, please. I've got a splitting headache."

"I didn't plan on playin' it in the car. It's all show."

"Fine," I acted hurried. "Let's just get this shit over with."

"Don't blame me. I got here as fast I could. Do you know where I was before Caracas called me? Hunting! I don't wanna be here any more than you do."

"It's not that I don't wanna be here," I clarified. "it's just that I have a deadline. My boy wants to see that you guys can come through at the drop of a hat."

"I don't know *why*. The main reason I'm even here is to show good faith and to prove we can come through with the ding . . ."

I stopped him before he could finish the word dinghy. Not only would that bring up more questions with JACNET than I was prepared to answer, but it might also have formed the basis of an entrapment defense later on. If he could demonstrate that I, and therefore the police, were persuaded that such a thing were possible, he could then use that information to suggest that the only reason he sold the drugs to me in the first place was because I promised many hundreds of thousands of dollars down the road. It was a stretch, given that he would probably have to admit to the fraud as well, but I wasn't taking any chances. "Doesn't matter. You got the crank?"

He popped open the CD player mounted at the top of the boom box and then turned the entire mechanism one and a half turns counterclock-wise. The innards of the CD player sprang up about a half-inch, and he quickly removed them. He then withdrew what was obviously consider-ably more than the few ounces I had ordered. Tossing the weighty bag onto my lap, he said perfunctorily, "You can pay us the remainder when we finish the rest of our business."

I knew I couldn't take anything on credit, but there were other issues to consider as well. The bag resembled a kilo and certainly weighed as much, but it was moist, and fresh crank tended to weigh significantly more than dried crank that had been cut fifteen times to Tuesday. But if I gave it back, I had to do so with as little discussion as possible of the amount being offered to me and for what purpose. If I would have taken the amount of drugs he was offering and stipulated, on tape, to that amount, he would have done some serious time in prison. I personally didn't think that such a severe punishment was necessary for him to learn his lesson.

I quickly made the judgment that the entire dinghy story was a ruse and that I wasn't going to pursue it any further. "I wasn't looking to build my credit rating with you guys. You got the ounces? Or am I to presume it's included in this package here?"

"You mean, do I have it separate from that there?"

"Ya. I presume you were prepared for me to say no? I don't wanna be cuttin' and weighin' this shit out here."

"Yeah, of course. I got it right here." He reached into the boom box and pulled out another package. "Why, you want it instead?"

"Yeah," I said, not wanting to say that I was keeping the kilo until I had what I was paying for in my hands. When he placed the ounces on the console between us, I counted out the money and then vaguely concluded, "That's all I need to pacify my boy at this time. I don't really need this bag here." If he made any further reference to my keeping the kilo, I would simply give it back. If he didn't, I would keep it and dump it out the window on the way back. He never uttered another word about it. Of course, he didn't have the luxury of knowing we were on tape.

The fact remains, if I had given him back the kilo he would have been suspicious. So unless I wanted to find myself ducking every time a car backfired, I preferred to play along. What would it matter, anyhow? I planned to be long gone before my first installment ever came due. More importantly, I also had the same excuse they intended to use on their dupes (investors) when they didn't repay. I would be arrested with the rest of my co-conspirators and therefore unable to consummate the deal. The beauty of the thing was that Devon could not go to the police, and, if this whole dinghy thing were all a ruse, this kilo would cut deep into their profits. And if it wasn't a ruse, at the very least this was a chunk of crank that would never reach the streets. If you think this seems a bit confusing, try assimilating all this information in about three seconds with so much at stake. In any case, I couldn't see the downside. At least not in the time I had to consider things. I took the kilo.

Now, how to get rid of it? As you will recall, when I rendezvoused with JACNET my vehicle would be searched top to bottom along with my person. There had best not be a kilo of crystal methamphetamine where there were only supposed to be a few ounces.

As Devon drove away, I inserted "Smuggler's Blues" into my CD player and, when I saw the JACNET vehicle backing out of its space, I gently pitched the kilo out my window into some shrubbery that bordered the parking lot. With their concentration diverted by my loud music (they would likely jump to turn the volume down on their receiver), the direction of Devon's departure (they would probably have him tailed and need to radio his present course to the surveillance vehicle) and the simple act of backing out of their parking space, I was certain they would not notice what I did. I was correct.

I returned to the park immediately following my meeting with JACNET and recovered the kilo. As I poured the contents slowly into a shallow creek that ran crookedly along the edge of the park, I thought not of the danger I was running, but rather the unethical depths to which I was willing to sink in order to strike a blow against this pandemic scourge called drug abuse. Like one pestilence afflicting another, I knew what it took to defeat them. It just so happens that in my covenant with my conscience, the firstborn son was named Ethics, not Morality. The cliché "It takes a thief to catch a thief" didn't become a cliché without having at least a shred of truth to it.

Joe got the report to the D.A. with about three minutes to spare, and my meeting with the grand jury was on the docket.

Chapter   29

When the D.A. and JACNET prepped me for the closed grand jury the following afternoon, I was less concerned about those I had investigated finding out than I was about the grand jury not cozying up to the notion of undercover investigators in their workplace. If the fundamental concept rankled with them, it didn't matter how many volumes of evidence we had in support of our case. They would not hand down a single indictment. And according to the district attorney, that was a distinct possibility.

After the district attorney laid the foundation and detailed my role in the investigation, she turned the floor over to me. With as much authority as I could convey, I presented the generic blueprint of an undercover corporate investigation.

When the questions began, they seemed innocent enough. There was a general consensus that everyone we sought to indict deserved it. In fact, the likelihood of guilt was never a point of contention. Our methods for determining that guilt were, however.

"You said you use cameras," a young woman began to explore. "Where do you place them? You mentioned the parking lot and in offices and such, but there aren't any offices where you worked, right? At least in the part of the mill *you* worked in, correct? So where else do you put cameras?"

"If your question is 'do we place cameras in areas where people have a legitimate expectation of privacy,' I gotta tell ya that's strictly prohibited by law. But you know, we put 'em in break rooms, anywhere where ya might find a phone, in all kinds of nooks and crannies throughout the workplace where people might hide. Places like that."

I never once said that we didn't place cameras in the bathrooms at Boise because she never actually asked. She asked about generic practices, and because this was my first case, I was not qualified to answer in such broad, sweeping terms. And besides, although it was highly inappropriate to do so, such cameras had no bearing on the grand jury's decision-making process because we never used any of that evidence against those we sought indictments against. It was as if that evidence was suppressed. Indeed, none of the recordings made by K and S, whether illegal or legal, were ever used as evidence. It was simply a tool for focusing the investigation.

A young man leaped in. "Now who . . . You work for the . . . Well, you're private, but you work for the police?"

"Not exactly. I work for a private company that was hired by Boise. Only when an investigator uncovers criminal activity are the police called in."

His face shriveled with confusion. The district attorney clarified the relationsip for him. "The police . . . that is to say, the task force, was involved from the outset. They, along with my office, mind you, gave strict parameters in which Mr. Bucchi was allowed to operate. It's very, very . . ." She held her hands out before her. "It's extremely controlled."

"So he's wired the whole time he's there?"

"Well . . . not exactly." The D.A. began to fumble over her words.

I explained. "What she's sayin' is that . . . Well, let me ask you this. Do you work in a big company?"

"Yeah, pretty big, I guess."

"If I were undercover at your company . . ."

"Not likely," he chuckled. "We don't have anything on the order of magnitude of Boise's problems."

"Don't count on it," I replied as I watched the D.A.'s face pucker. "There's no such thing as a drug-free company, I assure you. But that's besides the point. Take your company, for instance. You wouldn't want me taping all your private conversations with me if you were not involved in any sort of illegal activity, would ya?"

"I would probably hate it even more if I *was* doin' something illegal," he said with a candid smile. Everybody laughed.

"Good point. But the point is, we try to focus our recordings, whether it be audio or visual, on areas and people and situations that have the highest probability of reaping rewards. It not only protects the innocent employees' privacy; it also saves the company and the state lots of money in the process."

"I'm satisfied with that explanation, but now I have another question. . . ."

"What's that?" I asked.

"What's to stop you . . . And I'm not sayin' that you personally did this. But what's to stop you from misleading and entrapping someone when you're not wired?"

"What's to stop a cop from doing the same?" I proposed hypothetically. "Nothing, I suppose. But if you listen to all these tapes carefully, you won't find a hint of impropriety. Not a hint. And the reason is simple: I'm good at what I do, and I don't have to cut corners or resort to shoddy tactics to get what is necessary for an indictment."

He nodded his head and raised his eyebrows as if to thank me. "And your pay? Does that go based on your results?"

"Doesn't yours?"

"No. I mean, like a head count?"

"Let me ask you this. If . . . Well, let's just say you have two homicide detectives. One solves ninety percent of his cases and the other solves thirty percent. Wouldn't you pay the first one more money?"

"No, I wouldn't. They're both detectives. Same job. Same pay grade."

"But you'd promote the better one first, wouldn'tcha?"

"Yeah, but . . ."

"But what? A promotion is just another form of compensation. If I catch twice as many drug dealers and users as the next guy, shouldn't I get paid more? It certainly makes the company and society a lot safer to have twice the numbers of dealers off the street. My motivation for catching them is irrelevant. What's relevant is that they're drug dealers, plain and simple."

A young white woman interjected, "But at what cost?"

"Do you have any brothers or sisters?" I asked.

"What does that haveta do . . ."

"Because one of those drug dealers I caught might just be the drug dealer that tries to sell your brother his first gram of crank. And one day when your standing vigil at your brother's bedside as he lies there dying of AIDS, you're gonna wish you had done your part to protect him when you had the chance."

The D.A. interrupted in an attempt to quash what she believed was a complete breakdown in the proceeding. "I think we're getting a little side-tracked . . ."

"I don't," a curmudgeonly sounding gentleman said. "I, for one, did not enter into this discussion very comfortable with what you did at this mill, and I think it's gonna take a little more convincing."

I replied, "Has anyone here ever heard of the RICO Statute?"

When no one responded affirmatively, I launched into a stream of consciousness. "No? Okay. Well, the RICO Statute was adopted as a means of dealing with criminal enterprises like the Mafia. That is to say, rack-eteering. I'm sure many of you have heard of that. People who form an alliance for the sole purpose of committing crime. A criminal enterprise, if you will. Not unlike gang members, these people—these names you see before you and the voices you've heard on the tapes—they've come to-gether . . . Hell, they're at that mill for one reason and one reason only: It's the safest place to sell drugs, and they've got a captive audience. Now you can microanalyze what we've done till the cows come home if you suffer from a guilty conscience, but I'm here to tell ya that everyone on that list before you is guilty of the crimes for which they're accused. You've heard the tapes. You've heard how I sound on them. It's not pretty, but to catch a criminal that's what it takes. Becoming like them in almost every way."

"The only thing you haveta decide here today is whether it's better to allow a drug dealer to continue to act with impunity or to send them a message that drug dealers are no longer welcome in Oregon and that this community is fed up with their disease and is willing to give the police whatever creative flexibility they need to eradicate this plague from our society. If you cast your vote against indictment here today, ladies and gentlemen, then don't squawk about the courts, or the cops, or the politi-cians the next time someone gets away scot-free with a heinous crime you and everyone else knows they're guilty of because today was your chance to be counted and you decided to hang your hat on some perceived no-tion of fairness or some technical violation."

When silence fell over the room, I thanked the jurors and excused myself from the proceeding, confident that not a single indictment would be handed down.

About an hour later, the district attorney came into the room where I was waiting impatiently with Joe and Bud and informed us that everyone on the list had been indicted and that the jury's trepidation had been allayed by my candor, albeit arrogant candor.

As I walked out with Joe and Bud, Joe imparted some words of wisdom about how to conduct myself in court if I ever had to return, and then he told me the most amazing thing. "I had the lab test that crystal you got from Linda," he said. "Sure would like to have nailed her. That stuff was the purest I've ever seen. Took forever to isolate that strange . . . ," his voice tapered off as he turned away, ". . . compound, though."

"What's that? What'd you say?"

"Oh, it was nothing. It's just that we had this incredibly powerful crank on our hands, and it had traces of a compound we couldn't identify in our lab. We've never run into that exact type before, and we'd kinda like to know where she got it, that's all. Nothing we can do about it now, though. It's water under the bridge."

"What exactly was different?"

"What's that?"

"The drugs. What was different about it?"

"You see, that's the strange part. When the lab cooked it down, they found this protein . . . it was a gelatinous substance. I think they call it a viscous solution or something like that. Anyway, they said it was a type of collagen. . . . No, collagenous. Yeah, collagenous material. It's consistent with glue. Who knows, maybe it makes the high *stick* with ya longer." He and Bud laughed. And Joe was *still* laughing when he slapped me on the back and walked away. "Call me before you leave town. And Ken? Great job. I know it hasn't been easy, butcha really hit a home run with this one. I hope your company knows that, because *I* sure as hell have appreciated all your hard work."

"Oh, my God," I thought while sustaining a natural smile. "They're gonna walk with all the money and the dinghies to boot. No. No. That can't be. That just can't be. Something's not . . . Could those sons of bitches have pulled this off? Oh my . . . Wait. Wait. Now that I think about it, it did sorta look like Devon was pointing that gun he took from me a fraction too high. Maybe he intended to shoot over my head into Caracas's wall. Maybe it's all been a ruse from the get-go. Except for the glue part. And the blood near the laser pointer—fake? Damn, that'd be tough."

"Are you all right?" Joe said, his head turned sideways.

"Huh?"

"You zoned out on . . ."

"Yeah, yeah, I'm fine. It's nothing." I was still in shock when I said my goodbyes. "Enjoy your retirement, Joe."

"More than you'll ever know."

"I'll catch you before I leave, Bud."

"Yes. We need to debrief," Bud said, consistent to form. There was a sweetness about his 1940s mentality that had me once again yearning for a good old-fashioned world war. Debrief? You gotta love that.

I started to cut across a stretch of matted grass when Joe, still not free of his badge, warned, "Hey! I wouldn't do that! They give tickets around here for that! Use the sidewalk!"

Still in a daze, I responded in a manner that came naturally and required little lucidity. "You know," I called from across the way. "I don't know why they just don't wait until people have beaten paths across the grass before laying these sidewalks and then just lay the sidewalk over the trampled grass! It would make more sense that way! At least the sidewalks would be in the most logical and convenient locations! Pedestrians know more about where to put a sidewalk than engineers!"

"Arrr, you Californians!"

"You frat boys!"

"Oh, and Ken?" Bud called out from the parking lot. "You egress the mill tonight."

"Good ComSec, Bud," I said to myself.

It was Gordon's plan to have me leave work early that evening under the pretense that I was rushing home to Massachusetts because my father had fallen deathly ill. (I bet my father will be thrilled about that.) An actual phone call would come into the mill office, and I would dash out of the building all distraught. The problem, in my opinion, was that once the proverbial crap hit the fan everyone would know that I was the narc. And the problem with that was that many of the accused would know where the incriminating evidence stemmed from. Simply put, the bluff that would eventually be employed concerning the various techniques used by K and

S to gather information would be severely hampered if the accused believed that the only information we had on them came as a result of their dealings with me.

Having carried my investigation full term, I embarked on a day pregnant with possibility, a day that I knew would quickly miscarry if I didn't preserve my cover to the bitter end. Knowing that a lame phone call would soon come into the mill labeling me as THE NARC, I began telling everyone that the word was out that the mill was poised to drop a net over the lot of us. That way, when I departed, it would appear more like I was running from the law than from the lawless.

Just before my shift was over, and indeed my entire stay there, the mill was awash with speculation and gossip. The stories that I had launched in those waning hours as a means of creating the appropriate level of hysteria were scarcely recognizable when they returned full circle to me at shift's end. The most common sentiment among those with much to hide was, "If the shit hits the fan, that S.O.B.'s goin' down with me." The person referred to as "that S.O.B." was different for each person I spoke with. These sentiments certainly suited the investigators who would be conducting interviews at the close of the case.

Shannon, with her eyelids stretched to meet her brows, charged sideways down the chain at me toting about fifty pounds of wood. "Did ya hear? Did ya hear?" she said in rapid succession. "Phil? He's gone! Checked himself into a sanitarium or something! To dry out!"

"No shit?"

"Yeah. Know why?" She barely gave me time to shrug my shoulders. "So he won't lose his job when they nail everyone for the drugs!"

The shock on my face was genuine and went well with what she was saying, but of course had absolutely nothing to do with what she was saying. How in the world did Phil find out about this particular rule of engagement when it appeared no other employee had? Even George, who I had already confided in about this rule, was still at work. If Shannon was right, and Phil really did voluntarily turn himself in, he would escape being fired as a result of his drug use, but he would not escape arrest. And if as a consequence of his arrest he were to become incarcerated for any length of time, he would wind up losing his job as well. Not for the offense itself, but for the unexcused leave of absence.

Many months later I discovered that Phil had been forewarned of the impending interviews by a Boise executive who had conducted unofficial business with Phil during his tenure at the mill. The only saving grace was that Phil's high-level customer didn't have the wherewithal to ascertain that Phil was in a legal quagmire as well. He also didn't realize, thankfully enough, that I was the undercover agent who had brought about those legal travails.

Having put to good use all of the damaging information I had acquired over the past eight or nine months, the reprehensible rumors that I birthed and that now spread throughout the mill took on a life of their own. Productivity must have dropped eighty percent that evening as chain after chain shut down intermittently and arguments flared. To keep up images, I instigated arguments with employees who were rumored to have "ratted me out" to management. The mill became a pandemonium of insidious accusations and cutthroat collusion.

At one juncture that evening, I stood in the eye of the storm and rotated slowly in circles, musing over what was once a tightly woven ecosystem now disintegrating before my very eyes. And then, to my complete surprise, I began feeling melancholy about the mill, the work and especially the people. It was as though I had become invisible or was viewing footage of an old silent film. The hardness of the place had already begun to fade and yellow. And because I knew there would be precious little time for such fond reflection once I fled, I did so likely before it was prudent. The denouement I was sensing was anticlimactic to be sure. Or was it?

Chapter 30

The highly anticipated phone call that would mark the end of my stay at the mill came at about 9:30 P.M. Stan was the carrier of the supposed bad news. "Ken? You got an emergency phone call! Follow me! It's in the office upstairs!" He then shouted over to Jim as we passed by. "Jim! Take Ken's spot on Four!"

"What's up?" I said as we began to trot toward the darkened offices that overlooked the entire operation from high above.

"Not sure! Your mom's on the phone! Says it's urgent!"

"Oh, God," I shouted gravely. "It's after midnight in Massachusetts!"

Stan looked genuinely concerned. "It's upstairs! Follow me!" I pursued him up a narrow, rickety wooden staircase that led directly into a large, barren office area. With glass comprising the better part of an entire wall and the room virtually pitch black, except for a dim green desk lamp and a flashing yellow light on the multiline telephone, I could see clearly all the activity below. "What a great place for a surveillance camera," I thought.

Stan gracefully dismissed himself, but not before offering to help me in any way possible. Stan was a good person at the core, and each time he demonstrated it I was all the more ashamed that my investigation would inevitably lead to his termination.

"Thanks, Stan," is all I said, but my facial expression said good-bye.

"I mean it," he said. "Anything you need . . . anything."

"Go ahead," I said into the phone, still looking at Stan.

"Is it safe to talk?" The voice on the other end said.

"Am I done here?" I said softly.

"I'll be down on the floor," Stan advised, apparently realizing the matter was private. I acknowledged him with a waving hand.

"Yeah, you're done," the voice on the phone said. "Bring me the car we gave you to the theater, tonight. Know where it is?"

"Sure. You gonna be anywhere in particular?"

"You know where the restaurant is that sells the pies? In the same parking lot facing the main drag?"

"Uh-huh."

"Right there."

"Okay. One other thing. . . ."

"What's that?"

"Who the hell is this?"

"It's Mike. Reed. You remember me. We met when you came out here to interview."

"Oh, yeah. Sure. I remember. When ya gonna be there?"

"I'm headed there now."

"Well, give me . . . Ummm . . ."

"Is everything okay?" he asked.

A sudden flurry of activity and commotion from the Spreaders caught my attention. "Hello?" Mike queried with a ruffled voice. But I didn't respond. "Are you okay?" he asked again, becoming even more agitated. But I still didn't answer.

As I gazed through the smoke-colored glass, I became riveted on the activity below. Caracas and company were milling about in a frenzied manner, occasionally pointing upward in my general direction. Although I couldn't see their lips, never mind read them, I knew what they were saying. I was fleeing with their forty thousand dollars' worth of methamphetamine, and they weren't particularly amused.

"Ken! Is everything all right?" Mike shouted.

"Yes. Everything's fine. Give me forty-five minutes. If I'm not there by then, call the police." I didn't wait for a response and immediately hung up the phone. Like ants transferring the scent of a kill along, one to another, the Finish End, where the Spreaders were located, became a bedlam of hyperactivity. In order to get to where my car was parked, I would need to pass directly through the Spreaders. There was a rear exit, but no feasible way to get to it and then out to my car before they nabbed me. So I stood . . . and I watched.

A small band of employees, maybe eight men, led by Devon, began marching in my very specific direction. I then saw George, mounted atop his Hyster, dart out from behind one of the Spreaders toward Chain Three. When he arrived at the chain, ahead of the lynch mob, he leaned over and whispered something in Chief's ear. The gaggle was now just twenty feet behind him and moving determinedly in my direction. I remained steadfast and still. This was not some macho display of temerity on my part, I assure you. I simply didn't have the will or the energy to fight any longer. Or escape, for that matter. All I kept thinking was, "What a bad time for that to happen." I continued to watch—and wait.

Just as George's Hyster disappeared behind Dryer Four, I saw Chief and Matthew move up to intercept the gaggle that was headed toward me. My eyes volleyed between them and George's Hyster as it flickered from sight each time it passed behind an obstruction that lay in its path. When George turned the corner behind Dryer Four, I knew he was coming to see me. Yet I did nothing.

By the time George charged up the stairs, the mob had pushed Chief and Matthew aside, apparently not dissuaded by whatever the two had said to them. George slapped open the door with such force that it shattered the small port window at its center when the door collided with the wall. "It's now or never," he said, winded.

"What's going on, George?" I spoke in a monotone.

He took a couple of short breaths. "You know what it is." He exhaled profusely, smacking his fist on his thigh. "Now let's get the hell outta here."

"Where we gonna . . ."

"I can get us out the back way. Now shut the hell up and let's go!" He approached the window and laid his hands on the glass, at about eye level. "Fuck! They're almost here! If you wanna go, Booch, you gotta come right now."

Motivated by little more than gratitude, I didn't utter another word and sprinted ahead of him down the stairs. We zipped through the mill aboard the Hyster and exited the building toward the rear. "They've probably figured out what we're doin' by now and have already headed back out to the front of the building," he shouted. "I don't think we can beat 'em to our cars!"

"There's only one way to find out!"

"Shit!"

"What?" I asked.

"My keys. I left 'em in the break room!"

"Big fucking shit! Go with me!" Just as the words left my mouth, I realized the investigative faux pas I had just committed. It probably wasn't a good idea to take an investigatee to a rendezvous with the top brass of the client company. It was probably better than the alternative, though.

Cutting across the side parking lot to the front of the building, I saw several employees bolt from the front exit. George took evasive action and turned the Hyster toward them. It would have been an excellent tactic had one of them not been packing. Turning the vehicle sharply to avoid careening into the posse, we slid about a hundred feet across a lush, grassy knoll that separated the mill from the parking lot. Just as we started to decelerate, on the cusp of my long anticipated sigh of relief, the vehicle flipped, ejecting us from its cockpit. Our bodies were hurled topsy-turvy to the ground. Fortunately the uncontrolled skid also scattered the mob and provided us with a glimmer of hope. Covered in earth and blood, we lifted our bruised limbs from the water-swollen turf and scrambled our way toward my car.

"We're not gonna make it," George shouted just as a bullet whizzed past us.

"Okay, then," I screamed while still running. "Let's stop and try an' reason with 'em!"

"No, no! Go! Go! Go!"

Diving over and under cars, we made it safely to within fifty feet of my car before coming to an unscheduled halt behind a rusted-out van. The fifty feet separating us from liberation was unobstructed and, consequently, unprotected. "We'll never make it," George said before being interrupted by a voice that called out from the dark.

"Warriors! Come out and play, warriors!"

"Oh, shit," George cringed. "We're dead. *You* for ripping them off, an' me for helping you escape."

"That's a pretty good impersonation he's doin'."

"What?"

"Nothing. Don't worry. We can make it."

"Are you nuts?" he said harshly, his voice swelling with indignation. "Tell me this. Did you lock your car?"

"Of course, but it unlocks automatically with this." I held out my alarm activator. "And better . . ."

"We still haveta open the damn. . ."

"Shush!" I whispered sternly. "As I was about to . . . This button here will open the doors, too."

"What? Literally open them? Are you sure?"

"It did when I first bought it. I haven't actually used it in a while because I was afraid it'd give me problems."

"It opens the doors? Of the car?"

"Supposed to."

"Warriors," the voice rang out again, this time sounding much closer. "Come out and play-ay!"

"You ready?" I asked.

"What the hell," he said with a tense grin and a shake of the head.

"When I say 'now,'" I instructed. I then leaned forward and began feeling about the ground just in front of us on hands and knees, searching for anything that could be thrown. "Wouldn'tcha know it," I whispered in frustration. "Not a fuckin' stone in sight. The only ten square feet of clean ground within a mile of this shit hole and we're sitting on it."

"Whatta ya need a rock for?"

"To distract them. I'm gonna throw it over there. Except there's nothing to throw."

"Here," he said decisively. "Use this." He twisted and tugged on his school ring. It was probably twenty-plus years old—and heavy. I didn't ask him if he was sure. There wasn't time. And we had no alternatives. I briefly shook it in my hand like a die, stood up and heaved it across the parking lot. Pay dirt! It struck a car window.

"Over there!" I heard someone holler. "They're 'jacking a car!"

"Now," I declared in a suppressed bark. At a distance of about twenty feet, I disarmed the alarm and disengaged the locks with my remote. The doors, of course, remained shut. Gadgets like that were reserved for PIs who performed investigations for divorce attorneys, not undercover grunts like me.

We reached the car with surprising swiftness and, more importantly, before the bullets began to spatter around us. Once inside, I depressed the clutch and put the transmission in reverse before attempting to start the engine, wanting to avoid any delays because of a sticky gearshift. The fact is, once a Porsche's engine begins to rev, there is little hiding it. With a single turn of the key, we were not only moving backwards, we were discovered.

With my engine turning at maximum revolutions per minute, it was hard to tell if we were being fired upon for all the high-pitch whining. Hitting the brakes, I slapped the car into first gear, all the while cranking the steering wheel hard right to get us headed on the most direct route out of the parking lot. I stomped the gas pedal to the floor and rifled through the first three gears, propelling the car like a rocket to the nearest exit. Before I knew it, two trucks and a motorcycle were in hot pursuit.

My car blazed down the wavy street leading away from the mill and flew through the air as it reached the apex of each paved crest. As we made firm contact with the road, the struts rammed up into the wheel-wells and sparks danced like fireflies about the exhaust, vanishing as quickly as the car's passing. The car jolted and jarred furiously until it finally came under control about a mile out of Boise Cascade.

"We got company," I advised, glancing up at the rear view mirror intermittently.

"The doors . . . didn't . . . open!" he shouted hysterically.

"They opened."

"Automatically! They didn't open automatically!"

"You gonna help me here?"

"Shit!" he vented. "They're comin' up on your side! He's gonna run us off the road!"

I glanced out the side mirror. "On a motorcycle?" I asked incredulously. "Watch for the damn trucks, please. I'll handle this yahoo on the bike." I then mumbled something like, "Run us off the road with a bike . . . Are you serious? Movies should come with a disclaimer, I swear."

"I think he's gonna ram us!" George warned as one of the trucks accelerated toward our rear bumper. Cutting the wheel hard to the left and veering across the center divider of the main drag leading back into Medford, I slammed on the brakes, causing the trucks to sail past us and forcing the motorcycle off the road, where it quickly flipped over. "Bikes don't run cars off the road," I said.

"Is he dead?"

"Does it matter?" I immediately banged a U-turn back in the opposite direction, churning gravel high in the air like molten lava from a volcano, and the chase was on once again. This time, fortunately, there was only one truck giving chase. The occupants of the second vehicle had apparently gotten soft and stayed behind to render first aid to their fallen colleague.

Looking through the mirror at the truck behind us just as I was about to negotiate a very tricky hairpin turn, it suddenly occurred to me that this was one of the vehicles earmarked for confiscation by JACNET. "Best not wreck it," I thought. Downshifting with the nimbleness of Mario Andretti, I spun the wheel hard left and then cut it back toward the slide as I powered on through the turn. Unlike many car chases seen at the cinema, this one was over almost before it began. With a zero-to-sixty speed of under six seconds, my Porsche zoomed down the road that ran perpendicular to the mill, and I didn't slow until we reached downtown.

"Well, that worked out well," George said. "That is, unless going home or being able to remain in the same state is important to you."

"You, too," I replied.

"I was talking about me!"

"Oh."

"What the hell is all this about, anyhow? If there's a God, why would he allow all this to happen? What's the fuckin' purpose? Is it all like a test or something?"

"You better hope not, because I think you're failing miserably."

"Gee, thanks."

"You ever read Matthew 13:24? The parable about the weeds?"

"Excuse me?"

"Yeah, it goes something like this: A man plants good wheat seed in his field and . . . "

"Are you fucking serious? You're gonna give me a Bible lesson? Now?!"

"Yeah," I said. "Give me a chance here and listen. It's pertinent. So he plants this wheat seed and then, while he sleeps, his enemy plants weeds among the wheat. When the wheat starts to grow, so do the weeds. The servants ask the farmer if he wants them to pull the weeds before they choke off the wheat, but the farmer says no because he's afraid they may also uproot the wheat along with it. The farmer asks them to wait until the wheat has fully grown and then to harvest the weeds at that point. He then has the servants tie the weeds in bundles and burn them all in one big pile. He tells them to gather the wheat and bring it into the barn."

"Mysteries of the Bible will return after this brief message from our sponsors," he said lightly. "The point being?"

"I'm getting to that. I'm thinking, for reasons known only to God, mind you, that back when God cast Satan out of heaven, there must have been some sort of commingling of good and evil. Like our carrying the original sin and all. The weeds and the wheat in this parable, if you will. And in order to separate the wheat from the weeds God must first allow them to grow, lest he uproot the wheat with the weeds. Once they've grown and shown their true nature, they are separated, and the weeds are thrown into the eternal fire. Meaning, good and evil are stuck having to grow up in the same field together in order to be distinguished from one another later on."

"People start talking about the Bible and next thing you know they're using words like *lest*, he snickered. "So this is where we show what we are? Wheat or weed?"

"I'm sure you've heard the phrase "weeding out.""

"So now what do I do?"

"Read your Bible and go to church and hopefully you'll look more like wheat than a weed come harvest time. But first you need to help me with something. It'll only take a minute."

"You're not hearing me here!"

"I'm hearing you, already. Butcha haveta be patient with me here. As nuts as all this seems, you haveta believe me when I tell you that this won't seem so bad tomorrow. And besides, those guys weren't gonna kill us. Do you really believe anyone could be that bad a shot? They're all hunters, for cryin' out loud."

"You got all that from a car chase and some bullets flying overhead?"

"Huh?"

His voice showed frustration. "How do you know all that?!"

"I just do. You have to trust me."

"Like I have a choice. Damn. Why did I lend them all that money?"

"To double it. Face it, you got greedy."

He ignored my frankness and kept on talking. "You know, I don't give a damn about that money anymore. I just wish it wasn't gonna be used to make more people as fucked up as me. And *you*. You stiff 'em for forty K so you can make even more blaze heads like me. What's the fucking point anymore? Either way I lose. We all lose! I should've let you shoot it out with them. Fuck. We shoulda all shot it out. No winners, just losers."

"You want the kilo I stole?" I said bluntly.

"Yeah, sure. Give it to me."

"No, I'm serious."

"Why would you wanna give me a key?"

"I don't know. You could recoup your money, straighten your life out. You saved my life. It's the least I can do."

"I thought you said they wouldn't have killed us?"

"But you didn't know that."

He laid his head back against the rest as we pulled into the parking lot just across the street from where I lived. "Nah. You keep it. I wouldn't be able to live with myself if I continued to make people as fucked up as I am." He popped his head up for a second and looked around. "What are we doin' here?"

"I've gotta return a car to someone."

"Do it some other time! We gotta get the hell outta here!"

I ignored his words. "Don't admit to anything if you're ever questioned about your involvement with drugs at the mill." We both remained reticent, allowing our stillness to fill the necessary gaps. If he had any doubt as to who I was or what I had been doing there at the mill, he would have lambasted me with accusations and questions. He didn't. "Okay, then," I said. "Let's get this car back to its rightful owners and get your life back on track. Shall we?"

We strolled over to the 1989 Cutlass Supreme that Boise Cascade had purchased for me at the beginning of the case for the expressed purpose of helping me "blend in." Needless to say, I didn't want to blend in, and consequently, the car we were now approaching was caked in dust.

"So why me? I mean, why not sink me with the rest?"

"You know that kilo of crank I offered you a few minutes ago?"

"What about it?"

"Don't ever drink water out of the stream that runs through the park."

"I don't get it. . . ."

"I knew you'd never say yes when I offered it to you."

"I'm glad *you* did." He giggled nervously. "So they're all going down?"

"Most likely."

"Then I did lose my money?" he asked. "Aaah, fuck it. I didn't deserve to make anything off of all that anyway." He smacked the hood of the Cutlass and walked around to the passenger side. "You know what a baby's first words are in Japan?" he said rhetorically. "Da da. They're da da. No significance. They just are." He laughed. "Perspective, right?"

"Right," I smiled sympathetically. "I need ya over here, Ace," I insisted. "You'll be following me in this." I then glanced at my watch. "Oh, shit. We need to get a move on."

"O-oh," he warned, looking over my shoulder toward the front of the parking lot. "We got company."

Devon's big black truck, with its lights turned off, came creeping into the lot and then abruptly stopped, its rear end still hanging in the street. By now George and I had safely ducked behind the Cutlass. Devon, accompanied by two other men, having apparently spotted my Porsche in the lot across the way, backed out into the desolate street and accelerated to the next intersection.

"They're circling around," I cautioned. "They'll park across the street and send two of 'em over to pay me a visit at my apartment."

"How the hell do you know that?"

"When you've been visited as often as I have, you just know. Now follow me." We ran just as fast as we could to the other side of the street and took refuge behind a dumpster that was filled to the brim with the ripest refuse imaginable. As augured, they drove to the rear of the parking lot and parked next to my car. Two of them jumped out—Steve and someone I didn't recognize—and headed straight for my apartment.

"I swear," I whispered to George. "This guy (Devon) is like the Rain Man without the savant part."

"Now whatta we do?"

"We get the hell outta here. Stay here. I'll be right back." Knowing that he would be too confident to lock his vehicle, I simply ran to the side of his truck in a crouched position, opened the passenger door and forced him out of the vehicle. "Turn around," I said crassly, my weapon leveled at his head.

"You're a dead man," he responded, a vile smirk crimping his cheeks unnaturally.

I clobbered him in the back of his skull with the butt of my gun. "Betcha

never been hit that hard by a dead man before," I said to what I had
hoped would be an unconscious man. His moaning and groaning told me
otherwise.

"You watch too many movies," George said, startling me half to death.

"You 'bout scared me half to death, you stupid . . . What the hell you
doin' sneakin' up on me like that?"

"Hit 'im again," he insisted.

"Sure, if I wanna kill him. Here, take these keys and get that heap (the
Cutlass) rolling. It'll probably start slow, so don't flood it. Hurry." We left
the area without further incident, and that was the last I saw of Devon
until his trial several months later.

*   *   *

"I guess this is good-bye," I told George after parting company with the
Boise executive.

"Aren't you gonna drive me home?"

"No. But I'm gonna call you a cab and have 'im take ya over to a hotel
in Ashland for a couple days. It'll all be worked out by the time you get
there, so don't ask me any questions. It'd probably be best if you laid low
for a few days. Maybe skip work for a day or two."

"I still don't get why you didn't nail me."

"I do, and that's all that matters. Just don't make me out the fool."

"I'll try . . . not to, that is."

"Good luck, George."

"You, too," he replied earnestly. "You, too." And with that, the investigation, at least for me, was over.

*   *   *

With little packing to speak of, I stayed in a hotel that evening and waited
for swing shift to begin before returning to my apartment. At around
4:00 P.M., about the same time that the arrests and interviews were to
begin, it started to rain. I walked outside a couple hours later and sat on
the curb, letting the rain beat down on me. Though I struggled to catch a
scent of the mill, I couldn't. It had washed away like so many memories.

A short while later, Macki's car came sputtering into the parking lot.
Although I'm quite sure she had an umbrella readily accessible, she came
to my side without one and sat next to me in the rain, her head resting

softly against my shoulder. "I saw it on the news," was all she said as we sat for almost an hour.

I took her inside to dry off, where I told her all the sordid details of my protracted visit to Medford, Oregon. She was not at all surprised, but I must say a bit relieved. Rumors about a person's activities and their associations tended to run rampant in Medford. The funny thing is, a community this size in any other region of the country would not have had such a small-town mentality. Gossip aside, however, Medford wore its small-town linens quite well.

"Send me a copy of your book when it comes out," Macki reminded me as we hugged near my car.

"I will, Mack."

"And don't forget to sign it."

"I won't." I pulled back from her, kissed her and said good-bye.

When the final tally was made, more people were fired as a result of this investigation than of any other case in Krout and Schneider's storied history. If I'm not mistaken, the number passed sixty. Everyone mentioned in this book associated with criminal activity was terminated, including that auxiliary cop in White City. Oddly enough, though, Caracas was eventually hired back. I hope it was due to my insistence that we did not have him directly linked to any particular crime. I sincerely doubt it, though. The boat lab, I hear tell, was seized by the Feds, but still no word on the disposition of its owner, Mr. Green. Devon, Shannon, Phil and Jim all went to prison, along with an assortment of suppliers, cooks and distributors, or so I'm told.

Chapter 31

When I left the home of my friend John Yearly in Moreno Valley, California, the following day, the sun was pressing down on me. I drove to Santa Monica, taking the scenic route on I-10. A solitary cloud smothered the California sun, holding the mercury below seventy degrees as my Porsche swept along the Pacific Coast Highway. The nomadic vapor gradually dissipated, allowing daggers of light to strike the sloping, opaque violet hood. As I stared transfixed into the resultant glow, ruminating with the hypnotic harmony of the underground band Venice and the haunting lyrics of the Crosby, Stills and Nash offshoot, Anastasia and John, I rehashed ad nauseam the events of the previous eight or nine months. Their music took me clear across the country.

I was on my way to Massachusetts, the location of my next assignment and a few unlucky souls. I say unlucky because when I finished pouring an entire bottle of cologne over my windshield to prevent water from freezing on it (cologne is alcohol-based) for the third consecutive time, it finally dawned on me that our lives are sort of like that car: a little neglect—I had forgotten to fix the defogger—and suddenly you're pouring a hundred-and-fifty-dollar bottle of cologne on your windshield. Not unlike my defogger, the people I was about to investigate had probably neglected their lives, not realizing on a day-to-day basis that it was the only one they would be given.

Like so many investigators before me and so many after, I'm afraid, I traversed the country for the next couple years exposing a wide range of criminal activity by employees to their employers and suppressing myself to the point of suffocation. It was once very natural for me to assume new identities, ones with less self-blame and less pain than I had in real life, but I came to realize that even my pseudonyms had their share of pain and blame. But more importantly, I was flat disgusted with the non-Christian way I was obliged to live my life. The two were simply no longer compatible, and, as the Bible says, a house divided will not stand.

Having spent several years sending scores of drug dealers and other derelicts to jail, I had grown jaded. It had become clear that to be an effective investigator, which I was, you had to set aside all emotion, which I could not, and divorce yourself from the lives of those you were tasked to investigate, which I no longer would.

An inescapable axiom of the undercover corporate investigator is that people *do* get hurt as a result of what the UCI does for a living. The better the UCI, the greater the hurt. The closer and more intimate a UCI gets with his or her target, the greater the likelihood that the investigation will be successful. Therefore, a good UCI is defined as an investigator who can parlay his or her personal relationships and trust into arrests and terminations. If this same investigator has any heart whatsoever, it ends up shattered time and time again.

Do I think UCIs are necessary? I absolutely do. Do I want to be a part of it any longer? Hardly. The fact is, a good investigation, even one fraught with the type of ethical dilemmas recounted here, can have a positive impact on safety, fairness and equality in the workplace while simultaneously affecting the consumer's wallet for the better. To be certain, increasing productivity, reducing injuries and lessening the incidence of lawsuits ultimately enables a company to deliver its services to the public at a much more competitive price, thus making investigations such as these beneficial for all society.

The caveat to all this, however, is that there needs to be stricter guidelines on the companies that perform such work, especially with regard to the gathering of information *not* used in court, the strategic targeting of certain races and the questioning of employees who don't already have a stack of evidence against them; that is to say, the endless grilling of employees only implicated by circumstantial evidence. If some of the many problems delineated in this book can be mitigated, undercover corporate investigations will become one of the most effective weapons in today's law enforcement arsenal. If not, look out Fortune 500; hello class-action lawsuit.

*   *   *

With all the fanfare of a ribbon-cutting ceremony for a trailer park in Wichita, Kansas, my career as an undercover corporate investigator came to an abrupt halt shortly after the publication of my first book, *CIA: Cocaine in America*. With the words "He resides in California and is now a private investigator" printed conspicuously on the back cover, K and S did what it decided was best for the company and what certainly was best for me in the long run—they terminated our relationship.

Gordon spoke with me shortly after I left the firm and told me that he had actually suspected that I had previously been involved in some sort of "extracurricular activities" with one or more government agencies. He came to this conclusion in part because the FBI informed K and S when they hired me that they had an extensive file on me but could not release the contents due to national security considerations. Gordon said that he just assumed it had something to do with the high-level security clearance I held in the Air Force, because the FBI specifically stated that the files had nothing to do with any sort of criminal activity on my part.

In a real shocker, he also told me that he considered me to be the best UCI Krout and Schneider ever had, Glenn notwithstanding. Needless to say, this mended much of the rift between us and gave me a much higher regard for his investigative acumen and wisdom. See how easy I am to get along with?

When I walked away from undercover work, I took my K and S employment contract, my engagement ring and a copy of my sister's death certificate, drove up to San Francisco and heaved them off the Golden Gate Bridge, the place I made my first marriage proposal. My reasoning was simple: my job and my engagement were over and probably never should have existed in the first place. Both were never right for me, yet neither was inherently bad, either. In fact, K and S has continued on just fine without me, and it appears that my ex, who was truly a lovely person at heart, found the perfect man for her as well.

My sister will never be dead to me because neither my sister nor I will ever truly die. At least not as we Christians define death. To quote Jesus

Christ, if I may be so bold, "Let the dead bury their dead." The death certificate represented finality and was therefore as invalid as my employment contract and as flawed as my engagement ring.

I should stipulate, however, that this all made perfect sense to me while standing on the edge of a bridge, one sibling short of a nuclear family, recently unemployed and no longer a fiancé. Admittedly, it lost some clarity the moment I saw the price tag of my wife's engagement ring a few years later. When the saleslady asked, "Will you be making a deposit on this stone today, sir?" I could actually see that discarded ring rise up from the sea like King Arthur's Excalibur. I must admit, though, it did feel awfully good to make a clean break and to start over. And if you're ever in the market for a slightly used one-carat diamond ring, you need only walk about a third of the way across the Golden Gate Bridge from the Sausalito side and look straight down.

Why do I mention all of this, you might ask? I suppose it's because, in the end, if you're involved in any sort of workplace activity that might be construed as inappropriate, I'd like to remind you, whether or not you think it's appropriate for your company to spy on you, not unlike my wedding engagement and the loss of my two previous occupations, "birds die." However, if this seemingly trite piece of advice happens to arrive on your doorstep a day and a half after you've already collected your first unemployment check, drive to the nearest bridge, toss that which cannot be changed over the guardrail and simply start anew. It works, believe me! Just ask my best friend and the love of my life, Joanna Bucchi, and our perfect little boys, "The Bean" (Noah) and "Lantern" (Jack).

Epilogue

On September 7, 1998, a fire erupted in a dryer at the Boise Cascade mill in Medford, Oregon. In fact, it occurred during the same shift that I investigated. Using the hose at the base of the dryer, the dryer tender quickly extinguished the flames . . . or so he thought. Hours later, just before 11:00 that evening, the fire reared its ugly head once again; only now it rolled over the rafters like an avalanche. Unable to reach the blaze with water from the inadequate hoses, the employees were forced to run for their lives. The fire quickly raced across the ceiling and within minutes had fully engulfed the mill. The inferno roared on for days, and when it was over, the Boise Cascade mill, which had been doing business in Medford for some fifty years, had been reduced to rubble and ash. Over five hundred families were affected by this very avoidable catastrophe, and many were left destitute.

Ironically, Stan, who saved the mill during the fire described in this book, would likely have been working during the 1998 fire had he not been terminated by the company. Against my advice, I might add. Even more ironic, though, is that the fire occurred on Labor Day. Not surprisingly, the mistakes made during this 1998 fire were identical to those we made in 1993 . . . except for Stan, of course, who seemed to do everything right that evening.

Yet another glaring example of why a UCI can never close the book on a case.